P9-EDS-114

FROM DEPORTATION TO PRISON

LATINA/O SOCIOLOGY SERIES

From Deportation to Prison

*The Politics of Immigration Enforcement
in Post–Civil Rights America*

Patrisia Macías-Rojas

NEW YORK UNIVERSITY PRESS

New York

NEW YORK UNIVERSITY PRESS
New York
www.nyupress.org

References to Internet websites (URLs) were accurate at the time of writing. Neither the author nor New York University Press is responsible for URLs that may have expired or changed since the manuscript was prepared.

Library of Congress Cataloging-in-Publication Data
Names: Macias-Rojas, Patrisia, author.
Title: From deportation to prison : the politics of immigration enforcement in post–civil rights America / Patrisia Macías-Rojas.
Description: New York : New York University, 2016. | Includes bibliographical references and index.
Identifiers: LCCN 2016017051| ISBN 978-1-4798-0466-5 (hbk : alk. paper) | ISBN 978-1-4798-3118-0 (pbk : alk. paper)
Subjects: LCSH: Immigration—Government policy—United States. | Immigration enforcement—United States. | Mexican-American Border Region. | Criminal justice, Administration of—United States. | Social control—United States.
Classification: LCC JV6483 .M265 2016 | DDC 325.73—dc23
LC record available at https://lccn.loc.gov/2016017051

New York University Press books are printed on acid-free paper, and their binding materials are chosen for strength and durability. We strive to use environmentally responsible suppliers and materials to the greatest extent possible in publishing our books.

Manufactured in the United States of America

10 9 8 7 6 5 4 3 2 1

Also available as an ebook

CONTENTS

ACKNOWLEDGMENTS

My father had a dream recently that he was hiding from the Border Patrol. At ninety-three, he shouldn't have to run from *la migra*, least of all in his dreams. My mother appears in my dreams. She died suddenly while I was doing fieldwork for this project, but I've felt her presence throughout the years it took to write this book. I'm grateful to them both for their courage and resilience.

My siblings—Martina, Graciela, Ernesto, Isabel, Julio, Bertha, and Pedro—have deeply impacted my life. As the youngest of eight, I've often felt that I'm a little bit like all of them. Channeling their strengths during tough times has been my most precious survival strategy.

Growing up, my family kept a dark brown particleboard shelf stocked with secondhand books. I remember reaching for the thickest book when I was barely literate, holding it in my hands, and wanting to make one.

At Sarah Lawrence College, Shahnaz Rouse and Priscilla Murolo, who introduced me to sociology and history, were the first to encourage my thinking and put the idea in my head that I could make a book. I'm thankful that they never told me how much work it would be.

At UC–Berkeley, Michael Burawoy and Laura Enriquez worked with me—even when I didn't fit the mold—and came through for me in ways that I could never repay. I am especially thankful to them for continuing to support me long after I left Berkeley. I also genuinely appreciated the support of other exceptional scholars like Evelyn Nakano Glenn and Peter Evans. Margaret Weir, Troy Duster, David Minkus, Michael Omi, Loïc Wacquant, and Raka Ray also supported me during critical moments in the sociology doctoral program. Irene Bloemraad, who arrived as I was leaving, provided a solid foundation in migration studies.

Students at San Quentin's Prison University Project sparked an urge to know more about how the immigration system and prison intersect. A decade-long correspondence with a childhood friend also compelled me to learn more. At fifteen, he was labeled a "gang member," was charged and convicted as an adult, and spent most of his adolescence and adult life in prison. He was deported as I was finishing my dissertation at Berkeley. I think of him and his family whenever I sit down to work on this project. Their untold story influenced this investigation into the root causes of the Department of Homeland Security's Criminal Alien Program and current enforcement priorities.

Learning about immigration enforcement from local families and residents in Douglas/Agua Prieta and Ambos Nogales was one of my most rewarding experiences in life. In Tucson, Jennifer Allen, Daniel Espinoza, Mark Adams, Gustavo Lozano, Tresa Thomas, Lupe Castillo, Todd Miller, Pati Valera, Zoe Hammer, Ginnie Jordan, Shura Wallin, Manuel Abril, and Amy Hagemeier shared knowledge and exposed me to "The Other Arizona." Residents often expressed that they had grown tired of seeing their communities represented in a negative light or defined by the border wall instead of the cross-border cultural, political, and economic exchange that border regions are known for. They might be a little disappointed that I've written a book about the Department of Homeland Security's Criminal Alien Program, the Tucson Border Patrol Sector's role in implementing and expanding it, and Arizona's impact on national immigration debates and border policy, more broadly. But I do believe this story is worth telling, and I could not have done so without their generosity and that of other veteran activists, scholars, teachers, clergy, Mexican officials, public officials, and law enforcement who took time to educate me about what border security actually looks like on the ground.

Funding from the National Science Foundation, the Andrew Mellon Foundation Program in Latin American Sociology, and UC–Berkeley's Latino Policy Institute made it possible to conduct research in Arizona-Sonora and El Paso-Juarez, as well as pilot research in the San Diego-Tijuana border region. Professional development grants when I was on the faculty at Sarah Lawrence College allowed me to conduct follow-up research in Southern Arizona, El Paso, and the National Archives and USCIS library in DC. In DC, I am especially grateful to INS historians Marian Smith and Zachary Wilske for their generous guidance and advice.

At Sarah Lawrence College, Sarah Wilcox helped me negotiate an academic leave necessary to focus on the book. Priscilla Murolo, Shahnaz Rouse, Rona Holub, Deanna Barenboim, Bill Shullenberger, and Mary Dillard read and/or encouraged early drafts of chapters, article manuscripts, and the book proposal. Barbara Hickey and Bobbie Smolow also offered assistance with research and funding, friendship and support. I learned a lot from and was heartened by the support of former students like Liz Perez, Sophia Clark, Donna Honarpisheh, Alyssa Manansala, Xochitl Sanchez, Jennifer Wong, Kristelle Jose, Razeem Zaman, Michelle Lewin, Akash Radia, Thea Michailedes, Tom Loder, Ren Rossini, and Jennifer Campbell.

Ruth Peterson and Laurie Krivo of the Crime and Justice Summer Research Institute at The Ohio State University and the Racial Democracy Crime and Justice Network, along with Cid Martinez, Victor Rios, David Hernandez, Marie Provine, Marjorie Zatz, and Kathleen Blee, provided much-needed encouragement, professional advice, and substantive feedback. In Henricka McCoy, LaDonna Long, Mia Ortiz, Waverly Duck, Kishonna Gray, Lorrie Burrington, and Anthony Hatch, the 2012 SRI cohort, I found friendship and inspiration.

That the book finally came together is due to an unexpected post-doctoral fellowship at the Institute for Research on Race Public Policy (IRRPP) at the University of Illinois, Chicago under the leadership of Beth Richie. The year I spent at this dynamic research institute exposed me to a broad range of racial-justice scholars modeling diverse approaches to publicly engaged research that transformed the trajectory of my work. That challenged me to write a different book than the one I thought I had to, using my data to engage public debates about deportation and incarceration. Michelle Boyd provided generous mentorship on research and writing. She helped me find my way and rescued me from being buried alive by the eighteen boxes of "data" I showed up with. Franscesca Gaiba believed in this project early on and offered generous advice on all things scholarly and practical. Beth Richie, Michelle Boyd, Erica Meiner, Francesca Gaiba, Kerry Ann Roquemore, Ivan Arenas, Xóchitl Bada, and Ralph Cintron provided honest feedback on early chapter drafts and the book proposal when I was a scholar-in-residence at IRRPP. Ryan Villoria, Delaina Washington, and Zachary Jensen made me feel at home every day I showed up at the office to chip away at the manuscript. An NSF-sponsored workshop on immigrant detention and incarceration at IRRPP also greatly pushed my thinking on these issues.

I also had the great fortune of spending a year, under Bob Nelson's leadership, at the American Bar Foundation in Chicago, where I received tremendous support on this project. Jothie Rajah made me feel incredibly welcomed, and along with Terry Halliday, Bernadette Atuahene, Elizabeth Mertz, and John Hagan, Laura Beth Nielson offered the feedback and encouragement necessary to finally get the manuscript off my desk. Pegeen Bassett at the Northwestern Law School is one of the most amazing librarians I've ever met. The chapter on detention bed space came together because of her guidance and expertise in government documents.

At NYU Press, Victor Rios pushed me to get the book done. Not letting him down was a major motivation for finishing. I am thankful to him and Pierrette Hondagneu-Sotelo, whose work convinced me as a struggling grad student to stick it out and made becoming a sociologist feel like a worthwhile endeavor. I am also deeply appreciative of Ilene Kalish, Caelyn Cobb, Emily Wright, Alexia Traganas, and the anonymous reviewers for their careful reading of the manuscript.

At the University of Illinois, Chicago, where I've recently joined the faculty, I've been deeply impressed by the work of scholars involved in Latin American and Latina/o Studies, African American Studies, Gender and Women's Studies, Criminology, Law and Justice, and, of course, the Sociology Department. Beth Richie, Andy Clarno, Lorena Garcia, Claire Decoteau, Nilda Flores-Gonzales, Amanda Lewis, Laurie Shaffner, Barbara Ransby, Pamela Quiroz, Andreas Feldman, Nena Torres, Xóchilt Bada, Gayatri Reddy, Amalia Pallares, Lisa Frohmann, and Teresa Cordova have in distinct and meaningful ways helped me make the transition from a teaching college to a research-intensive university and to my hometown. Each of them embodies the kind of scholar I hope to be. I've also had the incredible honor of having students like Gabriela Benitez, Luz Acosta, Jorge Mena, Jose Herrera, Herrica Telus, and Debbie Patino. With their activism and engaged scholarship, they are transforming the conversations about incarceration and deportation in ways that I never thought possible when I began this work.

Many other people have helped along the way, even when the process felt immensely solitary. Maria Aguilar, Hong Luu, and Christopher Kasprzack have been there for me. Mark Toney, Sujatha Jesudadson, and Lynn Rivas offered tremendous inspiration and camaraderie in an early writing group. Rebecca Gordon and Jan Adams, Mizue Aizeki and Joe Nevins, Rima Vesley-Flad and Ethan Flad, Michelle Foy and Fernando

Marti, Maria Elena "Beba" Castaneda, Norma Martinez and Daniel Hosang, Robyn Rodriguez, Jennifer Chun, Angelina Godoy, Maria Cristina Morales, Leisy Abrego, Bob Wing, Alfredo DeAvila, Corina Pineda, and Lynnea Stephen also urged me on in one way or another over the years.

Special thanks to Tiyi Morris, Badia Ahad, and Michelle Boyd, who were there during the final push to finish. Rebecca Gordon, Sujatha Jesudadson, Joe Nevins, Rima Vesley-Flad, Ivan Arenas, Andy Clarno, Xóchitl Bada, and Joseph Margulies took time out of their busy schedules to read portions of the manuscript and to offer much-needed feedback. Each in their own way provided support, encouragement, and feedback on the writing process of a kind I'd never really known. Thank you so much. Nina Clements helped with the bibliography. Tara James helped with the index. Rudy Medina and Alyx Christensen helped me with the cover design. The folks at La Catrina Café and Café Jumping Bean in Pilsen also created a safe and empowering space in which to write.

My deepest gratitude goes to my children—Joaquim, already a better writer than I could ever be, and little Paloma, whose imagination inspires me. I love everything about them. My in-laws, Jack and Madeline, have also been greatly encouraging and supportive and provided a home away from home while I was conducting archival research in Washington, DC. I'm especially grateful to them for John, my *compañero*. To know John is to love him. I'm so thankful for his kindness and optimism, for his commitment to equality in the home, where it counts, for his willingness to uproot dozens of times so that I could do this work, for standing by me unconditionally and without criticism or judgment, for not letting me quit, and for helping me to get back up countless times. The larger struggle of which this small work is part is not mine to give away in a dedication, but this book that I have longed to make is in no small way dedicated to you.

Introduction

This book is about how mass incarceration transformed immigration enforcement and border policing. It is about how incarcerating over two million people in the United States gave impetus to a federal immigration initiative—the Criminal Alien Program—designed to purge noncitizens from dangerously overcrowded jails and prisons. Expanded in the 1980s to relieve prison overcrowding, the Criminal Alien Program quietly set off a punitive turn in immigration enforcement that has fundamentally altered detention, deportation, and criminal prosecutions for immigration violations. When I began researching this book, the Border Patrol had recently expanded the Criminal Alien Program in Arizona under a high-profile border enforcement campaign known as Operation Safeguard, launched in 1995. In an internal memo on Safeguard, the Border Patrol referred to Arizona as "critically important to the Administration's multi-phased border control and criminal alien removal strategies."[1] Safeguard infused the Tucson Border Patrol Sector with federal funding for one hundred additional agents, one thousand more detention beds, and biometric technology for criminal background checks, and it established the Institutional Removal Hearing Program to carry out fast-track deportations directly from Arizona prisons and jails.[2] Arizona quickly acquired some of the highest levels of apprehensions and "criminal alien removals" along the U.S.-Mexico border.

Alongside "criminal alien removals," the Arizona-Sonora border had also become the epicenter of migrant deaths. Anticipating a rise in migrant fatalities as border policing pushed unauthorized flows further into the hostile desert, Safeguard also included funding for search and rescue operations. By 2001, immigrant- and border-rights activists convened a border summit in Tucson, Arizona, denouncing migrant deaths and what they called a "humanitarian crisis" caused by U.S. immigration and border policies. This was the context I stepped into over a decade ago—a post–civil rights enforcement arena that drew as much on civil- and human-rights discourses as it did those of crime.[3]

In 2002, I volunteered to go door to door in five Southern Arizona border communities to survey residents about their experiences with the U.S. Border Patrol. Border residents, I quickly learned, are at once regulators and regulated. As law enforcement agents, suspected smugglers, immigrants, or long-term residents, they have become directly and indirectly involved in policing even as they are themselves policed. Going door to door, I met several residents of Mexican ancestry who were the immediate relatives or friends of law enforcement agents, or perhaps were employed in some aspect of security-related industries, and many more who had been pulled over on allegedly criminal grounds, as suspected smugglers. I met U.S. citizens under house arrest for immigration offenses like smuggling and some residents whose family members had had their legal status revoked and had been retroactively deported after president Bill Clinton signed the 1996 Illegal Immigration Reform and Immigrant Responsibility Act (IIRIRA), which greatly expanded criminal grounds for deportation.

Border residents' testimonies differed from historical accounts and my family's nearly one-hundred-year history of migration and enforcement. My grandfather migrated to Chicago from Mexico in the 1920s and was among those deported in the mass repatriations of Mexicans during the Great Depression.[4] My father migrated to the United States in 1942 as one of the first contract workers under the Bracero Program, a bilateral labor-recruitment program invented to meet wartime labor shortages. This was during the Jim Crow era when it was not uncommon to labor in towns where shopkeepers posted signs that read "No Dogs, No Negros, and No Mexicans."[5] For two decades, he migrated to (and was deported from) the United States as both a contract and an undocumented worker, eventually settling in racially segregated Chicago with my mother and siblings as legal permanent residents. My family's immigration status shaped my own transnational upbringing in the United States and Mexico throughout the seventies and eighties. And although I am a U.S. citizen, I have had to prove to border agents time and time again that I'm not an immigrant, or a foreigner, and that my papers are "legal," whenever I have reentered the United States from Mexico.

The post-1996 enforcement I witnessed in Southern Arizona defied my expectations of how border policing works. I'd stepped into a complex field—one in which the Border Patrol played a more direct role in local crime control and worked in partnership with local law enforcement, immigrant-rights advocates, and, at times, migrants and border residents themselves. Enforcement extended beyond the traditional relations among white Border Patrol agents, growers, unions, and Mexican migrants or between inspectors and border crossers. Instead of historical practices to regulate labor migration and cross-border commerce, I observed enforcement actions designed to manage crime. Security-related industries also played a more prominent role in local economies. And, instead of an overtly racial language of keeping out "wetbacks," agents— some of whom self-identified as "Hispanic," "Latina/o," or "Mexican-American"—and other players involved in border enforcement drew on a language of "rights" and "crime."

To navigate this complex enforcement field, I dug into archives in order to understand what legal changes and processes had led the Border Patrol to evaluate immigrants and border crossers in terms of criminal history. I knew from conversations with Border Patrol agents that detention beds determined the capacity of the system. The availability of beds influenced the daily decisions of agents about whether or not to enforce the law against someone. Taking the advice of INS historian Marian Smith, I "followed the money" and traced the history of the detention-bed quota. That story, buried in congressional hearings and INS records, uncovered the roots of the Criminal Alien Program, which, I discovered, emerged from the prison-bed crisis that began in the eighties and the post–civil rights crackdown on crime. That crackdown particularly targeted African Americans through disparate sentencing and, I argue, fueled a need to pull noncitizens out of regular prisons in order to create space for newly criminalized people of color.

Today, the Criminal Alien Program relies on biometric information technology and detention beds to target what are referred to as "priority aliens," or those with criminal records, for arrest and removal, and for criminal prosecution for unauthorized entry and reentry after deportation.[6] In fact, reentry after deportation has become a leading charge in sentencing people to federal prison.[7] Latinas/os make up almost half of all sentenced offenders, mostly for immigration violations such as reentry.[8] What began as a program to purge criminals from jails and prisons, which was CAP's original mission, has become one of the chief mechanisms driving federal criminal prosecution and imprisonment for immigration offenses.[9]

Combining a short history of CAP and "street-level" observations of its implementation, I also embarked on an ethnography of criminal immigration enforcement in Arizona-Sonora border towns.[10] In the field, I became less interested in the spectacle of the corrugated metal wall, stadium lights, and deployment of the National Guard, turning my attention to invisible sites where the merger of immigration and crime control forged ahead—a migrant shelter for deportees, the port of entry, a federal courtroom, or a detention center. The most memorable observations, however, occurred on remote desert roads and public spaces of Southern Arizona border communities, through my own experiences with immigration enforcement. In Southern Arizona, I was often stopped, pulled over, searched, and interrogated—by both white and Latina/o border agents—as a potential immigrant or suspected smuggler at the port of entry or on the street, as if to put me in my place. This occurred with regularity, which I logged along with other public observations of arrest and policing, prosecution and incarceration, detention and deportation.

Following a local campaign to block construction of an immigrant prison, I began visiting three migrant shelters in Mexico once or twice a week in order to help gather the testimonies of formerly incarcerated migrants.[11] My early visits were admittedly awkward.[12] I was often the only woman in a room filled with new migrants in transit and recent deportees from U.S. correctional facilities. I remember my first visit vividly. I was embarrassed to look, afraid of meeting their eyes, of seeming disrespectful because I wasn't in the kitchen with other women volunteers who had prepared the food. I couldn't help but look at the ground, notice their feet—old shoes, sandals, and no socks. I looked up slowly, noticing their dusty clothes, hands, and, finally, their eyes. I recognized them not as the immigrants represented in public discourse but as young men from my family's hometown in Mexico where I was raised. I was relieved and yet so uncomfortable, haunted by the thought that some of them might end up dead or in prison.

The shelters serve first-time border crossers and former deportees, mostly men from Mexico and Central America arrested on the border and in the interior.[13] I met deportees with criminal records and those without. I met migrants processed through civil proceedings and others who were criminally prosecuted for immigration offenses. I met first-time border crossers and English-speaking deportees with a long history of settlement in the United States. I met migrants removed on criminal grounds (under CAP) and others who were granted voluntary departure—a form of relief with fewer penalties and greater possibilities of future migration.

Migrants' perspectives on enforcement practices were essential, particularly when they shared their experiences with the border agents, Mexican officials, local law enforcement, smugglers, and vigilantes. Among them I also interviewed smugglers, mostly low-level employees, after meeting deportees in Mexican shelters who had been convicted on smuggling charges in the United States.[14]

Agents from the Tucson Sector of the U.S. Border Patrol and what became Immigration and Customs Enforcement (ICE), officials from the Instituto Nacional de Migración, Grupo Beta, and the Office of the Mexican Consulate also generously shared their perspectives and expertise on arrest and repatriation of migrants with and without convictions, antismuggling initiatives, and the impact of border security on local economies.[15] I also interviewed the directors, staff, and founding members of migrant advocacy NGOs, particularly those involved in providing legal services to detained migrants in removal proceedings as well as those monitoring human- and civil-rights abuses.

At the time of my fieldwork, anti-immigrant and militia groups were actively mobilizing in Southern Arizona. As much as I'd tried to ignore them, I couldn't, as they were also key players. To better understand their perspective and actions, I attended their local meetings and interviewed local ranchers, the Mexican Consulate, and migrants themselves regarding vigilantism in Southern Arizona.

Throughout the fieldwork, I shuttled back and forth between Arizona and Sonora, Mexico. For transportation, I relied on local makeshift shuttles, or *camionetas*, which transport border commuters to and from the border, and which border agents often associated with the smuggling industry. From the predominantly Latina/o border towns of Douglas, Agua Prieta, and Nogales, Arizona/Sonora, as well as, to a lesser extent, Altar, Sonora, and Sasabe, Arizona, I would go up the interstate to observe deportation hearings in a detention center in Florence, Arizona—a prison town sixty-one miles from Phoenix. With a population of twenty-five thousand, half of whom are imprisoned, Florence is home to an assortment of nine federal and privately run correctional and detention facilities.[16] There, I witnessed deportation proceedings and know-your-rights workshops for detained migrants from all over the world, as well as removal proceedings for formerly incarcerated Mexican and Central American immigrants under the Criminal Alien Program. In Tucson, I sat through criminal prosecution hearings under Operation Streamline, which is a federal prosecution program that charges immigrants with illegal entry and reentry in criminal courts. I talked directly to law enforcement officials from the police and sheriff's departments, as well as public defenders and prosecutors from the U.S. Attorney's Office for the District of Arizona, which in a post–civil rights context included whites and "racial minorities."

The research for this book spans a decade, the bulk of it conducted between 2001 and 2005. During one of my earliest meetings at the Tucson Border Patrol station, only weeks after 9/11, I wasn't allowed to enter the building for security reasons. The agent kept apologizing for having to meet with me outdoors in the hot sun. (I was pregnant at the time.) But by 2005, I'd collected over 150 interviews with immigration agents, law enforcement officers, elected officials, judges and public defenders, NGOs, migrants, and border residents.[17] Between 2007 and 2009, I conducted primarily archival research at the National Archives and the USCIS library in Washington, DC. I continued archival research and resumed fieldwork in the summer of 2010 after the passage of Arizona's "Papers Please" law (SB1070), and have returned one to two times a year since then.[18]

I often felt that I was chasing a moving a target, conducting my research in a state of flux, constantly shifting my observations between the migrant shelters, immigration and criminal courts, border communities, and the archives. This multisited approach (over a ten-year period) undoubtedly offered a unique perspective on immigration law enforcement and border security; however, it also limited my relationships in the field. Every time I returned to a site, there were new faces and accounts of death, smuggling, vigilantism, and hyperpolicing—new cases for criminal prosecution, new prison sentences, and rotating cases of detainees and deportees. I constantly had to reorient myself to my surroundings.

Despite my own border crossing history and my fluency in Spanish and English, I felt like an eternal stranger and outsider, until it finally occurred to me that the border had rendered us all strangers and foreigners in one way or another. With the exception of long-term border residents, most people knew one another, more or less, about as long as I had known them. Even many of the Border Patrol agents were strangers, as many of them had been transferred from other regions or hired quickly when Congress began investing more heavily in border security.

Though I was fully committed to this work, it often felt both wrong and necessary to approach people in those vulnerable moments just after they were deported or released from prison, as I was fully aware that my U.S. citizenship protected me, to an extent, and granted me unequal freedom to move back and forth between Mexico and the United States. In other ways, I felt compelled. Border activist Maria Jimenez once joked that Mexicans are the only ethnic group in this country with their very own police.[19] She was referring to the historical connection between U.S.-Mexico border policing and the social standing of Mexicans in the United States. But her observation also speaks to the power that immigration agents have been given to evaluate and "process people," then confer a public status.[20] This partially explains why I made federal mandates, legal processes, and enforcement decisions—in which everyone is implicated—my object of study, as if to reorient my gaze or shift the analytic lens for a change.[21]

I overcame my initial misgivings about observing and interpreting what I was seeing when I realized that I too was being watched. The border agents made this very clear each time they stopped and interrogated me. Smugglers let me know when, on more than one occasion, they followed me. One incident stands out in my mind: I had stepped into a church to take field notes, and a smuggler followed me in to let me know that he knew I was watching. The taxi drivers, also associated with the smuggling industry, became suspicious and questioned me when I asked them to drop me off at the Border Patrol station. The Border

Patrol agents also seemed suspicious when I arrived for interviews in a taxi. Border residents surprised me when they casually mentioned that they saw me or heard that I had been in Mexico the day before. Policing permeated every aspect of social life; everyone seemed to be watching.

* * *

For many, the punitive turn in immigration enforcement stems from the attack on the World Trade Center on September 11, 2001. After the reorganization of the Immigration and Naturalization Service (INS) under the newly created Department of Homeland Security in 2003, the agency revised the national border security strategy to "prevent terrorists and terrorist weapons from entering the United States" (alongside unauthorized migration and drugs).[22] However, the day-to-day operations of Border Patrol agents do not involve intercepting terrorists or chemical weapons, nor are border agents apprehending migrants from countries on the "state sponsors of terrorism" or "terrorist safe haven" lists. As Mexico's drug-related violence makes clear, weapons are more likely to go from the United States to Mexico than the other way around. Although 9/11 linked immigration and national security, this link occurred more in the national imagination than in practice. From a street-level perspective, the most salient feature of border security is not counterterrorism, but a blend of immigration and crime control that began well before the events of September 11.

Despite the rhetorical conflation of immigration with terrorism and national security, then, what border enforcement looks like in practice is little more than domestic crime control extended to an immigration context.[23] A typical day for Border Patrol agents is not intercepting chemical weapons but prosecuting illegal entry and reentry or deporting legal permanent residents, with the support of ICE, on criminal grounds.[24] Agents have yet to apprehend noncitizens on national security charges along the U.S.-Mexico border, much as the weapons of mass destructions failed to materialize in Iraq. Yet in stark contrast to public scrutiny of military expenditures and operations overseas, less is understood about what border security actually looks like domestically, despite widespread bipartisan consensus. Certainly, the border walls, barricades, and deployment of the Border Patrol agents tell a familiar story about national security and terrorism, but the mundane, less visible practices on the ground tell another.

* * *

This book examines America's new immigration regime, or what scholars have referred to as the "crimmigration crisis," "criminalization of migration," and "'immigrantization' of criminal law."[25] What brought on such an unprecedented approach to migration control that both aggressively punishes and recognizes "humanitarian" principles and procedural protections? How has the focus on criminal history as an enforcement priority affected the on-the-ground policing practices in border communities? What are the ways in which Border Patrol agents, local law enforcement, residents, ranchers, activists, and migrants themselves have come to contest, accept, and enforce growing distinctions between rights-bearing immigrants and "criminals"?

I argue that new enforcement priorities under the Criminal Alien Program fundamentally transformed detention and deportation in ways that merged the immigration and criminal justice systems. CAP expanded in the 1980s to relieve prison overcrowding by deporting noncitizens from jails and prisons. In order to fully implement the Criminal Alien Program, Congress restructured detention and deportation through the passage of the 1996 Illegal Immigration Reform and Immigrant Responsibility Act (IIRIRA), which—among its many controversial provisions—expanded criminal enforcement priorities, enacted retroactive deportation for immigrants with criminal records, instituted mandatory detention, and appropriated the critical funding for information technology and detention beds necessary to make the entire program workable.

My findings show that prison overcrowding in a post–civil rights era of mass incarceration in the United States played a critical role in ushering in many of the changes that merged immigration and crime control. In order to free up prison beds in the rapidly expanding prison system, Congress ordered the Immigration and Naturalization Service to begin targeting noncitizens with convictions for deportation. These new criminal enforcement priorities soon spread from jails and prisons to all other aspects of immigration enforcement.

At the U.S.-Mexico border, agents began processing people according to their criminal history and not just their immigration status. New enforcement mandates directing agents to identify and track "criminal aliens" in their arrest statistics gave border agents authority to distinguish "criminal" from "undocumented aliens." The new directives established and expanded a criminal alien category that differs from "illegal" status.

New enforcement priorities (that inflict criminal stigma) institutionalize a form of criminalization that differs from illegalization (the act of imposing illegal status).[26] Illegalization imposes a status of nonbelonging. It relegates people to "spaces of non-existence."[27] It marginalizes people. But it is not inherently a permanent status. Presumably one could alter or adjust immigration status, becoming a legal resident and eventually a naturalized citizen.[28] Unlike "illegal status," criminal status sticks. The criminal stigma, which for Black and brown youth gets assigned well before arrest and lasts beyond the initial punishment, inflicts "permanent marginalization."[29] The punitive turn in migration control, particularly the way it imposes a lasting criminal stigma via new enforcement priorities and criminal alien classification, then, must be understood in the context of a historically imposed connection between blackness and criminality.[30]

However, criminalization is not just the application of laws and policies from above. Federal immigration agents' relation to local players in the field (civil- and human-rights activists, the Mexican Consulate, or local law enforcement, for instance) shapes enforcement actions—at times in the opposite direction of stated policy goals. In the post–civil rights borderlands, local (and national) struggles over migrants and border residents as criminals or rights bearers have created a different enforcement landscape than post-9/11 terrorism and border security discourses would have us believe.

Overview of the Book

Arizona has played a historic role in immigration politics and criminal justice policymaking. It is an important site for analyzing post–civil rights border policing that combines some of the most punitive approaches to migration control with seemingly contradictory practices to safeguard migrant rights. The Arizona-Sonora borderland straddles state and federal laws that target immigrants, predominantly Latina/o citizens, and residents in border communities. It has some of the highest levels of arrest, prosecution, sentencing, and deportation along the U.S.-Mexico border. Yet it is also home to one of the most dynamic border- and immigrant-rights movements in the country.[31] Chapter 1 draws on theories linking civil rights and mass incarceration to interpret how the Arizona-Sonora borderlands became ground zero for "prosecutorial" approaches to migration control that aggressively punish while purporting to safeguard rights.[32]

Today's federal mandate to target immigrants with criminal records has roots in the Department of Homeland Security's Criminal Alien Program, for which Congress used its legislative discretion to set new enforcement priorities and resources to purge noncitizens from jail and prisons in order to relieve prison overcrowding in the post–civil rights era of mass incarceration. CAP's success lies in congressional funding for biometric technology and detention beds necessary for "criminal alien" tracking and removal. Chapter 2 foregrounds the story of the current thirty-four-thousand-detention-bed mandate—which permits an unprecedented four hundred thousand deportations each year—in order to show the role that the Criminal Alien Program played in *centering enforcement priorities on criminal history* and blurring the lines between immigration and criminal law enforcement. However, the punitive turn in immigration enforcement is not necessarily a "backlash" to civil rights. Rather, the new immigration regime in place today operates within post–civil rights "antidiscrimination" constitutional frameworks in ways that recognize rights for certain "victims," while aggressively punishing and banishing those branded as criminal.

Implementing criminal enforcement priorities—even in a punitive state like Arizona—has not been automatic. On the contrary, the federal mandate evoked tensions among border agents, local law enforcement, immigrant advocates, and Mexican officials on the ground. Along the Arizona-Sonora border, this includes migrant-rights advocates such as NGOs or the Mexican Consulate, who publicly oppose the criminalization of migration and pressure the DHS to comply with civil- and human-rights norms. It also includes local police and sheriff's departments along the border whose budgets depend on revenue from cross-border commerce and do not see migration as a criminal act, or public defenders in the U.S. Attorney's Office—already overburdened by drug cases—who pushed back on criminally prosecuting unauthorized entry in mass hearings. Chapter 3 highlights the ways in which local actors eventually adopted DHS's criminal enforcement priorities while also engaged in humanitarian interventions and safeguarding migrant rights, within a post–civil rights enforcement terrain.

The criminal alien mandate requires that border agents direct enforcement resources toward high-priority targets, principally those with a criminal record. Rather than processing migrants according to explicit "racial" and "national" criteria, they now distinguish between victims and criminals. Chapter 4 examines how enforcement priorities rooted in the Criminal Alien Program have transformed arrest and removal practices on the border. Because agents apprehend only a small percentage of migrants with a criminal record, they must move to the next priority—such as violating a deportation order—in order to maximize use of detention beds. As new border crossers, first-time apprehended migrants are often those *least* likely to have a criminal record. They were able to leverage that noncriminal and "victim" status to access justice and other forms of relief. Those *most* likely to have a criminal record were border crossers with a longer history of settlement, particularly those who violated a deportation order in order to reunite with families in the United States. In this way, deportation emerges as a pipeline to prison.

New enforcement targets and deployment of more border patrol to the Arizona-Sonora borderlands have inadvertently involved agents more directly in local crime control. This is the flip side to the more familiar scenario of local police and sheriffs who carry out immigration enforcement. Chapter 5 considers the *overreach* of enforcement priorities on citizens and legal permanent residents in predominantly Latina/o border communities who are suspected of or charged with immigration crimes. This differs from the more familiar ways in which law enforcement in Phoenix explicitly (and unapologetically) engages in racial profiling to police brown people. In communities along the international boundary, enforcement practices target residents on criminal grounds, as suspected smugglers. This deflects the racially disproportionate impact on border residents of Mexican ancestry, who are U.S. citizens and legal permanent residents, and generates local support for crime control, even by those it targets.

What does it mean to link "citizenship rights to a person's criminal history"?[33] Previous chapters having laid out the history and street-level practices surrounding new enforcement priorities, chapter 6 reflects on the Department of Justice's recent criminal justice reforms, and the Department of Homeland Security's new Priority Enforcement Program, designed to target "felons, not families." Evaluating border crossers and borderlanders on the basis of criminal history institutionalizes new forms of criminalization that differ from historic practices of illegalization. The concluding chapter reflects on this shifting enforcement arena and on the global diffusions of criminal enforcement priorities and considers the implications for migrant advocates and academics concerned with race and democracy.

1

The Post–Civil Rights Borderland

The Arizona-Sonora Border

"In this country, you have a number of rights in the court if you are accused of an offense," explains a judge to a group of sleep-deprived and handcuffed undocumented migrants in a federal courthouse in Tucson, Arizona. "You have the right to remain silent, not incriminate yourself. You have the right to a trial to contest charges. The federal government must prove you're guilty through witnesses and documents. A judge then determines whether you are guilty based on evidence. By pleading guilty today, you are giving up those rights."[1]

"But there are other consequences of your guilty plea," the judge goes on to say. "You will be deported and removed. Your fingerprints were taken, entered into a computer. If you come back, violate the law again, the charge becomes an aggravated offense." Through a translator the judge asks the group, "I have your plea agreements that you signed. Did you sign your plea agreements?"

They respond with a prerehearsed "sí."

"Did your attorney explain your charges?" asks the judge.

"Sí."

"Did anyone have difficulty understanding?" the judge continues.

"No."

"Are you pleading guilty to reentry?" he asks.

"Sí."

"Are you agreeing not to appeal your case?"

"Sí."

Since 2005, U.S. Border Patrol agents have referred apprehended migrants, mostly men from Mexico, Central America, and other Latin American countries, to the United States Attorney's Office for criminal prosecution under a federal program known as Operation Streamline.[2] In clothes still dusty from running through the Sonoran Desert at night, they fill polished courtroom benches, waiting to plead guilty to unlawful entry or reentry. Since these are criminal trials, migrants, now criminal defendants, are entitled, by law, to a court-appointed attorney.[3] The U.S. Attorney's Office assigns a federal public defender to represent multiple defendants in a single hearing.

Federal district courts don't have the capacity to criminally prosecute every undocumented migrant caught crossing the border without authorization. To manage the volume, magistrate judges conduct "fast-track" hearings en masse, and, in the case of Arizona, process around seventy migrants a day. Through a translator, the judge addresses every exhausted migrant individually. "Mr. Zaragoza-Galvan. Are you a citizen of Mexico?" The defendant responds affirmatively in English—an indicator that he'd been living in the United States for some time. The judge turns to the court interpreter and insists that the defendant respond in Spanish.

"Are you a citizen of Mexico, sir?"

"Sí."

"Did you enter through Sasabe, Arizona?"

"Sí."

"Were you previously removed from Nogales, Arizona?"

"Sí."

The magistrate judge turns to the next defendant. "Ms. Vargas-Lopez, are you a citizen of Guatemala?"

"Sí."

"Did you enter near Sasabe, Arizona?"

"Sí."

"Did you make an application or request permission to enter [the United States] with an immigration official?"

"No."

The judge questions each defendant individually. "Mr. Zaragoza-Galvan, how do you plead?"

"*Culpable*," he responds.

"Ms. Vargas-Lopez, how do you plead?"

"*Culpable*."

One after another replies, "*culpable*," "*culpable*," "*culpable*."

The judge orders prison sentences ranging from 65 to 165 days, admonishing some with stern words: "Didn't I tell you in this same court that if you came back you would be sentenced to prison?" After the hearing, the men and women exit the courtroom in single file, their heads hanging as they shuffle, still in shackles, through a side entrance to serve their prison sentences, then be deported.

* * *

The punitive turn in immigration enforcement is unusual even though unauthorized entry and reentry after deportation have been on the books as a misdemeanor and felony, respectively, since Congress passed the Immigration Act of March 4, 1929. Throughout the twentieth century, Border Patrol agents largely handled unauthorized entry as a civil rather than criminal offense.[4] Even when the former Immigration Service fell under the Department of Justice, the immigration and criminal justice systems operated independently.[5] Immigration enforcement's objective has been to regulate, not punish, migration across international borders.[6] Criminal law enforcement, on the other hand, relies on punishment, imprisonment, and has been oriented toward local crime control.[7] Even the rights that each system affords differ.[8] The immigration system mostly recognizes due process rights—the right to a trial, or protection from "arbitrary" or "capricious" enforcement—whereas the criminal justice system presupposes the substantive rights such as protection from unreasonable search and seizure (the Fourth Amendment), double jeopardy (the Fifth Amendment), or the right to be represented by an attorney (the Sixth Amendment).[9]

This "tough-on-crime" approach to migration control embodied in Streamline is most puzzling, because it is occurring at a time when the federal government is scaling back on the "lock 'em up" policies of the last forty years.[10] After a ravaging War on Drugs campaign created a prison system that locks up African Americans at a rate eight times higher than that of whites, for the first time in forty years, even punitive states like Texas have begun to reduce their prison populations. Other states have introduced or passed legislation reducing mandatory minimum sentences for low-level offenders, opting for drug treatment over incarceration, allowing early release for good behavior, limiting solitary confinement, and abandoning the death penalty.[11]

In 2013, former attorney general Eric Holder declared that "we cannot prosecute our way to becoming a safer nation. . . . [I]t is time to rethink the nation's system of mass imprisonment." Yet criminal arrests and prosecution for immigration offenses were trending upward, even as the attorney general publicly announced a commitment to "reforming the criminal justice system in the twenty-first century."[12] This occurred despite a 47% drop in migrant apprehensions after the Great Recession in 2008.[13]

Immigration has surpassed drug violations as the leading charge that sends people to prison, precisely when Congress enacted long-overdue reforms to reduce sentencing disparities between crack and powdered cocaine under the 2010 Fair Sentencing Act.[14] It is immigration prosecution, not drug laws, that is increasingly driving incarceration trends. And these arrests occur mostly on the U.S.-Mexico border.

Today, frontline Border Patrol agents have been given tremendous power to decide whom to stop, question, and arrest, as well as whom to criminally prosecute, detain, or deport due to prior criminal history. The political choice to go after certain enforcement targets is not new. What is new is the shift from explicitly racial and ethno-national to criminal enforcement priorities.[15] Never before had the former INS relied so heavily on criminal processes to enforce immigration law or used criminal history as the primary criterion on which to base enforcement actions. Agents, as opposed to judges, have been given tremendous discretion to confer criminal stigma on some, while exercising favorable discretion toward and administering rights to "vulnerable groups." Such classifications as *criminals* or *victims* influenced who would be subjected to "legitimate" state violence during arrest and who would not; who would have access to basic procedural rights and who would not; who would be formally deported and barred from further entry and who would be granted a "voluntary return"; who would be released from detention and who would be mandatorily detained, criminally prosecuted, and incarcerated.[16] This shift in enforcement priorities away from exclusively "catching illegals" to also "tracking criminal aliens" is significant, marking new classifications and procedures, new funding streams, new institutional arrangements between the criminal justice and immigration systems, and ultimately a new enforcement terrain.

The Punitive Turn

Over the last several decades, federal immigration laws have turned immigration offenses into punishable crimes or have expanded the immigration consequences for criminal convictions.[17] State laws have also imposed additional criminal penalties for federal immigration offenses by making it a state crime to be undocumented or by defining unauthorized entry as "self-smuggling."[18]

What is driving the punitive turn in immigration? To understand this, I had to look outside the immigration literature. Though I am trained as a migration specialist, I think the most compelling explanations are found in scholarship on punishment and society. Explanatory theories of this punitive turn fall into three general categories: instrumentalist (policy-oriented, efficacy-based arguments); constitutive (poststructuralist approaches that place greater emphasis on symbolic language or discourse); and structural approaches (that give equal if not more weight to material, in addition to discursive, dimensions of power). I shall examine each of these approaches in turn.

Legislators and policy makers typically justify the punitive turn as a security or crime-reduction measure.[19] Policy makers often refer to it as a shift from "catch-and-release" to "consequence-delivery" strategies.[20] Such crime-reduction logic is strikingly similar to that used to justify the "tough-on-crime" policies of the 1980s and 1990s, the very policies that legislators and policy makers are now beginning to scale back in other arenas.

In fact, critical criminologists, sociologists, and legal scholars have shown that the upsurge in mass incarceration was unrelated to crime rates. Incarceration rates were rising as crime itself was in decline, and vastly increased rates of imprisonment had no effect on crime levels.[21] Rather, it was a change in the laws themselves, the shift to mandatory minimum sentences or "zero tolerance" measures, that created the present conditions of mass incarceration. Similarly, migration scholars have shown that punitive laws, and not crime levels or security threats, are driving the rise in federal sentencing for immigration offenses.[22]

Another approach, which is attuned to the power of language and classification, considers punishment's cultural and expressive aspects.[23] Jonathon Simon and Malcolm Feeley's "new penology" framework interprets the punitive turn toward mass imprisonment as both a cause and an effect of new discourses, objectives, and classifications, all concerned with predicting dangerousness and managing risk.[24] In later work, Simon associates this focus on risk management with social anxiety over transnational flows of immigrants and refugees, vanishing jobs, labor protections, and a safety net in the global economy.[25] Some scholars have adapted Simon and Feeley's "new penology" framework to an immigration context, while others have drawn on Simon's later work that theorizes the so-called War on Crime as generalized form of governance, extending beyond the criminal justice system to families, schools, and the workplace.[26] Others have taken a risk-metrics approach that critically analyzes how statistics are used to "determine" the offending levels of specific social groups, with particular focus on how classification techniques create new enforcement targets.[27]

Related perspectives focus on how language and discourse have the power to create "moral panics," or public anxiety over an issue, and fear of crime, which lead to more punitive social control in order to "evaluate, classify, and react" to those perceived to be a threat.[28] Similarly, securitization scholars examine how political actors and the media or other institutions construct migration as a criminal threat by associating immigrants with smuggling, trafficking, and terrorism; as an economic threat to employment, wages, and welfare; as a social threat to national culture and identity; and as a political threat to existing power structures enacted through elections and other forms of political participation.[29]

Yet another approach considers economic and social forces shaping the field of punishment alongside the cultural and political.[30] Scholarship on neoliberalism and punishment identifies the links between a "neoliberal remaking of the state" and hyperincarceration in the United States.[31] Sociologist Loïc Wacquant argues that it is not "generic 'risks' and 'anxieties'" but "specific *social* insecurity" generated by the deregulation of wage labor, rising income inequality (and shifting racial hierarchies that once gave exclusive honor and social status to whites) that is driving the punitive turn. "The sudden expansion . . . of the penal state after the 1970s," says Wacquant, "is but a ruling class response aiming to redefine the perimeter and missions of [the state] so as to establish a new economic regime based on capital hypermobility and labor flexibility and to curb the social turmoil generated . . . by the public policies of market deregulation and social welfare retrenchment that are the core building blocks of neoliberalism."[32]

For scholars of neoliberalism and punishment, the punitive turn, and the concurrent growth of prisons, emerged to manage "deregulated labor" or to "warehouse" workers who have been marginalized by labor deskilling, welfare reform, and disinvestment in impoverished neighborhoods.[33] Similarly, migration and border scholars have argued that punitive approaches to migration control arose in order to manage global flows of migrant workers displaced by neoliberal reforms, particularly the expansion of free trade agreements and the adoption of free-market policies that lower labor protections and wages, cut back safety nets, and displace traditional industries unable to compete with global competitors. Others have gone further to argue that neoliberal discourses of individual moral responsibility have reorganized immigration and border enforcement in ways that produce distinctions between "responsible," "law-abiding" citizens and "irresponsible" and "deviant" noncitizens.[34]

A related perspective, and one that migration scholars seldom consider, concerns historical intersections between democracy and punishment. Here I refer to a growing literature that theorizes the links between civil rights and mass incarceration. The most common argument presents the punitive turn as a backlash against civil rights, codified in landmark legislation such as the Civil Rights and Voting Rights acts. Others see mass incarceration as a response to the civil rights movement and rights revolution.[35] Katherine Beckett, for instance, analyzed how politicians cast civil rights protests and urban riots as street crimes. This racial rhetoric linking civil rights protests to crime, she argues, led to the era of mass incarceration.[36] Jonathon Simon argues that out of "the crisis of the New Deal," crime emerged as a vehicle through which conservative elites would construct a new political order.[37] In her theory of "frontlash," Vesla Weaver shows how the punitive turn "developed out of the struggles of the 1960s" as opponents of civil rights mobilized new issues (e.g., crime) to alter the playing field in a way favorable to their interests.[38] Such perspectives on race, punishment, and democracy reframe policing and enforcement, taking it from a law-and-order issue to one of the most important racial-justice and civil-rights issues of our time.[39]

These studies invite further theorization of the connections between civil rights and mass incarceration, turning this seeming paradox on its head and suggesting that the two trends (expanded civil rights and greater punishment) might actually go hand in hand. Political scientist Naomi Murakawa's groundbreaking work, for instance, shows how civil rights liberalism helped to build what she calls a "civil rights carceral state."[40] Liberal demands to do something about racial violence committed by whites culminated in reforms that ultimately *expanded* the criminal justice system. Such liberal reforms, she argues, took the form of punishing individual hate crimes as opposed to addressing the root causes of systemic violence, and eliminating bias in the criminal justice system by instituting race-blind procedural reforms rather than addressing the criminal justice system's historic and systemic role in racial violence. Similarly, feminist criminologist Beth Richie's work examines how the professionalization of the antiviolence movement—particularly mainstream liberal feminists' use of the criminal justice system to advance women's rights—also expanded the prison system in ways that disproportionately target, and perpetuate state violence against, Black women.[41]

Such connections between civil rights and punishment resonate with my own observations in an immigration enforcement context, where struggles over due process and procedural protections in the immigration system are directly linked to the criminalization of migration. The recent rise of "race-neutral" criminal enforcement priorities in the immigration system are rooted in civil rights struggles over due process and equality under the law. Criminal classifications give the illusion of a race-blind immigration system that, considering the United States' history of racial immigration quotas on admissions and similar bars to citizenship, has never been race-blind. Classifying immigrants under the apparently race-neutral rubric of "criminals" masks a long history of systemic racial violence in border policing and immigration enforcement. It creates apparently race-blind distinctions between legitimate forms of state violence against "criminal aliens" and illegitimate forms of violence against migrant "crime victims" and "vulnerable groups" deemed worthy of state protection.

* * *

Theorizing the links between mass incarceration and civil rights provides a useful lens through which to analyze the punitive turn in immigration.

At the core are struggles over whether immigrants are "criminals" or rights-bearing individuals. And yet this perspective has been largely overlooked in what some scholars call "crimmigration" studies. There is a widespread assumption that immigrants are outside the political system as noncitizens or undocumented migrants. There is a tendency to conceptualize criminalization (of immigration) *in opposition* to rights. In "The Crimmigration Crisis," for instance, Juliet Stumpf states that ex-offenders experience an exclusion parallel to that experienced by noncitizens, marking an "ever-expanding group of outsiders by denying them the privileges that citizens hold, such as the right to vote or to remain in the United States."[42] Similarly, Lisa Marie Cacho theorizes the ways in which race and gender structure the political exclusion of "illegal aliens" and "criminals" from society through processes of criminalization and "racialized rightlessness" that devalue human lives.[43] However, this does not accord with actual immigration enforcement on the ground. In practice, not all undocumented immigrants are uniformly denied rights and classified as dangerous or punishable by the state.[44] Indeed, some are deemed "worthy" of state protection, while others are branded permanently "rightless" by virtue of a criminal conviction.

"Crimmigration" scholars argue that the convergence of immigration and criminal law undermines rights.[45] This is not a fact I would dispute, and it is one I return to in this book's conclusion. However, in the day-to-day practices, criminal branding of some noncitizens happens alongside recognition of rights for others. There are ways in which criminalization operates within, not in opposition to, a constitutional framework and appropriates civil rights norms.

Here I am not referring to actual laws, because on the books noncitizens have few guaranteed substantive rights. But on the Arizona-Sonora border, for instance, I was struck by how local struggles over immigrant rights and security influenced enforcement decisions on the ground. Local actors—including border agents, NGOs, vigilantes, and even migrants themselves—simultaneously drew on rights protocols and crime-control measures, often leaning on the criminal justice system as a way to administer or gain access to rights and justice. Border agents in both the United States and Mexico mobilize these discourses when they act as prosecutors and protectors. Immigrants draw on these frameworks when they plead guilty to illegal entry in exchange for their liberty from immigrant detention or prison. Even vigilantes draw on both crime and rights discourses when they define their "citizens' arrests" as "enforcing the law through the rule of law." In other words, the political and economic terrain in which Border Patrol agents, detention and removal officers, and others make decisions about enforcement has been profoundly altered by civil rights struggles, on the one hand, and, on the other, by crime as a political solution to demands for equality and justice.[46]

Drawing then on the historical connections between mass incarceration and struggles for civil rights, I conceptualize the relation between criminalization and civil rights *not as antithetical or directly opposed, but as integrally linked and complementary.*

This carceral liberalism perspective," a phrase I use to refer to the multilayered symbiosis of criminalization and rights, frames my own analysis of the transformation of enforcement—from the roots of new criminal priorities to the transformation of policing practices and the economic and political landscape in which this all plays out. By adopting this perspective, I am not only interested in interplays of rights and crime as political rhetoric or discourse. In my view, rhetoric and discourse are never far removed from the social relations and power dynamics that created them. Rather, I draw on both symbolic and structural approaches in order to understand the material, social roots of new enforcement priorities and how these new criminal classifications in turn create a new enforcement context.[47]

In Arizona, for example, elites succeeded in describing a desire to be free from a fear of crime as a "civil right." In doing so, they successfully reframed civil rights as a law-and-order issue. This law-and-order platform brought conservatives to power in Arizona and the United States. The "get-tough" policies and prison boom that ensued played a critical role in creating the INS's Criminal Alien Program, which instituted new, "race-blind" criminal enforcement priorities and led to a convergence between the immigration and criminal justice systems.

These new criminal enforcement priorities rooted in the Criminal Alien Program made their way back to Arizona as a way to manage unauthorized border crossings in the 1990s. Some Arizona politicians have embraced enforcement priorities, and prosecutorial approaches to managing migration more broadly, as a strategy to stem immigration's impact on the state's changing demographics, economy, and electorate. But new enforcement priorities have not been easy to implement, since Arizona is home to one of the most dynamic immigrant- and border-rights movements in the country. The Arizona-Sonora border, then, is an important site at which to examine how criminalization takes hold in a post–civil rights context.

Before turning to a short history of the Criminal Alien Program in the next chapter, followed by an ethnographic account of how it was implemented and how it transformed immigration enforcement, it is necessary to provide some background on Arizona's historic role in immigration politics and policymaking.

Goldwater's Arizona

Arizona's political and economic landscape looks very different from the way it did when copper mining, cotton and citrus farming, and cattle ranching dominated Arizona's economy. In the early twentieth century, its racial hierarchy placed "whites" at the top, followed by "foreigners" from Southern and Eastern Europe, and Mexicans and indigenous Arizonans at the bottom.[48] This racial hierarchy for workers maintained a dual wage system for Whites and Mexicans, who dominated the labor force in smelters and local farms and ranches.[49] Railroads transported seasonal migrant workers and minerals between U.S.-owned mines in the neighboring state of Sonora, Mexico, and smelters in border towns like Douglas, Arizona. And by 1920, Mexicans were 60% of the labor force in smelters.[50]

Copper, cattle, and cotton industries and growers' political power in the early twentieth century shaped enforcement priorities and discretion at the time, which fluctuated between looking the other way when labor demand was high or deporting radical immigrant workers during some of the most violently repressed labor strikes in history.[51] Tremendous labor radicalism and strikes throughout Arizona during this period eventually won workers the eight-hour work day, child labor laws, workers' compensation, and even a commission to regulate businesses.

In the postwar period, business elites in Phoenix pushed to diversify and transform Arizona's economy by competing for government defense contracts and attracting high-tech manufacturing to the state.

Between 1950 and 1977, high-tech manufacturing firms from aerospace and electronics industries like General Electric, Motorola, IBM, Intel, Garret Corporation, and Hughes Aircraft began operating in Arizona. By the 1960s, manufacturing, spurred by successful bids for government defense contracts, had become a major growth industry in Arizona, concentrated primarily in the Tucson and Phoenix metropolitan areas.[52]

Arizona's service economy grew. Rapid population growth stimulated a demand for clerical, sales, managerial, transportation, food preparation, banking, legal, health, and maintenance services in the Tucson and Phoenix metropolitan areas, where 75% of the state population resides.[53] Financial, health, hotel and restaurant services, and retail trade expanded to serve one of the fastest-growing states in the country.

To cultivate a "pro-business" climate, Phoenix-based business leaders first had to dismantle the old New Deal political structure and its philosophy of government regulation. Arizona had been staunchly Democratic in the 1930s and 1940s, and it had one of the most progressive constitutions in the union.[54] Reviving the Arizona Republican Party was the vehicle through which local elites successfully launched a political offensive against New Deal liberalism.[55]

"Pro-growth" elites in the Phoenix Chamber of Commerce successfully mobilized to revive the Arizona Republican Party by launching campaigns to unseat Democrats in city and state government.[56] Among them, Barry Goldwater, whose family owned a chain of department stores (Goldwater's), campaigned to elect more Republicans into city government and the state legislature. Goldwater himself ran for Senate and won in 1952 on an anti-union platform challenging New Deal liberalism. Once they dominated the state legislature, Republicans pushed free market policies of low taxation, minimal government intervention, anti-unionism, and cheap land for industry.[57] Historian Elizabeth Shermer refers to this as a state-dependent brand of neoliberalism that drew on government to create a political climate favorable to business.

Arizona Republicans successfully ran their campaigns on anti–New Deal, law-and-order, "tough-on-crime" platforms, partly in response to struggles for civil rights. In Phoenix, multiracial progressive alliances challenged discrimination and segregation in schools, employment, housing, and public accommodations. In 1967, race riots broke out against police brutality and economic and political marginalization of minorities.[58]

Well before Reagan passed what is known as the biggest crime bill in U.S. history—the 1984 Comprehensive Crime Control Act—Arizona introduced its first mandatory minimum sentencing reforms in 1975 and, as a result, struggled with prison overcrowding.[59] In 1977, the American Civil Liberties Union won an injunction to stop admitting new inmates into the main prison in Florence, Arizona, where severe overcrowding provoked extreme violence against inmates, prisoner strikes, and riots.[60]

Long before the United States began to imprison African American and Latinas/os at a disproportionate rate, Arizona's prison population was already predominantly Latina/o, Black, and Native American. In 1959, whites made up less than half (45%) of Arizona's prison population even though they totaled over 90% of the population at the time.[61] "Spanish Americans," "Negroes," and "Indians" made up 35%, 11%, and 9%, respectively.[62] Despite the federal injunction to relieve overcrowding, the Arizona legislature passed sweeping sentencing reforms in 1978 that dramatically increased prison sentences and diminished judges' discretion to reduce sentences or release inmates to relieve overcrowding, and did so again in 1982.[63] This greatly exacerbated the existing prison bed shortage, to which the Arizona Department of Corrections responded (with support from the state legislature) by releasing some noncitizen inmates to the INS, erecting tents acquired from the U.S. military, and building new prisons around the state.[64]

Prison construction—which the Arizona state legislature funded generously while promoting fiscal conservatism, limited government, and low taxes—became a viable economic development strategy in border and rural communities. In the 1970s and 1980s, the Douglas, Bisbee, and Nogales, Arizona, border economies experienced steady decline. Traditional industries like mining, agriculture, and retail were losing ground. By 1984, twelve mines had shut down, costing thousands of jobs. In 1987, the Phelps Dodge Corporation, a major employer in Southern Arizona, closed its operations in Douglas and Bisbee, Arizona, resulting in hundreds of lost mining jobs and white flight. The agricultural sector showed similar downward trends. In 1940, there were 18,468 active farms; by 1982, there were 7,334, most of which were concentrated in Maricopa and Yuma counties.[65] The Mexican economic crisis in the

early 1980s and peso devaluations further weakened the retail industry that depended on shoppers from northern Mexico, who crossed the
border on foot to shop in border towns, spending over $300 million
yearly.[66]

Arizona's growth model created disparities between Phoenix and border towns, like Douglas/Agua Prieta and Ambos Nogales, whose populations are predominantly Latina/o and poor. In 1985, Maricopa County
(Phoenix) had among the lowest unemployment rates in the country
at 3.8%, while Santa Cruz County (Nogales) reported a 21% unemployment rate. Even in 2000, Arizona border counties were designated "high
poverty areas" where at least 20% of the population lived in poverty.[67]

Though still dependent on tourism and retail from cross-border
shoppers, border towns increasingly depended on government-sector
employment and the underground economy. By the 1990s, the federal
government was the largest employer in the border counties like Cochise and Santa Cruz. This included the Arizona Department of Corrections, the Department of Homeland Security (formerly the INS), the
Department of Justice, city and county offices, and local school districts.
A former mayor of Douglas, Arizona, summed it up this way:

> The city of Douglas has gone through a lot of transformations. The major
> employer here for years was the Phelps Dodge Mining Company. They
> had a smelter that employed the majority of people in town. It was the
> biggest source of income as far as salaries were concerned. . . . When
> they closed the smelter down they lost all those jobs and, uh, other little
> things have happened here like the cattle industry . . . and mining. . . .
> [W]hen those things waned and they went away we became more and
> more dependent on northern Mexico. . . . The major industry here now
> is the [Arizona] Department of Corrections. We have a state prison here.
> We have a DUI center. They're responsible for all the local jobs. . . . That
> is not good news to us because all of those are publicly funded agencies.
> We don't have the one private industry that we really need to give us the
> impetus to take off.[68]

Arizona border towns continue to serve as transportation hubs for both
licit and illicit trade, which also impacts border economies. Today the
railroad lines and commercial vehicles transport human cargo and nar-

cotics. In the 1980s, drug interdiction operations on the Florida coast redirected drug flows to the Mexico border.[69] Arizona-Sonora border towns' history as a transportation and trade route made them particularly suitable for the drug industry. Even after the government stepped up interdiction efforts at the border, smugglers continued to transport shipments by hiring local residents to transport smaller shipments through and between ports of entry with backpacks and on foot. "Let's take a cartel that specializes in cocaine," explained a local law enforcement official:

> Cocaine is grown and produced in South America. Then it has to be transported through some kind of clandestine means from there to Mexico, where it's staged. On the other side it's warehoused and then distributed and transported across the border to another stash house somewhere in this country. Most of the contraband that comes through us is ultimately warehoused in Tucson, where it's distributed to all points—north, south, east, and west from there, mostly to the East and West Coast. . . . It involves tremendous criminal networks. . . . We had a network whose primary transport—people who were actually being paid to transport narcotics that were brought across the border—were high school kids, students getting anywhere from five hundred to twenty-five hundred dollars to take daddy's car, load up a truck load of marijuana, and drive it to Tucson.[70]

By the late 1990s, Arizona had become a major staging ground for unauthorized border crossings and human smuggling. Border Patrol operations in El Paso, Texas (1993), San Diego, California (1994), and Nogales, Arizona (1995), shifted migratory and smuggling routes to the Arizona-Sonora desert. From there, local smugglers, or coyotes, transported migrants through to Tucson and Phoenix, where they coordinated transportation to destinations throughout the United States.

As the federal government escalated its immigration control, organized human smuggling networks proliferated, generating significant employment and revenue in these economically marginalized areas. The fact that Agua Prieta was the largest staging area for illegal crossing was a tremendous boost to its economy, explains a government official:

[C]asa de huespedes, or hotels . . . went up all over the city of Agua Prieta. . . . They were of the very, very cheapest kind. A lot of them didn't have restroom facilities. They'd be simply one room—you would be astounded how many people they would fit in one room. . . . Near those hotels or casa de huespedes they put up all kinds of restaurants with cheap food. . . . They also had a lot of what they call changarros—changarro is a food stand, a movable food stand—and they were all over the streets here. And the food was burritos and aguita [water] . . . and it was all those people needed. It wasn't anything extravagant and far from it. It was just enough to sustain them until they jumped the border. They sold cheap canned goods and bottled water. Generally all that was bought over here in Douglas and taken back across the border.[71]

Today, cross-border consumption, law enforcement, and drug and human smuggling sustain border economies.[72] A high-ranking law enforcement official summed it up in this way:

Fifteen years ago there were maybe forty Border Patrol agents in Cochise County. Today in the entire Tucson sector there are fifteen hundred. DEA has a fully staffed office. FBI has a fully staffed office. [U.S.] Customs has built up an enormous contingent. . . . None of this existed fifteen years ago. The point that I'm trying to make is that government is the major employer in Cochise County, with very little industry . . . but there's a tremendous amount of industry built up around combating illegal drug trade and the people-smuggling trade that really has helped maintain the economy. That's why you'll never see legalization of marijuana and other substances, because the economy would collapse. [Chuckle.] There's too much money in it, built on both sides of the industry—both smuggling and combating, hundreds and thousands of jobs depend upon that element of the economy.[73]

Rapid growth and economic change in Arizona generated major population shifts in the Arizona-Sonora borderlands. Phoenix's population was 65,000 in 1940 and had grown to 105,000 in 1950. It is now the fifth-largest city in the United States, with a population of 1.6 million. Tucson's population grew from 35,000 to 213,000 between 1940 and 1960. By 2010, its population was 520,000. High-tech manufacturing jobs drew middle-class whites to the state, but they also drew immigrants to fill low-wage jobs in the service sector. Arizona continues to be one of the fastest-growing states, with net immigration accounting for the increase.

Migration patterns have also changed, not only in terms of increased volume but also in terms of character. Regional migrants from Sonora no longer dominate migration flows. With fewer jobs, regional migrants no longer labor in farms, mines, or cattle ranches and then return to their communities. The dominant flows through the Arizona-Sonora border are long-distance migrants transiting through border towns en route to major cities throughout the United States or settling in Phoenix or Tucson. "I've lived here all my life and there was a time when there wasn't even a fence down there," explains a local official.

> People would come across the border to work or visit, but then they would go back. Few would come across to go to other destinations. That changed drastically. . . . [T]he people that we're looking at now are not coming to stay in Douglas, Arizona. They're coming to go to all the factories and the agriculture and the hotels and the motels, and all the service jobs that they are largely responsible for now. They're transitional, you know. They're just moving through.[74]

The neighboring state of Sonora also experienced rapid population and migratory shifts. Like the businesspeople in Phoenix, Mexican elites in Sonora also supported a "pro-growth" neoliberal agenda. They supported the Mexican government's move to create deregulated, anti-union free trade zones along the border that attracted *maquilas* or assembly plants for foreign export. In 1979, there were 75 plants in Sonora employing 16,705 Mexican migrant workers.[75] By 1990, there were over 100 plants employing an estimated 37,000 workers, 90% of them women working long hours at low pay and living in unincorporated *colonias*, or squatter settlements without potable water, paved roads, or electricity.[76] The *maquiladoras* drew migrants from all over Mexico and also spurred rapid population growth in north Mexican border cities.

Demographic shifts have produced particular tensions for Arizona. On one hand, its rapid growth gave the state greater influence in national politics through more representation in the House and votes in the Electoral College.[77] On the other hand, immigration and population growth generated from its neoliberal model is shifting the state's demographics. Arizona's Latina/o population doubled between 1990 and 2010 and is expected to become a majority-minority state over the next two decades. That Latinas/os now account for over 20% of the state's electorate, with over 60% of Latina/o voters (and as high as 80% in recent elections) supporting Democratic candidates has important political ramificatons for a Republican state like Arizona.[78]

Border security operations and agents' day-to-day practices on the ground must be understood within this network of power relations, an arena vastly different from that of 1924, when Congress established the Border Patrol. Growers' political influence in Arizona has waned; labor demands alone cannot fully account for an agent's decision to prosecute criminally for an immigration offense. New economic and political landscapes have introduced actors to which Border Patrol must be accountable—new elites, anti-immigrant-rights groups, and border-rights groups. Yet this new enforcement terrain does not end at state lines. Arizona is and has been an important player in national politics, and its political and economic history has deeply informed national immigration debates and congressional action.

"Arizonafication" of U.S. Immigration Politics

In 1964, Arizona Senator Barry Goldwater ran for president on a conservative, pro-business, law-and-order platform.[79] Though he lost, Goldwater's outspoken views on low taxes, anti-unionism, small government, and law and order made him the national spokesperson for the modern conservative movement. His presidential campaign ignited a spark that reshaped the Republican Party, gave rise to the New Right, and laid the foundation for Ronald Reagan to win the presidency in 1980.[80]

Goldwater's prestige and connections gave Arizona Republicans access to political and business elites, CEOs and politicians in Washington who would influence federal policy in order to promote and protect a "business climate." Goldwater and Arizona Republicans took their political and economic agenda in Arizona to a national scale.

Goldwater's influence also gave Arizona Republicans access to prominent positons in the GOP.[81] Under the Nixon administration, Goldwater recommended William Rehnquist and Richard Kleindienst for posts within the Department of Justice. In 1969, William Rehnquist, who practiced law in Phoenix and was active in the Arizona Republican Party between 1953 and 1969, became assistant attorney general to the Office of Legal Counsel. Sharing Goldwater's views on law and order, Rehnquist supported pretrial detention, wire tapping, and capital punishment. Nixon appointed Rehnquist to the Supreme Court in 1971. Goldwater also recommended Richard Kleindienst, who had served as chairman of the Arizona Republican Party, to the Department of Justice. Nixon promoted Kleindienst from deputy to attorney general in 1972 during the Watergate scandal. Showing his loyalty to Nixon, Kleindienst resigned in 1973. Kliendienst was also a close friend of Rehnquist, who recused himself when the Supreme Court reviewed the Watergate case.[82]

Goldwater also influenced Ronald Reagan's appointment of Sandra Day O'Conner, a two-term Republican senator and former assistant attorney general in Arizona, to the Supreme Court in 1981, as well as Rehnquist's promotion from associate to chief justice of the Court in 1986.[83] Both shared the economic and political views for which Goldwater became famous. They were free-market conservatives known especially for devolving federal power to states on issues ranging from criminal justice to immigration. Arizona's political trajectory then has greatly influenced the direction of the country as a whole—particularly the rise of neoliberal reforms marked by privatization, deregulation, devolution, cuts in social spending, and mass incarceration.

Arizona Republicans' position on national immigration issues, however, has been more nuanced. Because of cross-border trade with Mexico and ties between Arizona and Sonoran economic elites, Republicans from Barry Goldwater to John McCain have supported immigration reform. Early Arizona Republicans like Goldwater did not campaign on an anti-immigration platform the way they do today. They maintained business relationships with Sonoran elites and depended on cheap Mexican labor for Arizona's booming service economy.[84] They also relied on Mexican American voters to put Republicans into office and to help undermine unions that had historically discriminated against Mexican workers. Goldwater himself was a member of the Alianza Hispanica.[85] Arizona Republicans then have not always had hard-line views on immigration. Historian Geraldo Cadava writes that in the postwar era, cross-border relations between Arizonan and Sonoran elites took precedence over border security. Back then Arizona politicians were more likely to push "to open borders than to close them."[86]

Still, Arizona's historic influence on national immigration debates should not be understated. In the 1980s, Reagan reinstated immigrant detention, prompting the Tucson Border Patrol to detain and deport, often to their death, Central American migrants fleeing U.S.-backed civil wars in Central America. This violated the 1980 Refugee Act, which former Democratic president Jimmy Carter had signed into law. At the time, the federal government refused to acknowledge Central American migrants as refugees because they were fleeing U.S.-backed torture regimes, which the United States had labeled "democracies."

Arizona became the birthplace for one of most important post–civil rights movements for immigrant rights—the Sanctuary movement.[87] In Tucson, the Manzo Area Council, a local War on Poverty program, began providing legal services to Central Americans crossing the Arizona-Sonora border after "a [Salvadoran] woman showed up to our office with a bullet lodged in her body."[88] Manzo members challenged Central American refugees' detentions and deportations in strategic alliances with local churches that would later become the stronghold of the Sanctuary movement.[89]

Arizona's political influence on national immigration debates, then, mostly aligned with more favorable attitudes towards immigration. As unlawful detention and deportations continued, activists began helping undocumented refugees cross the border, as an act of "civil disobedience" whose inspiration was drawn from the Underground Railroad that helped enslaved African Americans reach freedom. In 1982, the Reverend John Fife declared the Tucson-based Southside Presbyterian Church a public sanctuary. Rendering aid to border crossers had long been customary in the Arizona-Sonora borderlands. After Manzo's public declaration, congregations all over the country followed suit in places like Chicago, Los Angeles, San Francisco, Boston, and New York. By 1987, hundreds of churches had declared sanctuary in twenty-eight cities, involving over seventy thousand volunteers.[90] Through litigation, legal services, and civil disobedience, they directly challenged enforcement practices on constitutional and moral grounds.

It wasn't until the 1990s that Arizona supported more punitive approaches to immigration control, when Border Patrol launched Operation Safeguard on the Arizona/Sonora border.[91] Safeguard is best known as a border control operation deploying one hundred more Border Patrol agents to Southern Arizona. It funded surveillance technologies such as low-level light cameras in Douglas and Nogales. It also procured helicopters, infrared radar equipment, and a comprehensive radio system and constructed a border fence in Naco, Nogales, and Douglas, made from excess landing strips from the first war with Iraq.

Safeguard's other aim was to strengthen criminal alien removal efforts. The operation provisioned staff and resources to prosecute and remove immigrants identified as criminal aliens. It funded computer equipment for fingerprint identification, for instance, to better identify criminal aliens. It allocated resources to fund the opening of a Mexico-based Grupo Beta office in Nogales, Sonora, with the intent to "reduce crime." (Grupo Beta began in Tijuana as the Instituto Nacional de Migración's enforcement arm, comprising Mexican local and federal law enforcement agents.) Safeguard also established a Law Enforcement Support Center (LESC) for information sharing between local law enforcement and immigration agents, as well as an Institutional Removal Hearing Program (IRHP) in the Eloy, Arizona, detention facility in order to allow detentions and deportations directly from prisons and jails. The IRHP removal hearings occurred within correctional facilities rather than immigration courts, under the Department of Justice, Executive Office of Immigration Review (EOIR). Furthermore, Safeguard expanded detention bed space for detained criminal aliens by one thousand, added new criminal penalties for immigration violations, and provided some money for reimbursement to local law enforcement agencies for costs associated with incarcerating aliens.[92]

Before Safeguard, the INS had already invested considerable resources for border control in Arizona and what it terms "criminal alien removal." By the 1990s, immigration agents were already enmeshed in drug enforcement along the Arizona-Sonora border, but it was Safeguard's launch in 1995, following the 1994 Violent Crime Control and Law Enforcement Act, that afforded the Tucson Sector the mandate—backed by more resources, personnel, and technology—to classify, prosecute, and deport immigrants on criminal grounds.

Safeguard arguably created more problems for Arizona than it promised to solve. Border agents' deployment to the border towns like Douglas and Nogales, for instance, pushed migration flows to remote desert areas, which are much harder to police. Human smuggling in Southern Arizona intensified, as did border crossings through the desert, straining local police and sheriff's department budgets, already taxed with handling drug arrests and convictions resulting from Arizona's harsh sentencing laws.

Police and sheriff's deputies in border counties complained that a substantial portion of their budgets went to immigration law enforcement. The Cochise County Sheriff's Office reported that 40% of the budget went toward responding to, investigating, prosecuting, and incarcerating immigrants. Nogales officials complained that citizens paid the price for enforcing immigration laws. According to a law enforcement official, "Illegal immigration is an issue between the United States and Mexico and yet local citizens pay for the cost of enforcing those federal laws. If one-third of our county budget is going for a federal issue, what's going for our schools? What's being invested into our streets, into our infrastructure? We just don't have the money."[93]

Deep tensions surfaced surrounding the state's changing population and its political ramifications, particularly as Border Patrol operations like Safeguard pushed migration and smuggling routes to Arizona. Safeguard incited conflict over civil- and human-rights issues closely linked with border enforcement—namely, racial profiling, raids, migrant deaths, and hate crimes. It triggered fiscal anxieties and deep-seated insecurities about immigration's impact on the state's social infrastructure—schools, hospitals, and the criminal justice system. Safeguard also reinvigorated debates about "state's rights," primarily to fend off constitutional challenges to state-level laws denying social services to immigrants or laws turning immigration offenses into state crimes.

In the late 1990s, conservative Arizonans responded privately to what they described as failed border policy by "taking matters into their own hands." In 1999, an Arizona rancher, Roger Barnett, made national headlines when he and his brother began privately arresting migrants and turning them over to the U.S. Border Patrol. Barnett helped found groups such as Concerned Citizens of Cochise County and the Arizona Ranchers Alliance in 1999 and the "Shadow Border Patrol" in 2000.[94]

In 2001, a congressional committee sponsored hearings on how the volume of unauthorized migration was impacting Southern Arizona. At the hearing in Douglas, Arizona, in Cochise County, public officials testified about the fiscal impact on the criminal justice and health care system, asking the government to cover expenditures related to immigration. Local ranchers dominated the hearing, voicing their anger at and criticism of the federal government for "not doing its job." Roger Barnett complained about debris, cut fences, and empty water tanks caused by migrant traffic on his leased land. "The only law enforcement out there is myself. . . . We need to take the law into our own hands"—a remark that was met with applause.[95]

In 2002, Chris Simcox, a former kindergarten teacher from California, founded the Civilian Homeland Defense and put out a call to form an armed militia group to patrol the border. That year "American Border Patrol" (not the U.S. Border Patrol) and another private border patrol group from Texas, Ranch Rescue, also began operating in Cochise County. In 2005, Chris Simcox and Jim Gilchrist, a retired CPA and Vietnam vet, created the Minuteman Project.[96]

Arizona's political climate in the 1990s also revived its immigrant- and border-rights movement. Local activists—formerly involved with Manzo Area Council and the Sanctuary movement—challenged Border Patrol misconduct and vigilante violence. In 1993, activists founded the Arizona Coalition for Human Rights/Coalición de Derechos Humanos after Border Patrol agents fatally shot Dario Miranda Valenzuela, a Nogales, Sonora, resident.[97]

In 2001, former sanctuary churches and newer organizations such as the faith-based Healing Our Border and the Southwest Alliance to Resist Militarization, founded in 1998, organized a Border Summit that gathered immigrant-rights activists from around the country to denounce national immigration and border policies. As border policing intensified and migrant deaths soared, new groups emerged, such as the faith-based Humane Borders (2000) and the Samaritan patrol (2002), founded after fourteen migrants died crossing the Arizona border in May 2001. In 2003, the Border Action Network (formerly the Southwest Alliance to Resist Militarization) launched grassroots organizing campaigns against Border Patrol abuses and vigilantism in the predominantly Latina/o border towns of Douglas and Nogales. In 2004, activists, including former Sanctuary and Manzo Area Council leaders, formed the "No More Deaths Coalition." Local activists joined national coalitions, lobbying in Congress and warning mainstream immigrant-rights groups in the interior against compromising and conceding to more border security.

The congressional response to political mobilization on immigration in Arizona was largely punitive. This included harsher sentencing for human smuggling, incentives for police/INS collaborations, stricter detention policies, and criminal prosecution for immigration offenses. Arizona politicians have also passed their own signature state laws that went beyond standard xenophobic anti-immigration ordinances to policies requiring state and local law enforcement to impose federal immigration law.

In 2004, right-wing state representative Russell Pearce drafted and helped pass Proposition 200, requiring proof of citizenship for anyone registering to vote or applying for public benefits in Arizona. Supporters criticized then governor Janet Napolitano, who publicly opposed it. To deflect criticism for being "soft" on immigration, Napolitano focused her attention on "criminal aliens" and instituted a Memorandum of Agreement under the 287(g) agreement, which deputized state personnel from the Arizona Department of Corrections and the Department of Public Safety to carry out civil immigration arrests and detention.[98]

In the same vein, the Arizona state legislature passed a state smuggling law in 2005 that made human smuggling a state-level felony. Local prosecutors interpreted the statute to include unauthorized immigrants as "conspirators" to smuggle. Maricopa County attorney Andrew Thomas and county sheriff Joe Arpio used the law to justify arresting and prosecuting undocumented immigrants on "self-smuggling" charges.[99] In 2006, Russell Pearce introduced and helped pass Proposition 100, which denied bail and instituted pretrial detention for immigrants convicted of crimes.[100] By 2006, the Arizona legislature had begun allocating state funds to criminally prosecute immigrants. In 2007, the Department of Corrections authorized ICE, under the DHS, to open an "ICE unit" within state correctional facilities.[101] In 2010, Pearce introduced the now-famous "Papers Please" law, or SB1070, which inspired similar state immigration laws around the country. SB1070 made it a state crime to be undocumented in Arizona and required all law enforcement to check immigration status during stops or arrests. The U.S. Supreme

Court upheld the "Papers Please" provision, while striking the measure that made unauthorized status a state misdemeanor.[102]

This then is the volatile context in which agents enforce immigration law on the Arizona-Sonora border. Front-line agents' enforcement actions reflect political pressure from above and below. From above, Congress and high-ranking officials in federal agencies, such as the Department of Homeland Security, impose mandates and resources that prioritize criminal aliens as high security risks. Agencies draft and circulate memos and operating instructions to regional directors in the Phoenix district and the chief Border Patrol agent for the Tucson Sector, which includes nine Border Patrol stations, each with its own supervisory agents. The memos outline agency priorities for arrest, given federal resources and political pressure to respect rights. Currently, DHS has bed space capacity that permits four hundred thousand removals a year. Such congressional mandates and agency directives, alongside the U.S. Border Patrol's relations to other players in the field, and the border political economies shape this new enforcement terrain.

From below, multiple political pressures also shape enforcement action. There is pressure on the Border Patrol from Mexican officials and business elites not to disrupt cross-border commerce, on which Arizona's service economy depends. There is also pressure from a dynamic local immigrant- and border-rights movement in Southern Arizona to respect rights and to do something about migrant deaths, vigilantism, Border Patrol misconduct, and deportations in the Tucson Sector. Lastly, there is pressure on the Border Patrol—mostly from local political elites and anti-immigrant forces—to go after "law breakers" and "criminals," broadly defined. Taken together, this interplay of punishment and rights encapsulates America's new immigration regime.

2

Beds and Biometrics

The Legacy of the Criminal Alien Program

At a crowded bus depot in Phoenix, people line up behind glass doors waiting to board buses. Others leave their bags on the floor to save their places in line. Several men talk about time they'd served in Arizona prisons. A man with braids chats with another about being "out" and doing good. "I'm working," he says. Another man chimes in. He's just out of prison too.

My attention turns to two uniformed Immigration and Customs Enforcement (ICE) agents who walk into the station with a young woman and a baby she's holding. Badges hang on their necks. Their weapons are visible. They hand the young woman a manila envelope, which I recognize from other times I've observed ICE agents parole migrants from detention. Her name and alien registration number are written across the envelope in blue marker. They speak to her politely as she holds a baby who looks to be no more than three months old. Despite the language barrier, she looks calm. They hand her a bus ticket and explain how to board. She listens. This is ICE in a humanitarian capacity. The agents walk out of the station looking pleased, relaxed even—not tense in the way agents typically are when making arrests.[1]

The formerly incarcerated men and the young woman paroled from ICE custody capture two faces of immigration enforcement. On one hand, the Department of Homeland Security (DHS)—in collaboration with the Bureau of Prisons, the U.S. Marshals, the U.S. Attorney's Office, and immigration courts (Executive Office for Immigration Review)— has a mandate to direct enforcement resources toward high-priority "criminals" and "national security threats." On the other hand, DHS has issued explicit guidelines on identifying nonpriority targets—families, nursing mothers, the elderly, and minors—for removal from the deportation and detention docket.

The #Not1More national conference on deportation in Phoenix, where I was headed, addressed precisely these issues.[2] When I arrived, the tents and canopies sprawled over the grounds of a community center were a welcomed counterpart to the "tent cities" for which the local Maricopa County sherriff, Joe Arpio, has become known. Instead of chain gangs, each tent hosted a workshop or training on an aspect of deportation policy. I walked toward the strategy session on deportation and the presidency, where the discussion centered on the Obama administration's record on deportation.

It was a historic gathering because, for the first time, critical players in the immigrant-rights movement met to talk about deportation instead of legalization, which tends to dominate immigration debates. Legalization seemed almost irrelevant to the conversation, since deportations often come with bars to reentry, which thwart any possibility of future legal migration. The focus was on immigration enforcement—the rising deportations, detentions, and criminal prosecutions, which the Arizona-based activists understand well.

Less than six months after that gathering, amid ongoing civil disobedience actions outside detention centers across the country, the Obama administration ordered the Secretary of Homeland Security, Jeh Johnson, to conduct an administrative review of deportations. In press conferences, the Obama administration contended that the president has no "power to stop deportations" and could face legal challenges for obstructing the enforcement of immigration laws. Antideportation activists pushed back, arguing that while the president waited for Congress to pass a bipartisan immigration bill, the administration continued its "ramped-up enforcement strategy of deportation."[3]

The Obama administration deflected mounting criticism from protestors by blaming the GOP for blocking immigration reform and for a bloated enforcement system inherited from previous administrations. According to a former deputy counsel for the Department of Homeland Security, ICE agents must enforce the law. There is a thirty-four-thousand-bed mandate. Agents must fill beds. Allegedly, ICE's "hands are tied" because "they cannot ignore the law."[4] However, the former INS, which now operates under the Department of Homeland Security, has always had the discretion to enforce or not enforce the law.[5]

And its enforcement priorities have reflected political choices of the time.

In the early twentieth century, the former INS prioritized race, nation, labor radicalism, or the demands of powerful industries for cheap labor more than criminal history.[6] During the earliest moments of racially restrictive immigration laws—the Chinese Exclusion Acts of 1882, 1892, and 1902, the 1921 Quota Act, the 1924 Immigration Act—criminal prosecutions, criminal deportations, and mandatory detentions were not prevalent in immigration enforcement. In fact, the INS maintained its distinction from the criminal justice system on grounds that immigration was a civil, not a criminal, matter.[7]

The recent turn toward enforcement priorities that blend humanitarian concerns and crime control stems from early challenges to immigration enforcement by Chinese antideportation activists, radicals, and reformers and a more recent scramble for detention beds in the post–civil rights imprisonment boom that gave rise to the Criminal Alien Program to purge "criminal aliens" from jails and prisons. I became interested in the history of CAP and the current thirty-four-thousand-bed mandate because congressional funds for detention beds are entangled with the politics of enforcement priorities that directly shape decision making about whom border agents arrest and prosecute and how they do so. This is that story.

Early-Twentieth-Century Enforcement Priorities

Criminal grounds for admission and expulsion have been on the books for over a century.[8] Yet deportation, detention, and attempts to criminalize migration were highly contested. Deportations of legal permanent residents with criminal convictions were difficult to carry out because of limited resources and time limits on deportations that protected noncitizens from expulsion after three to five years, on the belief that deportation would cause undue hardship on long-term residents.[9] And detention, which was used administratively to hold migrants in exclusion or deportation proceedings, could be and was legally challenged, since the Constitution protects all persons against constraints on individual liberty.[10]

In the early twentieth century, race, radicalism, and labor politics—not crime—drove enforcement priorities. The 1924 Immigration Act established the U.S. Border Patrol to enforce restrictions against "Asians, prostitutes, anarchists, and many others categorically prohibited from entering the United States."[11] This was a period of tremendous labor radicalism and unrest, as a great many immigrant workers fought for and eventually won the eight-hour workday, collective bargaining rights, and health and retirement benefits taken for granted today.[12] Strikes were brutally repressed by police, sheriffs, and militia groups, and radical immigrants were targeted, often in collaboration with the former INS, which operated under the Department of Labor.[13] The most well-known enforcement operations were the Palmer Raids, which occurred in 1919–1920, when Attorney General Palmer drew on the immigration system for deportation warrants needed to conduct raids and expel hundreds of labor activists in thirty cities.[14]

Throughout the early twentieth century, radicals and reformers mobilized against deportations and the criminalization of migration as political tools designed to weaken the rights of poor and working people. They directly challenged public perceptions that associated immigration with criminality, using statistics to show that the "foreign-born commit fewer crimes than the native born" and that deportation, therefore, would have no impact on crime levels.[15] And they pushed for equal protection and due process rights in both the criminal justice and immigration systems. They mobilized against bills proposing to criminalize migration and expand criminal deportations on grounds that they targeted long-term residents, mostly European immigrants, with long-standing ties to the United States.[16]

When in 1929 Congress proposed a bill to criminalize illegal entry and reentry that included a provision to expand criminal grounds for deportation, radicals and reformers pushed back. The American Civil Liberties Union (ACLU) lobbied against the bill, arguing that "no matter how wrong it is for an alien to come here without inspection, . . . once he has become part of our society, he should not be thrust out to the country that may be his native land but which may have become alien to him."[17] An Illinois senator proposed amendments to the bill calling for deportable migrants charged with criminal offenses to have access to a hearing and counsel as well as time limits on deportations that "may result in breaking up a family acquired after [an immigrant's] arrival in this country and years after the offense alleged was committed."[18] And the governor of New York threatened to "issue pardons to those convicted deportable alien criminals coming out of New York penal institutions—to pardon them to prevent their being deported by the Federal Government."[19]

Reformers struck down the criminal deportation provisions in the bill. In the final version of the law, only the criminal penalties for re-entry and illegal entry at sea and land borders remained. [20] Yet even after its enactment, criminal prosecution was rare. The commissioner of immigration noted that implementing the law was expensive. And the U.S. Attorney's Office decided which cases to prosecute. The result was that very few prosecutions actually occurred. As the Justice Department reported,

> Not all violations result in the institution of criminal proceedings against the offender. Because of the realization that some illegal acts are committed through ignorance of the law or without fraudulent intent, many cases are closed by the administrative officers of the government, even though the investigation established that a crime has been committed. A district Director of the Immigration and Naturalization Service is authorized to close any case insofar as prosecution is concerned. . . . All other cases must be presented for determination to the United States Attorney. . . . That official is not required to institute criminal proceedings in every case presented to him. . . .[21]

In 1936 Congress debated a bill that included measures to give the INS, then under the Department of Labor, the authority to deport immigrants convicted of any crime and to exercise discretion to "guard against the separation from their families of the non-criminal classes."[22] The commissioner of immigration testified to the challenges of deporting long-term residents, mostly European and Canadian immigrants, with criminal convictions.[23] At the time, the law required deportation in cases involving crimes of moral turpitude, with a prison sentence of one year or more within five years of entry into the United States. The INS was unable to deport long-term residents whose conviction exceeded the time limits on deportation. Or often the judge or magistrate would recommend against deportation, particularly in cases of long-term residents. A 1934 INS training manual stated that "every effort is made, consistent with law, to insure the elimination of the criminal alien from the United States. Unfortunately many cases have developed in which it has been found impossible to deport even habitual criminals because they are not comprehended within the terms of the present deportation statutes."[24]

Before Congress, the commissioner argued that having more discretion to deport some criminals would prevent the deportation of those with strong ties and roots. In stark contrast to today's punitive rhetoric, the commissioner stressed that the bill targeted "habitual criminals" and was not intended to

> deport a man who might have been in the country for 20 years, deport him for some purely minor offense, which was classified technically as involving moral turpitude, such as minor theft, for instance. He may have been a good citizen during all this time, and have had one slip, and yet, he would be met with this terrible penalty for that single offense. Now, neither the present immigration law nor any other statute dealing with criminals is so severe and unyielding as that.[25]

This sentiment also circulated in training materials of the period.

> Consider the case of the honest industrious alien whose only offense has been illegal entry into the United States. In the natural course of events, he marries an American citizen, establishes a home, and becomes the father of American-born children. Then comes his arrest on deportation charges. Deportation will probably mean the separation of the family—that his home will be broken up forever and that his wife and children will have to depend on charity for their support. Under the existing law deportation is mandatory if the charge of illegal entry is sustained. There is no discretionary power vested in the department that would avert it no matter what suffering may ensue or how meritorious or appealing the case.[26]

The ACLU and more radical segments of the labor movement were vocal in their opposition to giving the Department of Labor more discretion, arguing that it would "strengthen the weapon of deportation law as a strike-breaking measure."[27] Others argued that "deportation . . . is not a solution for crime. When you put in this bill here provisions for the deportation of foreign-born people and non-citizens who commit crimes, you are not going to the bottom of what causes crime, what causes both the native and foreign-born to commit crimes."[28]

Even official government reports at the time showed that immigrants had lower crime rates than the native born and that those with a longer history of settlement were more likely to commit crimes.[29] Opponents successfully defeated the bill because of how it would affect mostly European immigrant families with established roots in the United States. That the bill, and subsequent measures similar to it, failed is a testament to the success of reformers in debunking the perceived criminality of European immigrants at the time, and generating public sympathy and opposition to the deportation of long-term residents, even those with criminal convictions.

These early-twentieth-century struggles over enforcement priorities and discretion show how reformers pushed forth pro-immigrant legislation. But they also illustrate the extent to which reformers fell short of fighting for racial justice. Historian Khalil Gibran Muhammad argues that urban progressives successfully decriminalized European immigrants through a social distancing from the perceived criminality of Black migrants from the South, by failing to directly challenge and ultimately reproducing an association between Blackness and criminality. "From the opening of the Progressive Era to its waning days on the eve of World War I and the Great Migration," writes Muhammad, "black criminality had become not just a universal tool to measure black fitness for citizenship; it was also a tool to shield . . . Americans from the charge of racism."[30]

In the southwest borderlands, Mexicans were also viewed as unfit for citizenship, and not fully "American," despite their historical presence in the United States. Yet in contrast to anti-Black criminalization, they were subjected to "illegalization" that associated Mexicans not with innate criminality but with perpetual foreignness as "aliens." Early enforcement priorities were not aimed at crime per se but were determined by the demands for seasonal, cheap labor by powerful local industries. Historian Kelly Lytle Hernandez provides a wonderful illustration of how powerful growers successfully influenced a *reduction* in congressional appropriations for enforcement.[31] Although Mexican migrants were exempt from quotas under the 1924 immigration law, agents arrested and expelled migrants in accordance with the labor needs of growers.[32]

When labor demands were low, the INS took pride in arresting migrants before they could establish roots. Border Patrol training materials instructed agents to target aliens

> who entered illegally before they had sunk roots in this country . . . in the name of American-born wives and children who would be the main sufferers of the almost inevitable event of their ultimate detection and deportation. In holding fast the line, the border patrol performs not only a vital national, but a *humanitarian* service. (emphasis added)[33]

Rather than criminally prosecuting undocumented migrants for illegal entry or reentry, the legacy INS relied on a voluntary departure system, established in 1927, whereby migrants signed a waiver agreeing to "voluntarily depart" and give up their rights to a removal hearing.[34] By giving up their rights to a hearing, migrants could return to Mexico the same day. Even during the historic Mexican repatriations during the 1930s, 1940s, and 1950s, voluntary returns greatly outnumbered formal deportations as the most cost-effective way to expel someone. And the INS prosecuted few migrants for illegal entry or reentry in criminal courts, with the exception of a "small class of undesirable migrants (radicals, prostitutes, smugglers, and 'repeaters')."[35]

What is striking about early-twentieth-century enforcement priorities, then, is that criminal prosecutions for immigration offenses and deportations on criminal grounds were not more prevalent. Criminal *deportations*—particularly for European immigrants—were publicly contested. Criminal *prosecutions* for immigration offenses were uncommon. And for the most part, the immigration system and criminal justice system developed independently of each other. Detention was controversial, reserved for "enemy aliens" during times of war, such as the unconstitutional detention, during World War II, of over one hundred thousand persons of Japanese ancestry, seventy thousand of whom were U.S. citizens.[36] By 1940 and 1954, respectively, two major detention and deportation processing centers on Angel and Ellis islands had closed.

Reformers had successfully swayed public opinion about deportation and detention and exposed the unchecked discretion of immigration officials and law enforcement. Herbert Hoover's National Commission on Law Observance and Enforcement (Wickersham Commission), on which several reformers served as lead investigators, uncovered widespread instances of police brutality, unlawful detention, and due process violations in the immigration and criminal justice systems. Zechariah Chaffee, Walter Pollack, and Carl Sterns, who were the three main consultants for the Wickersham Commission's *Report on Lawlessness in Law Enforcement*, for instance, were well-known civil liberties attorneys and founding members of the ACLU.[37] Chaffee was a coauthor of the ACLU's famous report on the Palmer Raids.[38] Walter Pollack represented the Scottsboro Nine in *Powell v. Alabama*.[39] One of the earliest national reports on police brutality, *Report on Lawlessness in Law Enforcement* documented widespread police abuse, including forced confessions, unlawful detentions, and police violence. Historian Samuel Walker notes that this report's recommendations were noticeably vague and brief, the likely outcome of political compromise.[40] Civil liberties attorney Reuben Oppenheimer's *Report on the Enforcement of Deportation Laws* criticized the immigration system, then under the Department of Labor, for serving as immigration inspector, investigator, and prosecutor, culminating in widespread unfair trials for immigrants in deportation proceedings.[41] These early-twentieth-century struggles over enforcement priorities and discretion show how reformers and civil libertarians championed liberal immigration policies with greater protections in the justice systems.[42] But they also illustrate the extent to which procedural reforms fell short of addressing the root causes of racial and police violence, a struggle that would be taken up by civil rights and antiracist activists.

After the Rights Revolution

Enforcement priorities shifted again in the post–civil rights era, when the federal government struck racial quotas from immigration law. The 1965 Immigration Act unleashed new enforcement challenges for the legacy INS when it imposed the same numerical visa quota limits of twenty thousand for every country, on justification of equality and "non-discrimination."[43] Until then, Mexico and other countries from the Western Hemisphere had been exempt from quotas. Once inspectors quickly issued all the available visas under the new quota limit, those unable to enter "legally" crossed the U.S.-Mexico border without visas, causing a surge in border arrests for unauthorized migration.[44]

The INS, operating under the Department of Justice, went to Congress for funds aimed at managing the rise in unauthorized border crossings. Before Congress, the INS explicitly attributed the rise to economic conditions in Mexico and to *federal polices* such the termination of the Bracero Program in 1964 and the 1965 Immigration Act: "Restrictions on the importation of Mexican agricultural labor, and the numerical limitation on Western Hemisphere immigrant aliens, all combine to produce a situation that results in increases in surreptitious entry without inspection, and other immigration law violations."[45] Anticipating the spike in unauthorized border crossings, the INS requested funding to establish its antismuggling program in 1965.[46] Funding for border policing grew steadily just as sweeping civil rights legislations opened a space to legally contest immigration law enforcement practices and as crime was becoming a major political issue in the United States. Barry Goldwater, who during the 1964 elections campaigned on a law-and-order platform as a response to the civil rights revolution, introduced crime as a wedge issue in U.S. politics.[47] President Lyndon Johnson beat Goldwater in a landslide victory and took on the crime issue as his own. By the late sixties, both conservatives and liberals had appropriated the issue. In 1968, the Johnson administration increased federal funds for state and local government to carry out crime control alongside the Great Society programs for which it is known.[48] Funding for state and local crime control jumped from $300 million to $1.25 billion.[49]

When Johnson signed the 1968 Omnibus Crime Control and Safe Streets Act that launched the so-called War on Crime, he expanded the Department of Justice's size, power, and funding, much of which went to police departments, criminal courts, prisons, and information management.[50] The Immigration and Naturalization Service, transferred to the Department of Justice after 1940, did not fall neatly into this broad mission, since it mostly handled matters related to citizenship and immigration, not criminal law. To access the massive funding pouring into the

Department of Justice for crime control, the former INS, in its budget requests before Congress, began to frame its own enforcement actions— long considered administrative rather than criminal—through a prosecutorial language of combating crime.[51] In a 1972 appropriation hearing, the INS commissioner requested funds to curtail the "large influx of illegal aliens on the Mexican Border," arguing that "[i]llegal aliens contribute to unemployment, increased welfare costs, and to the increased crime rate."[52] The language, almost verbatim to that used in political speeches to mobilize public support for a "war on crime," provided budget justifications for more Border Patrol agents, workplace raids, and "intensified liaisons with federal and local jails holding deportable aliens who are serving sentences so that immediate deportation may be effected upon their release from confinement."[53]

Yet in practice, the INS did not regard unauthorized immigrants as criminal nor did it have the resources to pursue criminal prosecution. "Most illegal aliens are not criminals," a former INS commissioner stated in a public speech. "[T]hey are good people who have the same concerns that you and I do: to provide for their families and gain some security."[54] Nor did the agency rely heavily on criminal prosecution. According to the INS commissioner, "Prosecution of persons employing illegal aliens is generally not effective because of the attitude of the public toward Mexican people. Those Mexican aliens found along the border more frequently than not are grateful for food and housing provided in detention facilities. The great bulk of those apprehended should not be treated as criminals."[55]

Here the commissioner indirectly referenced the upsurge in prison reform litigation in the 1960s and 1970s that grew out of the civil rights movement and successfully challenged the constitutionality of deplorable prison conditions.[56] Drawing from the law-and-order rhetoric of the times, conservative critics contended that raising prison standards "coddled criminals." The commissioner disassociated unauthorized immigrants from criminality by juxtaposing an image of impoverished Mexicans "grateful" for detention conditions with that of "criminal" activists in the prisoner-rights movement.

To the extent that the INS pursued criminal prosecution, it was not for illegal entry but for "aliens of the criminal, immoral, and narcotics classes." In the Border Criminal Identification Program, agents used a paper copy of an FBI "[be on the] lookout list" in determining admissibility.[57] During the 1968 budget hearings, the Border Patrol reported that out of 4,000 "lookouts," 600 were excluded or denied admission.[58] During the 1971 budget hearings, the Border Patrol reported that of the 12,400 cases it referred for prosecution, the U.S. Attorney's Office accepted only 7,300.[59]

Although the former INS drew on crime discourse to justify budget requests, criminal deportations and detentions were less prevalent and more contentious. And as the INS drew on law-and-order rhetoric, immigrants drew on the civil right laws to challenge their deportations.[60] During one budget appropriation hearing, a former INS commissioner complained that Mexican aliens had learned to ask for trials instead of accepting voluntary departures. "Aliens are no longer willing to accept voluntary departure as they have discovered that by surrendering to the Service and applying for various benefits under the law, they may remain in the U.S. until all remedies have been exhausted."[61] In oral histories, Border Patrol agents deployed during the 1970s also complained that undocumented migrants were no longer docile, temporary workers, but settled U.S. residents unafraid to assert their constitutional rights:

> The UDAs, undocumented aliens, have turned into a different group of people. . . . Most of those we dealt with in the early days were the working class. Very rarely did you have a problem with those people. They were polite to me and I was polite with them, and did my job. . . . [T]he working class I was talking about would be like farmer workers. . . . As time went on we ran into people who didn't intend to work on farms. It was just a different class of people. They were belligerent; they wanted something for nothing. If we arrested one, the first thing he wanted was water or food. It was always "Give me something." And then we ran into a lot more that wanted to escape from being arrested.[62]

Mimicking law-and-order critiques of the welfare state and Great Society programs, this wistful agent notes that in the past, unauthorized (Mexican) immigrants who crossed the border to work in the fields were more like the early, industrious (European) immigrant "working class." The unauthorized border crossers he encountered in the seventies were more like native-born minorities (i.e., Blacks and Latinas/os).

They made demands ("give me something") on the federal government for "food and water" during detention and relief from deportation in exchange for "nothing," at the expense of taxpayers.

In a 1976 speech delivered in Phoenix, Arizona, former INS commissioner Chapman similarly noted,

> There are some built-in advantages for anyone who is illegally residing in this country, and additional major barriers to enforcement of immigration laws. Unfortunately, the advantages to the illegal seem to be increasing while at the same time barriers to law enforcement are being erected even higher. . . . Court orders and decisions make a difficult job even harder. . . . Our constitutional guarantees of privacy, freedom and the right of due process all work to the advantage of the illegal alien.[63]

Here the commissioner invoked the legacy of the Warren Court that expanded the rights of criminal defendants through a series of landmark Supreme Court cases in the 1960s. Appropriating the language of civil rights, critics decried that such procedural reforms "handcuffed" police and violated victims' rights.[64] The commissioner warned that such constitutional constraints advantage immigrants and victimize border agents.

During this period, multiple lawsuits legally challenged the constitutionality of immigration arrests, deportation raids, and detentions.[65] In appropriation hearings, the Department of Justice sought funding to aggressively target immigration litigation that legally challenged enforcement practices. Again, court rulings and legal opinions by INS general counsels affirm that deportation and detention are civil, administrative matters and not a punishment for a crime. Thus, various lawsuits challenging the constitutionality of key enforcement practices such as search and seizure or area control operations (i.e., workplace raids) ultimately upheld different sets of rules for immigration versus criminal enforcement.[66] Yet all the cases affirmed procedural rights of due process as evidenced in Border Patrol handbooks and training manuals of this period.

A 1975 Border Patrol handbook explicitly states, "An Immigration officer's powers . . . are subject to constitutional, statutory, and judicial restraints, which require him to take a reasonable and humane approach in performance of his duties."[67] The handbook includes a chapter on "Civil Rights in Law Enforcement" that explicitly warns agents that

[i]n addition to a moral obligation to uphold constitutional guarantees of personal liberty, patrol agents must be aware that failure to grant due process of law . . . exposes the officer to the possibility of a civil suit for damages or criminal prosecution. . . . The principal areas of concern are illegal search and seizure, brutality, protracted questioning, illegal detention, and use of confessions made without proper warnings.[68]

Despite the onset of a federal "war on crime" in the post–civil rights era, criminal history had not yet become the primary criterion guiding enforcement discretion. The INS had established protections for long-term residents. Intra-agency operating instructions in the 1970s refer to a "non-priority program" recommending "non-priority treatment" in certain deportation cases.[69] In fact, out of 1,843 in 1975 that varied across nationality, nonpriority status had been granted to "aliens who have committed serious crimes involving moral turpitude (9%), drug convictions (7%), fraud or prostitution . . . communists, the insane, and the medically infirm."[70] The vast majority of cases—32%, or 590—were for "those who would be separated from their families." The program's main purpose was to "avoid an unwarranted hardship upon the subject alien or members of his family."[71]

Criminal deportations were difficult to execute because among those with convictions, many were long-term residents. Immigrant detention was also unpopular.[72] During budget hearings before Congress, the INS commissioner testified that "emphasis is placed on parole [from detention] proceedings whenever possible to avoid detention expenses."[73] Training manuals of the time instructed agents to avoid illegal detention, citing "the Constitutional guarantee that a person shall not be deprived of liberty without due process of law" and noting how "one of the most easily aroused emotions of the American public is sympathy," particularly for the mistreatment of people in INS custody.[74]

Crime-centered approaches, then, did not yet dominate immigration enforcement actions. Nor did a criminal conviction carry the same lasting and unshakeable stigma that it does today. Post–civil rights enforcement discretion emphasized nonpriority categories for enforcement based on "humanitarian" considerations. Such practices continued throughout the 1980s, under a practice of "nondeportation," which often involved letting the file sit on a desk, or paroling migrants from detention, not only as a cost-saving measure but also because of the political pressure to minimize hardship for certain immigrant families with long histories of settlement.[75]

The Prison Boom and the Scramble for Beds

Prison expansion under the War on Crime played a critical yet understudied role in shifting enforcement priorities in the immigration system. During the Reagan era, the 1984 Comprehensive Crime Control Act intensified a prison bed shortage. Considered "the largest Crime Bill in the history of the country," it set into law pretrial detention for certain offenders, imposed mandatory minimum prison sentences, and expanded forfeiture laws that provided incentives for state and local governments to carry out arrests and prosecutions, all of which increased the likelihood of imprisonment, mostly for federal drug offenses.[76] Until then state and local governments had seldom prosecuted federal crimes, but the funding provided both the resources and the incentive to do so.[77]

Anticipating that a rise in convictions and prison sentences would trigger prison overcrowding, the Department of Justice (DOJ) budget request for FY 1984 included $6 million to create additional bed spaces in federal prisons. The Appropriations Committee questioned top Department of Justice officials, including former U.S. attorney Rudolph Giuliani and assistant attorney general for administration Kevin D. Rooney, about how the Bureau of Prisons calculated the need.

> DOJ (GIULIANI): The need was calculated really over a period of two
> fiscal years, 1983 and 1984. . . . We realized that the Federal Prison
> System was operating over capacity already before you added any
> additional agents or prosecutors, and we also realized that the kinds
> of cases we were going to be asking them to concentrate on are the
> kinds of cases where federal judges would be likely to give long
> prison sentences. We estimated what we believe to be, again it was
> a rough estimate, and a conservative one, the number of additional
> drug defendants we would have over the course of the next year or

two or three years, to try to build up the number of bed spaces that
we would have available for those respective defendants.

CONGRESSMAN: Why do you use beds? Why don't you use cells?

DOJ (ROONEY): The Bureau of Prisons has a renovation rehabilita-
tion plan . . . with respect to expansion of bed space, by renovation,
et cetera. These particular beds are . . . the first group of beds or cells
that would open up through renovations at existing facilities.[78]

Prison overcrowding had become so severe that the attorney general
and director of the Bureau of Prisons were no longer requesting funding
for cells, but for beds. Cells harken back to older approaches to reha-
bilitating offenders. Beds signified a "new penology" designed to "warehouse" and isolate "dangerous" populations, taking them off the street.
Yet they also invoke a benign image of adhering to federally mandated
prison standards that prison activists fought and died for. From that moment on, in appropriations hearings and budget line items, "beds" and
"bed space" had become a catch-all phrase for "humanitarian" conditions as well as prison overcrowding, prison construction, and mass imprisonment as an accepted policy solution to social problems.

What began as a political strategy to win elections became a dominant policy approach for years to come. During appropriation hearings
throughout the 1980s and early 1990s, the attorney general routinely
requested additional funds for prison beds and construction projects.
The Bureau of Prisons instituted a cooperative agreement with state
and local facilities to provide bed space. The Department of Justice borrowed the idea to use private contracts from the INS's historic use of
nonservice facilities.[79]

Mass incarceration and prison overcrowding also led to a bed space
shortage in the immigration system when the Reagan administration reintroduced detention as a strategy for managing the flow of Cuban refugees of the Mariel boatlift, which began in the final year of the Carter
administration when Fidel Castro allowed Cubans to leave through the
Mariel harbor. In line with public fears about crime, the media portrayed
the Cuban exiles as criminals.[80] In 1981, the INS abandoned its practice
of nondetention and instituted an internal policy of detaining all deportable migrants, including those seeking asylum, with the exception of
pregnant women and certain juveniles. The INS detained over one hun-

dred thousand Cuban and forty-five thousand Haitian refugees, fleeing political repression under the Jean-Claude Duvalier ("Baby Doc")
regime (1971–1986), in prisons and detention facilities.[81]

Many Cuban detainees were housed in the Atlanta Penitentiary and
in state prisons throughout the country. Most Haitian detainees were in
custody at the Krome detention center in Florida and other detention
centers in Brooklyn, New York, Fort Allen, Puerto Rico, and Port Isabel, Texas, as well as in federal prisons throughout the United States.[82]
However, bed space in state and local jails and prisons became limited,
as prison overcrowding worsened.

Prior to Reagan's detention policy, the more common practice for the
INS was to release migrants on parole or bond.[83] As the INS detained
more people, it encountered a detention bed shortage of its own. In congressional budget hearings, the INS effectively linked enforcement capacity to detention bed space in order to secure more funding. Between
1975 and 1985, detention funds jumped from $2,451,113 to $36,474,375.[84]
In 1968, bed space capacity was at 858. In 1982, it more than doubled to
1,800 spaces. In 1985, bed space grew to 2,265.[85] In 1986, the Department
of Justice secured funds to build a one-thousand-bed-capacity detention
facility for Cuban detainees in Oakdale, Louisiana. It also contracted
with over a thousand nonservice facilities in forty-six states, mostly jails
and some private facilities.[86] Historically, the INS contracted with small
boarding houses, and later with local jails, but the security industry had
become a growing market by the 1980s, and the INS began contracting
with larger corporations.[87]

In addition to Cubans and Haitians, the INS detained El Salvadorans, Hondurans, Guatemalans, and Nicaraguans all fleeing U.S.-backed
civil wars, often in violation of the recently signed Refugee Act of 1980
that aligned U.S. refugee and asylum protocol with international human
rights law. Mexicans also grew in the population of detainees, particularly when they challenged their deportations. Many testified to being
coerced into signing voluntary departures "without notice of rights,
legal information, or access to legal counsel."[88] Faced with mounting
pressure from legal advocates, the INS eventually paroled many Cuban
detainees but continued to detain those charged with criminal conviction under the drug war. The INS was unable to deport them, because
there was no repatriation agreement with Cuba.

Cuban repatriation was central to debates about bed space. The attorney general routinely updated Congress on efforts to negotiate a repatriation agreement with Cuba as "the only long-term solution for about 6,000 or more, many of whom are in custodial institutions, and who *exacerbate the prison problem.*" (emphasis added)

> ATTORNEY GENERAL: There will not be an end to it until we can somehow get these people back to Cuba where they belong. And as I say, we are continuing our efforts but, they have not been very fruitful unfortunately.
>
> CONGRESSMAN: What should I tell my folks who say, "Just put them on a boat and push them off the shore?"
>
> ATTORNEY GENERAL: Well, I have got to be candid with you. We did consider this at one time, but we were worried. There were some rather elaborate plans to head the boat in the direction of Cuba and just let it beach itself there. Unfortunately, that did not turn out to be practical.[89]

For the Department of Justice, Cuban detainees "exacerbated" prison overcrowding. So dire was the bed space shortage that the attorney general was willing to expel them without documents and in violation of international repatriation agreements and asylum and refugee law. That such a proposal turned out to be impractical was due to intense political mobilizations on behalf of detainees.

The INS's mandatory and indefinite detention policies unleashed an onslaught of litigation and legal advocacy campaigns. Legal advocates challenged the selective and arbitrary enforcement of detention for Cuban and Haitian refugees. The Sanctuary movement took on aspects of the Underground Railroad and hid migrants from the INS. It also challenged the discriminatory denial of due process and of asylum for Central American refugees. Other lawsuits challenged forced voluntary departure imposed on Mexican detainees. To counter legal challenges, the Department of Justice established the Office of Immigration Litigation in 1983.[90] Throughout the eighties, DOJ requested funds for "aggressive litigation" in budget appropriation hearings alongside funds for prison beds to address the overcrowding.[91]

The 1986 Anti–Drug Abuse Act exacerbated the bed shortage by expanding mandatory sentences for drug offenses. In 1987, the director of the Federal Bureau of Prisons testified at a budget hearing that

> [w]ithout question, the single most important issue we face in the Bureau of Prisons today is the rapid increase in the prison population and the overcrowding that has come about as a result. . . . The fact that Congress enacted the Anti–Drug Abuse Act last session undoubtedly is going to have a major and significant impact on the federal prison population. . . . The Bureau of Prisons is in the midst of *the largest expansion program in the history of the organization* . . . . If we do not increase the capacity of the Federal Prison System, I think we will find that the lack of prison space will become a *constraint on the criminal justice system* . . . . We will develop *a gridlock situation* where there is *simply no room available* for those defendants who are sentenced by the U.S. District Courts and committed to the Attorney General's custody. (emphasis added)[92]

Prison overcrowding, the bed space shortage, and the "gridlock situation" it threatened to create pushed Congress to reintroduce measures to expand criminal deportations. Congress proposed deporting "alien felons" swept up in the drug war as a way to free up more detention space and prison beds for native-born Black and Latina/o youth who would fill them. In order to free up beds and mitigate prison overcrowding, the 1986 Anti–Drug Abuse Act expanded the grounds for excluding and deporting noncitizens charged with drug offenses.[93] It also authorized the federal government to reimburse states for "incarceration costs of alien felons" and included a measure requiring the secretary of defense to deliver a report to the attorney general on unused military buildings that could be converted into detention facilities, including the suggestion to use "land at Guantanamo Bay, Cuba, to build a prison."[94]

In budget hearings, the INS routinely updated Congress on the status of detention and deportation.

> CONGRESSMAN: It has been reported that INS has not been able to detain aliens who are subject to deportation because of lack of facilities.

INS: Yes, it's true to some extent. INS has requested 15 million dollars in the 1987 supplement budget request for detention facilities to help alleviate the problem. Another major effort, which will reduce the problem of detention in non-INS facilities [jails and prisons], is being pursued by the INS, the Executive Office for Immigration Review (EOIR) and state and local officials. *This program will identify incarcerated criminal aliens* for the purpose of conducting hearings in identified state or local facilities in order to remove these individuals from the United States expeditiously upon completion of imposed sentences. . . . . *This will help free up existing detention space.* (emphasis added)[95]

The 1986 Immigration Reform and Control Act (IRCA) first introduced the idea of a criminal alien program designed to deport convicted felons. But it was the 1988 Anti–Drug Abuse Act that further expanded criminal penalties for drug offenses, requiring more prison beds. It also included a provision for deporting noncitizens convicted of aggravated felonies, which at the time included a much narrower list of major offenses such as "murder, drug trafficking, and illicit traffic in firearms."

In 1988, the INS also instituted two pilot projects—the Alien Criminal Apprehension and the Border Patrol Criminal Apprehension programs. That year the INS established an Institutional (removal) Hearing Program in state and federal prisons and a Criminal Alien Program (CAP) to handle INS litigation involving criminal deportations involving any "alien who has been convicted of a crime."[96] CAP established "criminal alien cases as the highest priority for resource allocation in all immigration cases before the Executive Office for Immigration Review."[97] It also required the secretary of defense to identify facilities "that could be made available to the Bureau of Prisons for use in incarcerating aliens."[98]

The INS's internal procedures handbook also confirms that detaining and deporting people under CAP freed up beds in the prison system.

An item of concern for many years is the lack of detention bed space and funding for the INS Detention and Deportation Program. It is advantageous for the INS and an efficient use of tax dollars to commence the lengthy deportation and exclusion process against criminal aliens who are serving sentences so that the final orders of exclusion and deportation can be obtained before the alien is released into our custody. *It appears to be the intent of Congress in its passage of the criminal provisions of IRCA to take steps to alleviate the nationwide problem of prison overcrowding by addressing expeditiously the large illegal alien population encountered in corrections systems in many states.* (emphasis added)[99]

Between 1980 and 1994, the prison population had grown 500%.[100] Democratic president Bill Clinton signed the 1994 Crime Control Act, which added an additional one million police officers to the streets. It increased death penalty crimes—no doubt to also relieve prison over-crowding. It also included a "three strikes" provision that imposed a life sentence for three-time offenders. The act also raised penalties for immigration offenses such as human smuggling and reentry after de-portation. It appropriated $9.7 billion for more prisons, $1.2 billion for more Border Patrol and criminal deportations, and $1.8 billion for the State Criminal Alien Assistance Program, or SCAAP. Funding for the high-profile border enforcement campaigns in the early 1990s further institutionalized the Criminal Alien Program.

Yet deporting people for mostly low-level drug convictions remained difficult to execute because many were not recent immigrants but long-term legal permanent residents swept up in the drug war. Legal perma-nent residents had been a "nonpriority" category for the INS, as were deportable migrants with long histories of settlement and family ties. In fact, among the 1986 Immigration Reform and Control Act's major provisions was an "attempt to deal humanely with aliens who established roots here."[101] It established a legalization program that provided legal status to persons who had been in the United States without authoriza-tion before 1982. The attorney general testified before Congress that "the policy of the INS is that if a person would qualify under the Immigra-tion Reform Act for legal residency, they are not deportable."[102] Internal guidelines on prosecutorial discretion confirm that the unauthorized relatives of those legalized under IRCA were also a nonpriority category for enforcement, explicitly stating that "the removal of spouses and chil-dren would be inconsistent with enforcement priorities."

Prison overcrowding was a powerful impetus behind proposals to deport noncitizens with convictions, mandatorily detain noncitizens in order to deport, and eventually criminally prosecute those who violate deportation orders. Yet even by expanding penalties for immigration offenses and grounds of deportability for those with drug convictions, "criminal alien removals," as they came to be known, were still difficult to carry out because they disproportionately targeted immigrants with longer settlement histories, legal permanent residency status, and access to forms of relief from expulsion. Congress would have to revamp the deportation and detention system in order to make a criminal alien program workable. This is precisely what the 1996 immigration law did.

Restructuring Detention and Deportation

Signed by President Bill Clinton, the 1996 Illegal Immigration Reform and Immigrant Responsibility Act (IIRIRA) targeted "criminal aliens" above those entering without inspection (EWIs) as a major enforcement priority, while putting in place the necessary infrastructure to carry out the new mandate. IIRIRA broke enforcement barriers by restructuring the deportation and detention process. Among its sweeping provisions, IIRIRA eliminated the distinction between exclusion and deportation. Prior to the law, persons entering without inspection and already in the country could contest their deportations in a hearing, whereas persons who presented themselves at the ports of entry were found inadmissible and, therefore, excludable.[103] Collapsing exclusion and deportation into one removal category was a way to narrow the ways in which immigrants could contest deportation.

But the law did not stop there. It greatly expanded the grounds for "criminal" removal by expanding the category of aggravated felony to include petty theft, DUIs, and minor drug offenses. Before IIRIRA, aggravated felonies were limited to major offenses such as murder, rape, or drug trafficking.[104] The law also imposed mandatory detention and instituted retroactive deportations, which applied to both unauthorized and legal permanent residents. IIRIRA included court-stripping measures that narrowed judicial review in immigration hearings. The law instituted an expedited removal process that fast-tracked formal deportations without a hearing. It also made it legal for the INS to detain and deport on the basis of "secret evidence."[105] In short, it unraveled many of the procedural safeguards developed over a century. It weakened procedural due process for immigrants with convictions and incorporated criminal processes into immigration enforcement without having to deliver many of the substantive rights found in criminal procedure for those classified as criminal aliens.

In many ways, IIRIRA can be regarded as a backlash against immigrant rights in a post–civil rights era. It did after all promise to curb illegal immigration by fortifying the border, curbing welfare benefits for "legal" immigrants (some of which were later reinstated), and ramping up deportations.[106] The law's most punitive aspects, however, were not necessarily put in place to restrict "illegal immigrants," as the name suggests. Rather, it was crafted to free up more beds in the prison system for Black and Latina/o youth incarcerated by harsh drug laws. The New Right, by then a congressional majority, proposed the law after the 1995 Oklahoma City bombing. Like the Anti-Terrorism and Effective Death Penalty Act and the welfare reform law—the Personal Responsibility and Work Opportunity Reconciliation Act enacted that year—IIRIRA stems from long-standing political mobilization, beginning with the Goldwater campaign, to regain or maintain political footing in the aftermath of the civil rights movement through a law-and-order agenda.[107]

Yet the punitive turn in immigration never abandoned a constitutional framework. On the contrary, the new blend of criminal immigration enforcement directly appropriated a "race-blind" language of rights. IIRIRA gave front line agents more discretion to confer or deny rights on the basis of criminal status. IIRIRA also constrained immigration judges' discretion by mandating retroactive deportation for prior offenses and making immigrants with past convictions ineligible for forms of relief such as adjustment of status or deferred action status. Restructuring detention and deportation was not so much a retreat from civil rights as a move to administer relief and protections on the basis of criminal history. It is precisely the fact that it operates within a constitutional framework that gives the criminalization of migration an air of consensus and makes it difficult to contest.

Much as with the funding that backed the War on Drugs, Congress vigorously funded IIRIRA's enactment, particularly by expanding high-profile border initiatives, efforts to remove a greater number of "criminal and non-criminal deportable aliens," and funding for detention bed spaces. In addition to pouring resources into Border Patrol operations,

Congress also funded the Criminal Alien Program. In 1998, Congress earmarked $109.7 million to detain and deport criminal aliens.[108] Congress also funded the U.S. Marshals and U.S. Attorney's Office to assist with prosecuting and deporting immigrants charged with drug offenses.

Similarly to the way in which the federal government created financial incentives for state and local police departments to enact federal drug laws, Congress also expanded the State Criminal Alien Assistance Program to incentivize local law enforcement's cooperation in detaining and deporting noncitizens with criminal records. The funds were primarily to reimburse state and local law enforcement agencies for noncitizen offenders in their custody. This marks an important shift in INS-police collaboration because, prior to this, it was the INS that was supporting federal drug enforcement efforts. The collaboration reorganized around immigration enforcement, namely, detention and deportation of criminal aliens.

This is a surprising turn of events, because it really was the War on Drugs, not illegal immigration, that was burdening law enforcement budgets. IIRIRA, which required mandatory detention for noncitizens who had completed their prison sentences, as well as the high-profile Border Patrol operations of the mid-1990s, drained local and county law enforcement budgets. Yet this never factored into congressional debates. Instead, Congress continued to fund detention beds in INS facilities, prisons and jails, and private detention centers.

By then the justification for expanding detention bed space was no longer to manage overcrowding in federal prisons but to manage the detention bed shortage that the 1996 law's mandatory detention provisions triggered. Between 1995 and 1997, INS beds jumped from 6,000 to 11,500.[109] In 1997, the INS commissioner requested funds for three thousand additional beds in FY 1998.[110] By 1998, bed capacity had reached 16,000. Yet even with the substantial increase in beds, the INS Commissioner reported that the agency "would be unable to meet the [mandatory] custody requirements of IIRIRA."

In addition to mandatory detention, IIRIRA expanded expedited removal, which bypassed the immigration courts, essentially "allowing lower level officials to make decisions which were once reserved for judges," as one senator put it. To counter criticism from migrant advocates that the expedited removal process ran the risk of "mistakenly sending some refugees back to persecution and torture," the INS commissioner requested funding for immigration adjudication under the Executive Office of Immigration Review (EOIR). The commissioner stressed that "INS removal goals are tied to EOIR adjudication efforts. . . . [E]nhanced detention is dependent on expedited caseload, the maximum number of aliens the INS is able to process through facilities."[111] The director of EOIR also requested funding to hire twenty-eight new immigration judges and twelve BIA (Board of Immigration Appeals) attorneys in anticipation of a thirty thousand caseload increase in response to the 1996 law.[112]

During a budget hearing for FY 1998, the Committee on Appropriations criticized the INS's progress on deportation.

> CONGRESSMAN: By recent INS estimates there are five million illegal immigrants now living in the U.S.; the same peak level of illegal immigrants in the country as of 1986, which was the reason we passed the Immigration Reform and Control Act of 1986.
> *We've given you triple the resources you had in 1986*, and despite the unprecedented increase in funding, a 105% increase over the last four years, your strategy has only made a dent. . . . Instead the population of illegal immigrants continues to grow.
> You seem to be making progress on the border in California, I admit; stopping illegal border crossings, though, is only one facet of the fight. And I'm talking about . . . removing illegals presently here, including criminals. You deported 68,000 last year. That's less than 1.5% of those living here.
> You fell short 37% of your own plan to deport 110,000 aliens in 1996. The Institutional Hearing Program—is 23% short of your own goal. There are 193,000 outstanding orders of deportation . . . where an Immigration Judge has ordered someone deported and they're still here; can't be found.
> Neither of you can say that your problem is because you don't have resources. *We shoveled money at you, gave you more money than you asked for year in and out.* . . . In 1997, we gave INS $78 million and 2,000 more detention beds; 2,000 more than you asked for. You said in 1996 that you would deport 110,000. . . . In fact there were 68,000 deported.

INS COMMISSIONER: Removals for last year are 36% higher than the year before. This year when we move up into the 93,000 range, that will be 37% higher than what we achieved last year. . . . That system rests not only on the removal action, but detention facilities and detention capacity which has also been funded generously by the Committee. *Using that detention space effectively is a major link that needs to be properly developed in order for removals to increase* at the level they've been increasing.

CONGRESSMAN: Why can't the INS find the 193,000 for which you've got orders of deportation and they're just staying here?

INS COMMISSIONER: We do very well on deporting those people who are in detention. It is very difficult and labor intensive to deport people who have orders of deportation and are not in detention. It's crucial. That's why we ask for it. That's why we look very, very closely at having the maximum turnover in that bed space so that we can remove the largest number as effectively as we can. (emphasis added)[113]

The testimony conveys challenges associated with implementing the 1996 law, even with "triple" the resources. Mandatory detention for people with convictions exacerbated a detention bed shortage in the immigration system. Yet there was political pressure to continue investing in detention (as opposed to adjudication in the immigration courts) as the necessary vehicle for executing deportations.

The INS also confronted various legal challenges from various advocacy groups that criticized the law, and how it not only hurt asylum seekers but also disproportionately targeted legal permanent residents. As the agency's commissioner later explained, "This was new. Until then green card holders had greater protections in the system. As enforcement went forward, people were put in the system who were never in before."[114] In August 1999, the National Immigration Forum, the ACLU, and other immigrant-rights groups officially launched the "Fix '96" campaign, intended to amend provisions in the 1996 law concerning judicial review, mandatory detention, the use of secret evidence, and expedited removals.

In November 1999, twenty-eight congresspersons, led by Lamar Smith of Texas, one of the 1996 law's main backers, sent a letter to Attorney General Janet Reno and INS commissioner Doris Meissner, urging the INS to refine its enforcement priorities and use prosecutorial discretion to reduce hardship for legal permanent residents with citizen children. The letter stated that

> [l]egislative reforms enacted in 1996, accompanied by increased funding, enable the INS to remove increasing numbers of criminal aliens. . . . However, some cases may involve removal proceedings against legal permanent residents who many years ago committed a single crime at the lower end of the aggravated felony spectrum, but have been law abiding ever since, obtained and held jobs and remained self-sufficient and started families in the U.S. . . . There has been widespread agreement that some deportations were unfair and resulted in unjustifiable hardship. If the facts substantiate the presentations that have come to us, we must ask why the INS pursued removal in such cases when so many other more serious cases existed. . . . We write to you because many people believe that you have the discretion to alleviate some of the hardship, and we wish to solicit your views as to why you have been unwilling to exercise such authority in some of the cases. . . . True hardship cases call for the exercise of discretion, and over the past year many members of Congress have urged the INS to develop guidelines for the use of prosecutorial discretion. . . . We hope that you will develop and implement guidelines for INS prosecutorial discretion in an expeditious and fair manner.[115]

In 2000, the INS commissioner issued an internal memo on the INS policy of prosecutorial discretion. The memo instructed district directors and chief Border Patrol agents throughout the agency to exercise discretion "at all stages of the enforcement process."[116] It listed factors for enforcers to consider—immigration status, length of residence in the United States, criminal history, and humanitarian consideration for vulnerable groups such as women, the elderly, and minors—when "deciding whom to stop, question, and arrest" and whom to detain or deport.[117] It also stressed factors *not* permissible, such as "an individual's race, religion, sex, national origin, or political association, activities or beliefs."[118] The commissioner affirmed protection from discrimination and "humanitarian" principles while also directing agency resources toward expansive criminal enforcement priorities under IIRIRA. The guidelines, continued under later administrations, are the basis for current prosecutorial discretion guidelines.

The attack on the World Trade Center on September 11, 2001, thwarted any efforts to repeal the 1996 law's detention and deportation provisions. On the contrary, Attorney General John Ashcroft drew on immigration law as a pretext to target and detain members of Arab and Muslim communities as potential terrorist subjects—the majority of whom were held in maximum security prisons without ever being charged with any terrorist crime.[119] On September 20, 2001, the Department of Justice and the INS amended detention custody procedures in order to allow for continued detention, even when there was no charge, during times of emergency. The PATRIOT Act of October 26, 2001, authorized indefinitely detaining immigrants if there were "reasonable grounds to believe" they were involved in terrorism. Prior to these amendments, routine detention and removal practices required that custody and removal occur as quickly as possible. Indefinite detention keeps persons in custody even after their cases have been determined and when there is no charge against the detainee. This went against the Supreme Court ruling in *Zadvydas v. Davis* that indefinite detention is unconstitutional.[120]

The controversial policy of preventative detention allowed the Department of Justice to detain 1,128 immigrants, mostly Muslim and Arab men, as potential security risks. The vast majority had been charged only with immigration violations and minor criminal charges, not terrorism. Additionally, the INS rounded up 6,000 Arab and Muslim immigrants with outstanding deportation orders. It also detained another 2,747 Arab and Muslim immigrants under a special registration program initiated after 9/11.[121] These numbers do not include the hundreds of "enemy combatants" detained in Guantanamo Bay, who were not under the custody of the Department of Justice but under the supervision of the Department of Defense.[122]

By 2001, the U.S. detention capacity had grown from six thousand to nineteen thousand over seven years and, in that same year, Congress appropriated $75 million for immigrant detention and construction projects.[123] The detention beds were used primarily for "criminal aliens"—mostly noncitizens charged with minor convictions during the drug war. Under Attorney General Ashcroft, the Department of Justice

also requested funds for additional prison beds for the growing population of incarcerated women and terrorist suspects apprehended on
minor criminal charges. Filling the beds with incarcerated Black and
Latina women and immigrants charged with drug offenses and Arab
and Muslim immigrants suspected of, but never charged with, terrorism
provided the body counts necessary to justify more funding for wars on
crime, illegal immigration, and terrorism.

The Detention Bed Mandate

In 2003, Congress transferred the INS to the newly created Department
of Homeland Security (DHS), separating immigration service from its
enforcement actions. Under the DHS, there are three main bureaus that
handle immigration matters. Citizenship and Immigration Services
(USCIS) receives applications of migrants seeking to enter the United
States or to adjust their immigration status, or those wishing to become
naturalized citizens. Customs and Border Protection (CBP), which
merged Inspections, Customs, and the Border Patrol, polices authorized and unauthorized flows in areas between and at various ports of
entry. Immigration and Customs Enforcement (ICE) concentrates on
interior immigration enforcement through detention and removal operations. The immigration courts and the Board of Immigration Appeals,
under the Executive Office of Immigration Review, remained under the
Department of Justice.[124]

The reorganization of the INS under the Department of Homeland
Security (DHS) transformed the funding structure for immigration enforcement. Before the reorganization in 2003, the INS commissioner had
more discretion over where and how to direct congressional funds.[125]
Since the creation of the DHS, funds for Citizenship and Immigration
Services come directly from user fees.[126] CBP and ICE, the main enforcement arms of DHS, derive funding directly from Congress. Most
federal funds are no longer pouring into the Department of Justice, but
instead are directed to the Department of Homeland Security, which
has since then become the government's largest law enforcement agency.

The importance of this shift in funding streams cannot be overstated.
For decades, INS commissioners complained of being the "step-child"
of the Department of Justice and of being underfunded. As one former

INS commissioner stated, "The Attorney General carried the agenda."[127] From the late 1970s onward, Congress funded the INS to play a supporting role to law enforcement and other agencies within the Department of Justice, mostly for *drug enforcement*, not immigration control.[128] After the reorganization, federal funding went directly to the Department of Homeland Security, which trickled down to state and local law enforcement agencies, the U.S. Marshals, and the U.S. Attorney's Office—this time for *immigration enforcement*, not drug control—to assist with criminal alien removal and criminal prosecution for immigration offenses.

The turn toward criminal prosecution, it turns out, was also a direct outcome of IIRIRA and the bed-space shortage it created. By 2004, detention beds along the border were filling up with "criminal aliens"— casualties of IIRIRA's expanded definition of aggravated felony—who had been stripped of their legal permanent residency status, and had been mandatorily detained and retroactively deported long after serving their sentences. This left fewer beds to detain unauthorized border crossers without convictions. Mexican nationals could be removed through voluntary departure, and they were. But the cases of Central American migrants apprehended at the border were more complicated and were more likely to result in detention, while immigration judges from the Executive Office of Immigration Review (EOIR), which remained under the Department of Justice, determined their cases.

DHS expanded criminal prosecution in order to minimize the practice of paroling eligible, mostly Central American, migrants from detention and to reduce a backlog of removal cases in the immigration courts.[129] Often when detention centers on the border were at capacity, the Border Patrol and Detention and Removal officers paroled apprehended Central American migrants without convictions, by releasing them on recognizance. This infuriated conservative critics in Congress who renamed the historic practice of detention parole as a "catch and release policy"— that encouraged migrants to abscond or go underground once they were released on recognizance. In a 2004 congressional hearing, the Committee on Appropriations berated DHS officials for its policy of "catch and release"—that is, releasing people "based on capacity, not merit."[130]

To put an end to "catch and release," Congress increased funds for detention bed space *and for criminally prosecuting immigration offenses*. The idea was to prosecute in criminal courts instead of the immigration courts and to avoid paroling migrants from detention.[131] Increasing the bed count was touted as a measure to reduce the level of "absconders" who failed to show up to their removal hearing once they are released on recognizance.[132] In 2004, the Intelligence Reform and Terrorism Prevention Act funded eight thousand detention beds each year between fiscal years 2006 and 2010.[133] In 2005, the Bush administration requested additional funds for criminally prosecuting immigration offenses, particularly under the federal prosecution program, Operation Streamline. Migrants criminally prosecuted for border-crossing offenses are deported directly from prison, which circumvents any additional strain on detention capacity.

Bipartisan support for immigrant detention–related bills had by then become commonplace, many of these calling for more beds. Those calling for constraint and discretion in the uses of detention often failed. Some proposals argued for more immigration judges, but Congress continued to invest in building detention capacity, much as it did during the era of prison expansion. In 2005, the Sensenbrenner Immigration Bill (HR 3477) included measures to increase detention beds and to impose mandatory sentences. Another bill debated that year, HR 4312, the Border Security and Terrorism Prevention Act, included provisions for more bed space and a line mandating that DHS "fully utilize bed space." The bill died and was reintroduced in 2006, again calling for more beds and repeating the mandate to utilize bed space.

That spring, mass protests broke out in cities throughout the United States, involving many of the very people the Sensenbrenner bill targeted.[134] That so many took to the streets, I believe, had less to do with what the bill proposed and more to do with the punitive detention and deportation practices, already firmly entrenched, that people experienced when crossing the U.S.-Mexico border. Other bills introduced in 2007 proposed expanding appropriations for criminal prosecution—HR 2630, 3283, and 3093 and the Federal Criminal Immigration Courts Act. The Sensenbrenner bill, HR 3477, and those that followed, failed. But immigration raids and a surge in deportations ensued.

In congressional hearings, ICE reported issues related to three major "categories" of people who made ending "catch and release" difficult: (1) the lack of detention facilities for family groups; (2) an injunction preventing the detention and deportation of El Salvadorans; and (3) problems with "really difficult countries," referring to the lack of a repatriation agreement with China over thirty-nine thousand Chinese nationals with final orders of deportation.[135]

At the time, detention bed capacity was at 20,800, and 85% of people in custody were mandatory detainees or those classified as "a national security threat or a criminal threat."[136] Rather than revisit mandatory detention provisions, Congress continued to fund more beds. During FY 2007 appropriation hearings, the Committee on Appropriations questioned the assistant secretary of ICE, Julie Myers, about bed space capacity, acknowledging that instituting a "catch and return" policy would require still more beds:

> CONGRESSMAN: Without Congress even acting on immigration reform, we now have a policy that's going to cause a need to detain them until they're returned. Sometimes that takes a while. . . . Are we utilizing what we can use? Is there anything you need to change statutorily to be able to use all the beds to detain as many of them as possible so that catch and return can be successful?
>
> MYERS: Well we are certainly looking to make sure we use the 20,800 beds we have . . . and squeeze every dollar we can out of those beds by making sure they spend less time in the beds.[137]

The testimony illustrates a law-and-order focus on maximizing resources, increasing efficiency, and processing as many people as possible, and marks a shift away from traditional adjudication in the immigration courts. Yet the testimony also reveals a disconnect between what Congress legislates and the enforcement reality on the ground and complicates the bed space issue. "Currently bed space is *not* limiting us except for the issue of families" (emphasis added), Myers explained.

> MYERS: We make over 1.1 million apprehensions a year and the majority of these are Mexicans who are returned to their country . . . and we do not detain them. The catch and release issues, the bed space issues, relate to what we refer to as other than Mexican.
>
> CONGRESSMAN: Well, my question relates to all of them. . . . The problem we have on returning Mexicans to Mexico or other than

Mexicans is that you have to recognize them in court without keeping them in custody until their court appearance.[138]

In the hearing, ICE assistant secretary Myers clarified that most Border Patrol apprehensions are of Mexican nationals, who are more likely to be "voluntarily returned" than detained and deported, at cost to the federal government. The "catch and release" policy most directly affected "other than Mexicans." As she explained, bed space was not an impediment to enforcement actions against Mexican nationals, who make up the majority of apprehensions and removals every year. Unable to grasp the complexity of migration flows and enforcement actions in the U.S.-Mexico border region, the congressman boiled the issue down to a shortage of beds.

Expanding bed space and alternatives to detention, as well as coming up with more sophisticated ways to deport by reducing court time or bypassing immigration judges altogether, had become a major focus in budget hearings when Barack Obama was elected president in 2008. That year, Congress approved funds for Operation Streamline. By then the bed capacity had risen to 31,500, up from 28,000 the year before. During a DHS appropriation hearing for FY 2008, then president Bush's budget included a request for $569,800,000 for three thousand new Border Patrol positions, $1 million for border fencing and biometric technology, and an increase of $118,000,000 for the Criminal Alien Program. The Committee on Appropriations expressed "disappointment" that the president had not requested funding for detention beds. It approved funding anyway.[139] Senator Robert Byrd, from the Committee on Appropriations, stated that

[t]he Committee is disappointed that the President's budget request does not maintain the linkage between requested increases for Border Patrol agents with a similar increase in detention beds. . . . Therefore the Committee provides an additional $146,451,000 for a total of $236,843,596, for 4,000 new detention beds. This is an increase of 3,050 beds . . . above the request and ensures a total of 31,500 beds.[140]

To prevent a detention policy rollback, Congress instituted a bed mandate in 2009, requiring that DHS maintain a bed level of no less than 33,400 beds. A Senate report on appropriations for the Department of Homeland Security in FY 2010, submitted by Senator Harry Reid, stated that

> [m]aintaining an adequate number of detention beds is critical to ensur-
> ing the integrity of our detention and removal system while at the same
> time preventing a return to the ill-advised "catch and release" policy. . . .
> The Congress took the lead and added funding for additional detention
> beds above the President's request the past 5 fiscal years. . . . Bill language
> is included directing that a detention bed level of 33,400 beds shall be
> maintained throughout the fiscal year 2010.[141]

Several bills came before Congress that year to "mandate" increasing detention bed levels.[142]

In 2009, following public scandals concerning medical care in detention facilities, ICE revised and publicized its new detention standards.[143] In response to protests against the Obama administration's record on deportations, ICE director John Morton released a memo on June 30, 2010, later revised on March 2, 2011, to field directors, special agents in charge, and all chief counsel outlining priorities for enforcement. The memo states that "ICE only has resources to remove 400,000 aliens per year, less than 4 percent of the illegal alien population in the United States. . . . ICE must prioritize its enforcement personnel, detention space, and removal resources to ensure that the removals the agency does conduct promote the agency's highest priorities" (e.g., terrorist suspects and "violent criminals, felons, and repeat offenders").[144] In 2011, Representative Lamar Smith introduced the "Keep Our Communities Safe Act of 2011," which would have authorized indefinite detention of migrants with orders of deportation who could not be deported due to a lack of repatriation agreements with the sending country.[145] The bill died.

By FY 2012, detention bed space in the United States had reached thirty-four thousand.[146] On May 23, 2012, the Committee on Appropriations stressed fiscal discipline for DHS, noting that "[w]hile the Department is charged with countering serious threats to our security, the

Nation faces another, perhaps even greater threat. This threat lies . . . here at home, where America's fiscal situation remains unsustainable."[147] Nevertheless, during this period of *fiscal crisis and government shutdowns*, the committee recommended $11,683,317,000 for Customs and Border Protection (CBP), $76,999,000 above the president's budget request. "This funding," the committee's report states, "sustains the highest level of Border Patrol agents and CBP officers in history. . . . The Committee also recommends $5,785,656,000 for ICE, an increase of $141,595,000 above the request, and sustains 34,000 detention beds— the greatest detention capacity in ICE's history . . . *denying the President's request for a reduction* in these crucial enforcement areas." (emphasis added).[148]

A dissenting Minority Report challenged the detention provisions in the bill, stating,

> [w]e strongly oppose inclusion of statutory language mandating that ICE maintain a level of not less than 34,000 beds through September 30, 2013, which is 1,200 more beds than the budget request. . . . While we have no problem funding the capacity at 32,800 beds, as requested, the use of those beds should be determined by enforcement actions and judgment of ICE on whether detention is required for particular detainees based on flight risk and danger posed to the public. . . . Further, in an environment of fiscal restraint, telling a federal agency that they are not permitted to spend less than a certain amount limits the ability of ICE to achieve its objectives with a savings to the taxpayer.[149]

Until then, challenges to the bed quota had been rare; detention-related legislation had the unexpected privilege of bipartisan support. The final appropriations act maintained a bed level of thirty-four thousand for FY 2013. In order to prevent the transfer of Guantanamo detainees to the United States, it also prohibited

> any federal funds from being used to construct, acquire, or modify any facility in the United States or its territories or possessions to house any individual who, as of June 24, 2009, is located at Guantanamo, and who: (1) is not a U.S. citizen or a member of the Armed Forces; and (2)

is either in DOD custody or control, or otherwise under detention at Guantanamo.[150]

In 2013, HR 2217, which passed in the House, called for "ICE funding to maintain a level of not less than 31,800 detention beds through September 30, 2014."[151] However, the final appropriations act of 2014 maintained the thirty-four-thousand-bed mandate, despite a letter to the president signed by sixty-five House Democrats calling for an end to the bed quota.[152] In May 2014, Representative Adam Smith of Washington State introduced the "Accountability in Detention Act" proposing that "the number of detention beds maintained shall be determined by the Secretary of Homeland Security and shall be based on detention needs. It is the sense of Congress that Appropriations Acts shall not mandate maintenance of a minimum number of detention beds."[153]

Filling Beds

The punitive turn in immigration enforcement must be understood in the context of the post–civil rights era of mass incarceration. Conservatives and, some would argue, liberal reformers helped spearhead law-and-order policies that exploded the U.S. prison population and created a crisis of prison overcrowding.[154] This chapter argues that the scramble for prison beds was a major force behind the Criminal Alien Program (CAP), which Congress pushed as a way to purge noncitizens from jails and prisons in order to free up prison beds. What is striking about this story is that the criminal alien mandate stemmed from a desire not to control migration but to free up bed space in the criminal justice system. CAP's roots, then, lie in the hyperincarceration of Black and Latina/o youth.

The Criminal Alien Program has transformed immigration enforcement on the border. It triggered a change in enforcement priorities. It transformed detention and removal. It led to developing integrated biometric technologies to track and measure risk, and it led to expanding detention bed space. The most seemingly benign aspects of CAP—beds and biometric technology necessary to identify and hold deportable criminal aliens—have played a crucial role in merging the immigration and criminal justice systems. CAP unleashed an onslaught of measures that institutionalized cooperation between immigration agents and local police, through interior enforcement programs like "absconder" initiatives, "fugitive" operations, 287(g) agreements, Secure Communities, and immigrant prosecution programs like Operation Streamline[155]—in other words, many of the punitive policies we associate with the criminalization of migration in the United States today.

However, punitive policies are not necessarily a "backlash" against rights and protections that reformers fought for for over a century. Rather, they operate within post–civil rights, "antidiscrimination," constitutional frameworks in ways that recognize rights for certain "victims," while aggressively punishing and banishing those branded as criminal. New enforcement priorities require that agents direct resources toward high-priority "criminals." Yet agents must also abide by guidelines for handling "noncriminals," nonpriority targets—nursing mothers, the elderly, and minors—to remove from the deportation and detention docket. This has created an enforcement terrain with new players acting as protectors and prosecutors.

3

Protectors and Prosecutors

Humanitarianism and Security

To the immigration agent, I must have looked suspicious. It was after dark and I was alone at the U.S. Port of Entry, rushing back after my first visit to a shelter for deported migrants in Nogales, Sonora. My quick and nervous pace—and no doubt my Mexican ancestry—set off a trigger. Instead of waving me through a turnstile, the agent questioned my whereabouts and the authenticity of my passport and U.S. citizenship. In that moment, one of thousands of inspections that day, I stood accused of document fraud, false claims to citizenship, and possibly other forms of immoral conduct. "Where are you coming from?" he asked sternly.

"Nogales," I replied.

"What were you doing there?"

"Visiting."

"Did you buy anything?"

"N-no."

"You didn't buy anything? So what were you doing there?"

"Just visiting."

"Where were you born?"

"Illinois."

"What's the capital of Illinois?"

"Huh?"

"I said, what's the capital of Illinois?"

"Springfield."

Outside the port of entry, a crowded shuttle van, or *camioneta*, pulled up to the sidewalk. *Norteño* music blared through a door flung open. "*Va pa' Tucson?*" the driver asked. I hopped into the passenger seat, greeted everyone, and before long, we were on Interstate 19 heading north.

Twenty miles from the international border, a tire blew out and the driver lost control. Within seconds, the van swerved across lanes, drove off the highway, flipped over, and landed on its side in the desert brush. In my field notes that night, I wrote,

> Adrenaline racing . . . I can't believe we survived. I could hear moans of the people in back. The driver stepped on my face trying to break the windshield to get out. Someone pulled me out quickly, afraid that the van would catch fire. I fumbled in the dark for my notebook with the notes I'd jotted quickly in the van before it swerved. We all got out safely. Only two people were seriously injured—a woman and a teenager—who had to be airlifted to the nearest hospital. . . . Border Patrol showed up even before the paramedics. I watched them from a close distance shine flashlights on people, no doubt trying to identify whether we were undocumented. They made everyone squat down and sit on the floor the way they do when they apprehend people. I refused to squat. Ignored their orders. A paramedic asked for my Social Security number. I declined to give it.[1]

The U.S. Border Patrol was the first to arrive on the scene, followed by paramedics, a sheriff's deputy, and firefighters from a station only a couple of miles away. Upon arrival, the Border Patrol agents ordered us to squat or sit in a subordinate position on the ground, a routine practice in apprehending migrants. All of us, including law enforcement and the paramedics, appeared to be of Mexican descent. All of us carried multiple forms of identification—green cards, visas, and passports. And all other passengers, including the driver, sat or squatted on command.

Once the agents sorted out our legal and criminal status, once they confirmed that the driver was not our smuggler, they turned the case over to the paramedics. Only then did the handling of the accident move from that of a crime scene to that of a humanitarian intervention. If someone had photographed the scene, the picture would show U.S. border agents standing over a line of suspects; a Santa Cruz County deputy sheriff giving a breath test to the driver and suspected coyote; EMTs taking vitals or strapping a body onto a stretcher; and emergency strobe lights flashing colors against the night sky.

Nothing about the way law enforcement acted seemed "illegal" or like an act of racial profiling. None of us dared to claim that our rights as racial minorities had been violated, even in our treatment as criminal suspects. On the contrary, the fire department and paramedics, also of Latina/o ancestry, were there to render emergency medical services, regardless of legal status. The unspoken presumption of rights to emergency medical care, to "equality under law," completely legitimized and normalized the handling of the accident, with which we all generally complied.

Since the 1990s, border agents carry out a federal mandate to track "criminal aliens." However, in a border region dependent on cross-border flows of people, goods, and money, implementing new crime-centered enforcement priorities did not generate the widespread consensus expressed in Congress. Even in a punitive state like Arizona, there was pushback from local law enforcement, the Tohono O'odham Nation, immigrant advocates, and Mexican officials on the ground.[2] Local law enforcement agents resisted enforcing immigration law in border communities dependent on cross-border exchange. The U.S. Attorney's Office for the District of Arizona, with court dockets filled with drug cases, was also reluctant to prosecute immigration cases. Mexican government officials and local NGOs publicly denounced the more punitive aspects of immigration and border policies resulting in unprecedented numbers of migrant deaths.

That DHS eventually garnered support for punitive approaches to migration control is partly due to the fact that politicians, policy makers, and former INS officials cloaked new enforcement priorities in what Jonathon Simon refers to as a "prosecutorial rhetoric" centered on punishing criminals and protecting victims' rights.[3] In *Governing Through Crime*, Jonathan Simon writes of how this rhetoric has influenced U.S. politics and culture. Mirroring the power of U.S. prosecutors to punish others, the prosecutorial model is a way of governing through laws, norms, language, or political discourse centered on championing victims' rights through aggressive punishment.

Privileging the crime victim reimagines civil rights as victims' rights or as a "right to safety" or "freedom from fear (of crime)."[4] Simon refers to the crime victim as "having emerged from the shadows of the civil rights subject as its own idealized political subject. In a kind of 'everyman extension,' the claims of crime victims adopted the complicity critique that civil rights and feminist activists had articulated concerning the involvement of the state in criminal violence [in the forms of 'lynchings, rapes, beatings']."[5] This reinterprets civil rights struggles against racial or gender violence as a battle against crime on behalf of crime victims, and masks the state's historical and systematic role in perpetuating racial violence through border controls and domestic policing. This deflects culpability away from state actors like police and border agents to individual "lawbreakers" and "wrongdoers."

In popular discourse the crime victim is typically the white, middle-class suburbanite or at times the police and law enforcement, more broadly. And this is certainly the case in places like Arizona, particularly Phoenix, where white "Americans" express feeling "victimized" by immigration and Arizona's changing demographics.[6] It is also evident when border agents or police charged with shooting and killing unarmed youth challenge proposals for any kind of law enforcement oversight or accountability mechanisms by asserting their "right to safety."

Nevertheless, in communities along the Arizona-Sonora border, the image of the crime victim is more complicated than in popular representations. On one hand is the image of the white rancher, the Native American tribal member of the Tohono O'odham Nation, or the Mexican American border resident who feels overwhelmed by the new volume of flows in Arizona directly resulting from U.S. border policy. On the other is the undocumented border crosser—victimized by smugglers, bandits, and the deadly, hostile environment—who also emerges as a crime victim in need of protection.

There is, then, local political pressure on border agents—from law enforcement agencies, Mexican officials, and anti-immigrant and migrant-rights advocates on the ground—to both *protect* and *punish*. In order to engage local actors in its criminal alien mandate, the Border Patrol must also acknowledge and give the appearance of safeguarding rights alongside meting out punishment. This chapter examines how front-line agents' relations to other players in the field shaped the ways in which enforcement priorities were implemented locally, and arguably in a different direction than Congress intended.

Enlisting Local Law Enforcement

Police and sheriff's deputies have become indispensable players in immigration enforcement. Although there was already a precedent of Border Patrol cooperating with police primarily on *drug* enforcement, they were not always directly involved in *immigration* control. Histori-cally in communities along the international boundary, like Nogales and Douglas, cross-border commerce took precedence over security.

Because police and sheriff's departments operate in economies heav-ily dependent on cross-border consumption, there is political pressure from local elites to "protect and serve" without disrupting international commerce. Officials explain that cash-strapped border communities "live or die" by revenue generated from cross-border exchange. "The most important thing that we think of as a community," explained one senior law enforcement official, "is that we *depend 100% on people cross-ing that border*. We encourage, we want, we need people to facilitate that border and to come across that border on a daily basis. . . . *We live or die by that*" (emphasis added).[7] He described the cross-border dependence in this way:

> The city of Nogales's major revenue source is sales tax. There is no prop-erty tax in the city of Nogales, so we live and die off of sales. Sixty percent of those sales are generated by visitors from Mexico. Every dollar that we collect in sales revenue, sixty cents comes from a Mexican shopper. So it is extremely important for us as a community to ensure that those Mexican shoppers are able to legally cross that border and come in here and purchase goods and return to Mexico.[8]

In communities with such cross-border linkages, then, police and deputy sheriffs don't automatically associate immigration with crime.[9] In contrast to federal immigration agents recruited from all over the country, local law enforcement officials often hail from border commu-nities themselves, and they don't by default see migrants as criminal.[10] Instead, they often define migrants by their economic status as shoppers or workers. One senior law enforcement official explains:

> Remember that the *majority of people crossing that border illegally are just decent people looking for a wage.* . . .
> If you think of the border town, you think oh my God there's all these illegal immigrants just running around . . . and it's lawless. It's going crazy, when in reality . . . they [migrants] come through here. . . . [T]hey get apprehended here. . . . [T]here's a *potential for more criminal activity*

because that's where the crossing point is . . . but the *majority are law-abiding people, they're just not here [legally]* . . . *They're not committing crimes.* They are usually *law abiding* . . . . They don't want to stand out because they don't want to get deported. . . . (emphasis added)[11]

Here, the agent challenges representations of border communities as "lawless." It is, according to the agent, the *border crossing* with multiple risks, rather than undocumented migrants themselves, that possesses "a potential for criminal activity." The agent also refutes popular images of "illegal immigrants" as criminal, referring to undocumented migrants as "law-abiding" *workers*, "looking for wage," as if to create social distance from unemployed native-born Blacks and Latinas/os warehoused in U.S. prisons.

In referring to immigrants charged with crimes, law enforcement, much like local elected officials, stressed the economic and social underpinnings of such offenses, most of which were in fact property crimes. Contrary to media portrayals linking Mexican immigration to border violence, local officials directly linked crime to the unemployment rate. Another law enforcement official explains,

If there are people who lose work in Nogales, Sonora, who can't come across, they are going to try and commit crime so that they can get money to go back home to the interior of Mexico. If we can do a good job of bringing jobs and making sure that the economy is strong on both sides of the border, then we reduce crime.[12]

In my earliest interviews with law enforcement officials in border communities, they made explicit distinctions between their mission and that of the Border Patrol and defined crime differently than federal immigration agents did. One senior law enforcement official clarified the distinction between the Border Patrol's definition of "criminal alien" and their own: "Now criminal aliens are defined in two ways, the Border Patrol defines criminal aliens as those who have reached whatever threshold they have . . . for having entered, been deported. We define criminal aliens as those who have been charged with committing crimes against the state, violating state statutes, burglary, theft, those kinds of things."[13]

The official makes clear that Border Patrol assigns criminal alien status on the basis of quotas ("thresholds") and internal policies of prosecutorial discretion that outline high-priority targets. For the Border Patrol, criminal aliens are those they decide to criminally prosecute for immigration offenses like "having entered" (illegal entry) or "having been deported" (reentry after deportation). By contrast, law enforcement agents in border communities differentiated criminal offenses ("violating state statutes") from administrative violations of immigration law committed mostly by undocumented migrants in transit and commuters. Police and sheriff's officials distinguish between what they describe as unauthorized economic migrants and those who commit criminal offenses.

The 1990s marked a major turning point in local law enforcement's eventually adopting "criminal alien" enforcement priorities. Major border operations in El Paso and San Diego diverted migrant flows to Southern Arizona in unprecedented ways.[14] Seemingly overnight, hundreds of thousands of migrants began crossing through the West Desert, including the territory of the Tohono O'odham Nation.[15] People smuggling proliferated, and a new law enforcement context emerged.

The massive influx frustrated local and tribal police as well as sheriff's officials who suddenly had to divert funds from their own budgets to manage the new flow of migrants.[16] A law enforcement official explains:

> Our current human smuggling dilemma, the illegal immigration that is occurring here, is the result of [Border Patrol] initiatives launched in El Paso in 1994 that funneled, that had the intent in fact . . . to limit as much as possible—and in fact close down major smuggling and trans-portation hubs—and to funnel and force as much of the immigration as they could . . . to the more hostile terrain of the southwest desert as deterrent to the illegal border crossers. . . . They believed that when people coming up from the south encountered that hostile environment, they would turn around and go home. Serious miscalculation. The end result is that more people are dying. . . . It hasn't acted as a deterrent at all . . . it's simply added a tremendous burden to sparsely populated areas like Cochise County that can ill afford to bear that financial yoke.[17]

They complained of "having to divert resources to something never intended."

We've always battled drug smuggling. . . . People smuggling became a significant law enforcement issue. . . . It's always been, but in terms of sheer volume, an unmanageable issue beginning in 1998—literally overnight, like a tidal wave. . . . While the numbers are down, there's still an unmanageable number of people coming through. . . . Prior to that it was a manageable issue. . . . It reached a point where it was unmanageable, overwhelming, and out of hand. We woke up—and keep in mind that we don't purposefully enforce immigration law. . . . Just as a consequence, just collaterally, we discovered that we were spending 40% of our budget on issues associated with illegal immigration.[18]

Where law enforcement officials had regarded immigration enforcement as a separate realm of law, the changing circumstances forced them to view migrant flows through a "security" lens rather than as cross-border commerce. The spike in migrant crossings through Arizona became a "public safety" issue for law enforcement, particularly when handling complaints by local ranchers about migrants running through their yards, leaving trash and depleting livestock feed.

We don't proactively enforce immigration law. But as a consequence of the sheer volume, the numbers of people passing through here . . . [T]ake a look at this map. . . . Cochise County is about the size of Connecticut and Rhode Island. . . . [A]ll those white squares are private property and the blue ones are state trust land, generally held in lease by the property owners for ranching and farming purposes. The quick observation is that when people cross the border, for the most part they are in someone else's land. . . . [T]hey're cutting fences, leaving gates open, leaving water supplies for livestock open and running . . . and the garbage that they leave in their wake. Most of them are carrying water bottles, and backpacks, and clothing that gets discarded and left behind and leaves a tremendous mess let alone the disturbance of seeing literally hundreds of people day in and day out in their backyards.[19]

Ranchers and other local residents were not the only perceived "victims." Police officials also recounted having to protect unauthorized migrants from "bandits," known locally as "bajadores." At the time, new migrant flows and local economic insecurity following the free trade-induced peso crisis created a situation in which the most marginal residents made a living by assaulting and robbing new migrants in transit.[20] According to law enforcement, the assaults typically occurred in the underground water and drainage tunnels for which Nogales is known. "Ten years ago when there wasn't all this technology and resources deployed by the federal government to protect our borders," explained an official, "there was uncontrolled, totally uncontrolled undocumented aliens crossing into the United States. There were points in time when we deployed our resources just to ensure the safety of the border." He went on to explain,

> We weren't so much worried about a person who was coming across the border per se because *that* was illegal, we were more concerned that if they're gonna do it and they are going to do it unchecked at least let's make sure that they're doing it safely and they're not getting robbed and beat up and stoned or raped in the interim. So we were deploying resources not so much to condone the illegal immigration, but since it was happening anyway, we had to make sure that there wasn't crime being committed in those areas. (emphasis added)[21]

Here the official acknowledges that the volume of flows, resulting from federal Border Patrol operations, put migrants at risk for greater victimization by the so-called border bandits. Yet he also implies that the "technology and resources" stemming from the same border operations that created the problem helped contain "border bandits" who prey on border crossers. Publicly, they credit the Border Patrol for reducing crime in border communities. Yet in interviews with law enforcement, officials complicated the story, stating that it was actually *the proliferation of smuggling*—also an outcome of Border Patrol operations—that displaced some "*bajadores*," referred to as "tunnel kids" or youth living in many of Nogales's underground drainage tunnels. "They were in the tunnels," one law enforcement official explained.

> They were stealing, robbing . . . and the county was paying for nothing but kids from across the line. They didn't have any room for kids from this side. . . . [Y]ou see the dynamics of this is that if they got caught, it was a better way of life for them than if they didn't. If you're living on the streets

and you rob, what is the penalty? A warm place to stay. Three meals a day. So it got to be a real problem. I mean I was working with the Mexican authorities and everybody on this side and actually I think it . . . we exceeded our expectations. You know and then another thing happened. Another part of the dynamic that happened is that *the smugglers started taking control . . . of the tunnels.* Well we had all these tunnels that are being discovered. All of a sudden they [smugglers] didn't want these kids in there. So you know, little by little they got edged out. (emphasis added)[22]

The law enforcement official characterizes the period just *before* the border buildup as a time when the local juvenile justice system performed welfare-like functions, like offering "a better way of life," "a warm place to stay," or "three meals a day" for homeless youth from Mexico. He implies that, prior to the buildup, the Mexican homeless youth arrests were taking up bed space intended for impoverished U.S.-born juvenile offenders in Arizona's overcrowded facilities. It was the buildup, particularly the proliferation of smuggling stemming from it, that ultimately displaced homeless youth from the tunnels. But it also transformed the Arizona-Sonoran border into one of the most highly trafficked smuggling corridors along the border.

As the intensification of policing made local law enforcement more directly involved in immigration enforcement, it also generated some friction over funding.

Local law enforcement departments in cash-strapped border counties commissioned studies on the impact of illegal immigration on the criminal justice system.[23] They testified before Congress, and they invited congressional delegates to Southern Arizona in order to secure funding to offset the costs of managing the rise in migrant flows.

Particularly after 9/11, law enforcement agents expressed concern that funding for law enforcement agencies would dry up once Congress appropriated funds directly to the newly created Department of Homeland Security. Officers complained that Homeland Security funds would go to Tucson and Phoenix even though "they aren't border towns." A law enforcement official explained,

In my business, time is money. Time is a finite resource. When my deputies are forced, having to respond to issues associated with illegal immigrants, saying yes to that means saying no to something else. I have seventy-five deputies to cover all the law enforcement needs of this entire county, and when you spread them over 365 days, those are pretty thin and when they have to respond to this significant increase in having to divert resources to things we never intended, never planned. . . . There's no more money . . . it's not like I can magically hire more people.

There's no permanent funding mechanism or pipeline for reimbursement costs, save one. And that is not in the president's budget this year. It's called SCAAP, State Criminal Alien Assistance Program. Five hundred and eighty-five million dollars in appropriations nationwide to reimburse local jurisdictions for costs associated with incarcerating criminal aliens.

Over the last five years we've been able to tap that fund for, uh, an average of about three hundred thousand a year, which is about 22% of what our actual costs have been. The amount has increased, but the amount per criminal alien we've been able to recoup has decreased because we've had more criminal aliens, more and more people have found out about it. When we first discovered it, it was kind of quiet. People have found out. More are applying . . . spread over a bigger piece of bread than it used to be.

But we're concerned that all this Homeland Security funding is not new money. It's money that is being diverted from existing programs and that proposes the demise of the SCAAP. In fact I wrote a letter to the president. I got a response. But in essence they said they think the money can be better used for deterring and preventing crime in their Homeland Security program.[24]

Criminal alien assistance funds under SCAAP never dissolved, but they have fluctuated from $130 million in 1995, when the funds first became available under the Violent Crime Control and Law Enforcement Act of 1994, to $565 million in 2002 and $400 million between 2006 and 2009 to $238 million in FY 2013.[25] The Department of Justice and the Department of Homeland Security jointly administer SCAAP. They reimburse states and municipalities "for incarcerating [or detaining] undocumented criminal aliens who have at least one felony or two misdemeanor convictions for violations of state or local law, and who are incarcerated for at least four consecutive days."[26] The 2005 Department of Justice Reauthorization Act required that funds be used "only for correctional purposes."

After the reorganization of the former INS under the Department of Homeland Security in 2003, the federal government began to allocate massive amounts of funding directly to DHS. Prior to the reorganization, federal funds went directly to the Department of Justice for local law enforcement and Immigration and Naturalization Service, which the attorney general oversaw. The channeling of federal funds directly to DHS for "criminal alien" populations transformed the relationship of local law enforcement in border communities to immigration enforcement.[27]

Funding to advance DHS's criminal alien mandate also provided additional revenue streams that offer incentives for local law enforcement agencies to provide detention bed space for the immigration system. It also created a new market for public and private prison expansion in Arizona.[28] In 2005, the Santa Cruz border county approved a sales tax increase to fund a new 372-bed prison in Nogales, Arizona, which opened in 2011. The county leases 170 beds for criminally prosecuting immigrants under Operation Streamline.[29] Cochise County is also pursuing an expansion of its jail in the Bisbee/Douglas area.[30]

Border Patrol and police collaboration on immigration enforcement has only deepened as the Arizona legislature enacted a series of state laws that punish unauthorized immigration status, such as SB1070.[31] To be fair, many departments in communities along the border came out against SB1070 but, generally, they have begun to implement DHS enforcement priorities that involve protection of crime victims as well as punishment.

In adopting DHS's criminal enforcement priorities, law enforcement officers don't exclusively or uniformly criminalize all unauthorized migrants. Rather, adapting the criminal alien mandate to a cross-border context, they increasingly process migrants in transit as either "victims" or "criminals." For instance, they assist with search and rescue operations and criminal investigations of crime scenes in remote areas (mostly migrant deaths or assaults).

In September 2002, three Cochise County deputy sheriffs recovered the decomposed body of a migrant woman and tied it to the hood of their SUV using the straps of the body bag. Douglas residents shared firsthand accounts of how the deputies acted irresponsibly when they stopped to get gas on their way to the morgue. Activists condemned the actions in a public statement charging that "[t]his incident clearly shows that these deputies had no regard for this woman as a human being." The county sheriff temporarily suspended the deputies without pay, calling the incident a "grievous mistake." He further noted that "[t]he discovery of the dead and dying is becoming all too common. . . . [T]hey take their toll on everyone involved, not least of which are the law enforcement personnel who have to gather them up."[32] The deputies publicly apologized to the family of the deceased and to the Mexican Consulate.

The deputies' punishment (suspension without pay) brings the migrant woman's victim (and rights-bearing) status into relief. The local newspaper noted that the woman, Janet Mata Mendez, twenty-four, from Veracruz, Mexico, had a bachelor's degree and had worked in an assembly plant in Ciudad Juarez before crossing the border. She was the 136th migrant body recovered that year. Calling attention to her university degree and employment history, a local paper even noted that when the deputies found her, she was wearing a sweatshirt, jeans, and tennis shoes, as if to emphasize her personhood.

Law enforcement agents, then, recognized that unauthorized migrants, rather than ranchers or border residents, are the population most at risk for victimization. Yet in addition to assisting with migrant protection, police and sheriffs were increasingly pulled into criminal prosecutions for immigration offenses by provisioning bed space for the Criminal Alien Program and assisting with criminal investigations. By taking on DHS's criminal alien mandate, then, they have been given broader discretion to sort and classify according to criminal *and* immigration status—to decide who is a "criminal" (e.g., smugglers, petty thieves) and who is an "illegal" (e.g., dead migrants, migrant workers). This is in tension with the more nuanced perceptions of border crossers as workers, students, or shoppers that law enforcement officers have traditionally held.

Partnering with the U.S. Attorney's Office

The Department of Homeland Security's criminal alien mandate has also transformed the Border Patrol's relationship to the U.S. Attorney's Office. Historically, the Border Patrol referred very few cases for criminal prosecution. With the exception of a small spike in prosecutions during Operation Wetback, the Border Patrol had prosecuted unauthorized entry violations as civil violations.[33] Even when I began this fieldwork in 2001, agents were more likely to treat unauthorized entry as a civil offense than as a criminal offense.

Over the past decade, the criminal prosecution rate for immigration cases has tripled.[34] Policy analysts attribute the rise in criminal prosecution for immigration offenses to DHS's "consequence-driven" enforcement strategy, which punishes immigration law violators. However, the spike in criminal prosecutions did not originate as harsher penalties for undocumented immigrants. Rather, it stemmed from the bed space shortage in immigrant detention and the prison system.

In the previous chapter, I discussed how the 1996 Illegal Immigration Reform and Immigrant Responsibility Act (IIRIRA) restructured immigrant detention and deportation in order to more easily expel "criminal aliens" and free up beds in overcrowded jails and prisons under the "war on crime." When I began my fieldwork in 2001, the mandatory detention and criminal alien removal provisions under IIRIRA pushed immigrant detention centers on the border over capacity. With detention beds often at capacity, there was limited space to hold migrants apprehended at the border.

The need to free up detention beds on the border, in turn, led to a greater reliance on federal prosecution for immigration offenses. Historically, a migrant's country of origin has influenced enforcement actions. As a detention and removal officer explained, "Voluntary returns are most common for Mexicans [because of proximity and cooperation with Mexican government]. OTMs ['Other than Mexicans'] are immediately sent to an immigration judge [for removal]."[35] But when the detention centers were full, agents would parole migrants by releasing them on recognizance pending a hearing before an immigration judge.

Between 2002 and 2005, when Congress authorized federal funds to criminally prosecute *low-level* immigration cases, the Del Rio Border Patrol Sector in South Texas experienced a 45% increase in apprehensions of non-Mexican nationals, mostly from Central American countries. Because the Border Patrol cannot return non-Mexican nationals they apprehend on the border to Mexico, agents issued a Notice to Appear (NTA) before an immigration judge and often paroled

"OTMs" without a criminal record, prompting intense criticism from Congress and political pressure to end the "catch and release policy."

In 2005, the Border Patrol began criminally prosecuting illegal entry and reentry in Del Rio, Texas, which became known as the federal prosecution program Operation Streamline. The origins and expansion of Streamline beyond the Del Rio Sector can be attributed to overcrowded detention centers, often packed with formerly incarcerated immigrants awaiting deportation and others mandatorily detained under the 1996 law. The Border Patrol utilized criminal prosecution as a way to bypass the immigration courts and the need to parole Central American migrants, or "OTMs," from detention. Streamline enabled the Border Patrol to issue fewer NTAs to non-Mexican nationals apprehended in South Texas and authorized agents to refer apprehended migrants to the U.S. Attorney's Office for criminal prosecution instead. By processing "OTMs" through the criminal justice system, Streamline made it possible to deport them after they served out a criminal sentence rather than parole apprehended migrants from overcrowded detention centers. Following criminal prosecution, they would be deported under the Criminal Alien Program, without their ever coming before an immigration judge to request any form of relief from deportation or detention.

To deflect legal challenges to Streamline, the Border Patrol drew on "race-blind," "nondiscriminatory" principles to implement the program. As one official explained, "the originators determined that Streamline would not work if it only targeted 'Other than Mexicans' for prosecution." To avert charges of discrimination based on nationality, he said, Streamline expanded its scope to Mexican and non-Mexican nationals: "Our concern was *equal protection* . . . . So Streamline became '*everybody gets treated the same*.' It became all inclusive" (emphasis added).[36]

Early implementation of Streamline involved hours of paperwork, including hand writing case numbers and preparing multiple copies for everyone involved. IT consultants reduced the processing time from hours to minutes. "With the push of a button," explained a Texas judge,

> it's in the system, it's on the calendar, it's made it to the defense attorneys and prosecutors, we've shipped it back to Border Patrol with all the information, Marshals have their jail lists. . . . The program accepts the

complaints and warrants from Border Patrol [and] sends them to the attorneys and to the judges to read. . . . Then when the agents come in,
they just use their thumbprint and it drops their signature in and the
judge does the same and puts a signature in on all eighty—we get them
in batches of eighty.[37]

Congressional funding for information technology (IT), personnel,
and detention and prison beds enabled the Border Patrol to expand its
partnership with the U.S. Attorney's Office. When Streamline extended
to the Tucson Border Patrol Sector in January 2008, Arizona was pro-
jecting a $1.7 billion deficit, one of the worst in the country.[38] At the
time, Arizona also experienced a surge in drug cases, possibly the result
of a reduction in the drug possession threshold for prosecution. Despite
initial opposition to Streamline, congressional funds for immigration
prosecution enabled the U.S. Attorney's Office for the District of Arizona to hire new attorneys, from 110 in FY 2008 to 149 at the beginning
of FY 2010.[39]

By 2009, federal immigration prosecutions had jumped to over 50%
of all federal cases, followed by drug prosecutions, which at the height
of the "war on crime" made up the majority of cases.[40] Illegal entry and
reentry (violating a deportation order) cases under Streamline made up
92% of all federally prosecuted immigration offenses.[41] Already overwhelmed by a rising immigration caseload, the U.S. Attorney's Office
in Arizona began turning away drug cases due to a lack of resources.[42]

The U.S. Attorney's Office now prosecutes more low-level immigration cases than drug cases, mostly illegal entry and reentry after deportation.[43] Before Streamline, agents in the Tucson Sector prosecuted less
than 1% of immigration cases. Because of the surge in Border Patrol
prosecutions, the District Court of Arizona now has one of the busiest
caseloads in the country and has grown 154% since 1994.[44] To compen-
sate for the increased caseload, ICE attorneys were deputized as prosecutors, and Border Patrol agents were deputized as U.S. Marshal Service
agents who provide courtroom security and transfer migrants to and
from courts, prisons, and other detention facilities. Private attorneys accepted contracts to represent defendants alongside public defenders.

The hearings occur en masse. During one hearing, as I entered the
courtroom I overheard an attorney speaking in Spanish on his cell

phone to the family of a defendant: "She's fine. The judge will give her thirty days. She has to serve thirty days from January 7. She'll be out by the seventh or eighth of February [pause]. . . . She was alone, lost in the desert. A [local] family helped her."[45] As I walked through the doors, the court was in session. Forty-five shackled migrants filled courtroom benches. Their public defenders wore fine suits but looked somber. There were two uniformed Border Patrol agents and two others from the U.S. Marshal Service. The prosecuting ICE attorney was also present.

The judge addressed the defendants:

> Each of you has had a lawyer appointed. . . . [Y]ou are charged with two counts: a felony for entry with a prior deportation, punishable from two to twenty years, and illegal entry, punishable up to sixty days. . . . Each of you signed a guilty plea. . . . [T]he felony charge is dropped, but the guilty plea means that if you enter again, you could be charged and punished. . . . All of you entered a guilty plea. If any of you don't want to enter a guilty plea and want a trial, please stand.[46]

No one stood.

The judge addressed the migrants through a translator, seven at a time. "Did you sign your plea agreements?"

"Sí," they all replied.

"Did your attorney explain your charges?"

"Sí."

"Did you have difficulty understanding?"

"No," they collectively replied.

"You are pleading guilty to reentry. By pleading guilty, you are waiving certain rights," explained the judge. "You agree to stipulated removal. . . . You agree not to appeal." The judge addressed defendants individually. "Mr. Hernandez-Flores? Do you have authorization to be here?"

"No."

"Did you enter through Naco? Were you previously removed in Calexico? Mr. Ruis-Vera, did you seek permission from a U.S. official?"

"No."

"Did you enter through Douglas? Were you previously removed from Calexico? Mr. Soto-Valdez? Did you receive permission to be here?"

"No."

"Did you enter through Sasabe? Were you previously removed through Nogales? Didn't your attorney explain that if you returned, you would serve considerably more time?"

The judge accepted the guilty pleas and ordered sentences ranging from sixty to ninety-five days. The entire hearing lasted twelve minutes. The attorneys helped migrants remove their translation headsets. They shook hands. Migrants shuffled out of the courtroom, their hands and legs shackled, and the judge called the next batch. After the hearings, U.S. Marshals and Border Patrol agents transferred them to prison to serve out their time and then face deportation.

"[We] didn't want to participate [in Streamline]," explained one supervisory attorney, "but [some felt] we could use some extra work. We agreed but it can't be done like in other places."[47] Judges and attorneys participating in Streamline did not necessarily regard unauthorized migration as criminal. Adapting DHS enforcement priorities to the local, cross-border enforcement terrain, they described their role in enforcement as one of *protecting and safeguarding the rights* of apprehended unauthorized migrants, whom they too regarded as being at risk for victimization (by smugglers, bandits, and immigration law and policy). One judge explained, "As horrible as this may look, it would be worse if it weren't for this guilty plea. If this didn't exist, they'd be doing twenty-four to sixty-four months."[48] They invoked a language of constitutional rights embedded in criminal procedures to diffuse criticism and legal challenges.[49] "The Public Defender's office tries to enforce the Constitution," explained a Streamline attorney. "We see ourselves as enforcers of the Constitution."[50] Another senior judge stated that

[w]e try in Arizona to make certain that rights aren't violated or trampled by this. . . . Operation Streamline isn't the same as assembly-line justice, it just means that there are a large number of cases at that particular level that are analyzed and heard each day. . . . I don't see it as our responsibility to tell the executive branch which cases they should prosecute or Congress what they should fund as far as that. . . . [I]t's our responsibility to hear the cases presented to us and to rule according to the law.[51]

Like local law enforcement, the U.S. Attorney's Office eventually adopted DHS enforcement priorities. They too appear to be sorting cases under a similar victim/criminal dichotomy, extending protection (from imprisonment) to unauthorized migrants without a criminal record and helping to prosecute those with a prior conviction, however minor, in accordance with DHS's criminal alien mandate. One judge explained how, in the Tucson Sector, Streamline went from targeting all unauthorized border crossers to prioritizing those with a prior record.

> When the program [Streamline] began we were doing about forty to seventy a day. . . . Some [cases] had felonies; some had none. There's been some change in policy. . . . Prosecutors decided to focus on bigger-issue cases. No more no [criminal] record people, just people with records. [On a given day], there will never be more than seventy.[52]

In a memo on immigration prosecution policy, an official from the Executive Office for the United States Attorney's Office noted that

> [a]ll of the United States Attorney's Offices (USAOs) prosecute the most serious offenses and *those offenders with established criminal records* as a priority. Along the SWB [southwest border], offenders entering the country illegally *but with no criminal record and no prior deportation* are almost certainly going to be voluntarily removed ("VR'd") numerous times before they are formally deported barring some unusual or aggravating circumstance in the case. Several factors contribute to this policy, the most pronounced being the lack of resources and bed space to detain and prosecute every illegal entry violator. Additionally there is also *very little punishment for first-time offenders*, and investigative agencies and the USAOs are inclined to spend their resources on the more serious offenses. Therefore, offenses in which aliens are smuggled for profit or where an alien with a serious criminal record reenters the country after being deported will receive priority attention. (emphasis added)[53]

The district of Arizona reports that

> [t]he Phoenix/Tucson/Yuma offices do not have an official policy on the number of times an illegal entrant alien must enter before being pros-

ecuted for the misdemeanor offense of 8 U.S.C. S 1325 [entry without inspection]. It is evaluated on a case by case basis but almost certainly *an alien would not be prosecuted on a first offense* unless there were aggravating circumstances. . . . The [District of Arizona] offices have guidelines in place to prosecute all provable 8 U.S.C. SS1326(b)(2) and 1326(b)(1) [illegal entry after deportation]. These offices also prosecute defendants who are currently on probation of federally supervised release.[54]

This is a new threshold for the U.S. Attorney's Office. Prior to Streamline, there were clearer distinctions between civil immigration offenses and nonimmigrant crimes. Like local law enforcement, judges, prosecutors, and public defenders are also processing cases according to who is or isn't an enforcement priority for DHS. Nonpriorities include unauthorized immigrants with "no prior record" or "first-time entrants." "Criminal aliens" are those typically charged with "reentry after deportation" or anyone with "prior contact with the criminal justice system."

DHS criteria informing who gets criminally prosecuted is becoming diffused and part of the lexicon of judges and attorneys. One judge distinguished between "economic illegals" and "criminal illegals," noting that most of those coming through Streamline have a criminal record. "The people here all have criminal history," he says. "They've had some previous encounter with the criminal justice system, whether it's through Border Patrol, U.S. [federal] courts, or state courts."[55] By "criminal history," the judge is referring to immigration offenses, charged as felonies "if they involve illegal reentry into the country after deportation, the smuggling of illegal immigrants, or illegal immigrants with prior criminal records."[56]

Another judge states, "You've got economic aliens. You've got criminal aliens. And until those two groups are separated and they're each dealt with separately, you're never going to have a resolution . . . and basically what happens is that the courts and enforcement become the only solution at that point."[57] Here the judge draws on the Border Patrol's criminal alien enforcement priorities as if they had always existed. There are moments when judges and attorneys challenged the classifications, but increasingly they have begun to adopt them. Just as police and sheriff's deputies have had to incorporate new thresholds to sort and classify undocumented migrants according to criminal status, such schemata and thresholds have extended to judges and attorneys to give legitimacy and a sense of consensus, masking the ways in which the political choice to go after "criminal aliens" makes up the very population that it targets.

Cooperating with Migrants' Advocates

As migrants' advocates, Mexican officials also played a key role in enforcement. They advocate for the protection of migrant rights in all aspects of enforcement, ranging from humanitarian assistance to migrants in transit to detention and deportation. Mexican officials have played a historic role in "protecting" Mexican nationals, though some argue that they primarily represent the interests of the state and not principally migrants per se.[58] During the Great Depression, they helped facilitate the repatriation of hundreds of thousands of Mexicans from the United States.[59] They played a similar role in "drying out wetbacks" during the Bracero Program, a form of repatriation in which U.S. immigration officials deported undocumented Mexicans and then, with cooperation of Mexican officials, readmitted them as Braceros with a labor contract.[60] Mexican consular officials have also advocated on behalf of migrants during major labor strikes, at times suppressing the more radical elements of labor organizing, to the benefit of growers.[61]

Officials from the Instituto Nacional de Migración and the Office of the Mexican Consulate still described their role as protecting Mexican nationals, but the focus has shifted from labor management to security—most visibly in the form of cooperating with the Border Patrol and local law enforcement on "migrant safety." The year after I began my fieldwork (2002) was an especially brutal one for migrants crossing the Sonoran desert. That year, apprehensions were half the levels of 1998, at three hundred thousand, but the death count had doubled.[62] In one weekend alone, the Mexican Consulate in Tucson had sixteen cases of dead migrants recovered from Tohono O'odham reservation on the border. "These weren't like the sixteen that died in Yuma [in 2001] *que crearon tanto escandalo* [that created such a scandal]," he explained.

These were sixteen that died separately [pounds the tip of his pen on scattered points on a map of the desert]. One here, another here, another there. . . . It began on a Thursday in June. "Sir, it's the sheriff. A *paisano* died. At 10:00 p.m. I get another call and at 12:00 midnight another, this time from the tribal police. "Sir, we found a dead girl." At 2:00 a.m. the Border Patrol called to inform us they found the body of a deceased woman. . . . It continued like that until Sunday. We ended up with sixteen corpses. . . . From January, February, March, April, May, we had a total of twenty-five cases and in those few days—sixteen [makes a slashing sound with mouth]. And from there they continued to rise. We stopped answering calls from the Border Patrol, from Instituto Nacional de Migración, because we were so backlogged with the task of identifying so many corpses.[63]

"Normally the body decomposes within seventy-two hours," the official explained matter-of-factly, "but in the summer months, in eight." Temperatures can reach up to 120 degrees Fahrenheit. Without shade, the Sonoran desert can feel like a vast ocean in reverse. There is a complete absence of water. The diverse vegetation and wildlife give a false impression of habitability. But the West Desert is more like the ocean's depth. A still, penetrating heat, not water, engulfs you. It suffocates you, slowly and naturally, drying up every fluid in your body. This is what it felt like the first time I walked in the desert, unaccustomed to the heat and with insufficient quantities of water. Away from the main roads or border towns, no one without water, a map, or a vehicle stands a chance.

When the Border Patrol launched Operation Safeguard in the Tucson Sector in 1995, it allocated resources for "criminal alien" removal as well as search and rescue, as the name suggests. The Border Patrol anticipated that under Safeguard, intensified policing in border towns would push migrant flows further out into the hostile desert. In an internal document on Operation Safeguard, the INS officials noted "special efforts to apprehend illegal immigrants and drug traffickers, but also decreasing violence and *preventing deaths* that occur when migrants cross desert areas."[64]

In 1998, the Border Patrol launched the Border Safety Initiative (BSI), which formalized and publicized its search and rescue operations aimed at reducing migrant fatalities. Invoking a language of human rights, one Border Patrol agent said of BSI's mission, "regardless of whether they are here illegally, they are human beings. . . . It's about producing a rescue as opposed to a fatality. Instead of having to recover a dead body, we find and stabilize injuries."[65] The Border Patrol circulated public service announcements and created BORSTAR, a search and rescue unit that trains agents as EMTs. "There are hundreds of tracks in the sand," explained the agent. "One search can take three and a half hours with a helicopter or agents on foot. By the time we find them, they are unconscious and dehydrated. . . . [S]ometimes we find them by the buzzards flying overhead."[66]

In search and rescue operations, the Border Patrol cooperated with Grupo Beta, established in 1990 by the Instituto Nacional de Migración (INM) with the purpose of "protecting and defending the human rights of migrants." As one agent explained, Grupo Beta is made up of federal, state, and local law enforcement officers who assist with search and rescue operations, educate migrants about the risks of crossing through the desert, offer legal and social assistance, and combat smuggling and other "crimes" against migrants. In Grupo Beta's new office in Sasabe, Sonora, a major "hot spot" for smuggling at the time, a map was hung showing all the major points of entry used by smugglers in the West Desert. In their one-room building on the outskirts of town, the agent went over the main smuggling points in the West Desert, the safety literature they disseminate, and search and rescue techniques and equipment they use. We drove over to the international boundary in a bright orange pickup truck with the Grupo Beta logo. The border was literally marked by a barbed wire fence with a makeshift gate on it. "The gate was put up because smugglers just drove right through the fence," he explained. "This way you don't have to fix it every time they knock it over. All they have to do is open it." We were surrounded by desert, barbed wire, and traces of crossings littered everywhere. In the distance he pointed to a group of ten people walking, with gallons of water in hand, behind their guide, the smuggler. "People don't usually begin to cross until nightfall," he said, "but it looks like the Border Patrol might be changing shifts because they are not around. The Mexican constitution says that people have a right to cross, so we can't actually stop them from crossing. La Ley General de Población [Mexico's immigration law] guarantees 'transito libre' [freedom of mobility]."[67]

That the Mexican border agent made no effort to intervene was due in part to the fact that the migrants were already on U.S. territory, but also that Mexican officials did not automatically view Mexican migrants, or their guides for that matter, as criminal. I once asked an INM official how he felt about receiving deportees released from U.S. prisons for immigration offenses like illegal entry, reentry, or smuggling, to which the official replied, "they haven't committed any crimes here." Similarly to the Grupo Beta agent above, Mexican officials invoked a fundamental right to mobility guaranteed in the Mexican constitution and international human rights law. But they avoided questions about whether that right applied to non-Mexican nationals crossing through Mexico.[68]

Like the Border Patrol and other players, Mexican officials invoked a language of rights, yet have also adopted DHS's prosecutorial rhetoric that constructs migrants as crime victims. The process of recovering and repatriating bodies was often part of a larger criminal investigation that targets smugglers (and non-Mexican nationals) for prosecution. The Mexican Consulate, for instance, was tasked with investigating cases of migrant deaths. Much of the work involved establishing the identity of a decomposing corpse. Once the Border Patrol identifies a body and transports it to the medical examiner's office in Tucson, the Mexican Consulate's office would begin its investigation, often with missing persons reports from the Department of Foreign Ministry in Mexico or with clues found on the body—an ID, a phone number—and with training, technology, and information acquired from DHS and U.S. law enforcement agencies. "When the process of identification is difficult because the remains are so decomposed," explained the official, "then we turn to digital fingerprints, DNA, or dental records. . . . It's like detective work. Once we establish the identity, we notify the family. . . . The majority of the *paisanos'* bodies are embalmed and returned to Mexican territory." Mexican officials then continue to assist with repatriation of Mexican nationals as they have historically done, but in this case of cadavers instead of workers, and through criminal investigation techniques.

In doing this investigative work, they too distinguished "victims" from "criminals," in accordance with DHS enforcement priorities. One consular official recounted a phone call from the Border Patrol. "'We have a minor, eleven years old. She has no family with her. One person from the group [of fourteen apprehended] says he's from her hometown,'" he said, quoting the border agent. When the consulate interviewed the young girl, she offered the following testimony: "'My father spoke with that man. He has my father's number.'" The consulate learned that the child's parents lived in Atlanta and "paid this man to bring her. He's a coyote." According to the consular official, the coyote initially denied the smuggling accusations when the consulate interviewed him (also a Mexican national) saying, "'*No que yo la conozco* [I know her].'" The consulate recounted that "[h]e [the coyote] said that when the Border Patrol apprehended him, they cleaned him out. He lost all the numbers." After helping to secure a confession from the coyote, the consulate said to the Border Patrol handling the case, "'I don't know what you plan to do with that one [referring to the smuggler]. I'm not interested. He's fine. He's healthy, but I want the girl to sleep in her own bed.'"

Here, the Mexican government official's retelling of this incident conveys the image of the young girl as a crime victim, a victim of smuggling. It also conveys the Mexican Consulate's day-to-day cooperation with U.S. authorities to track down the parents of unaccompanied minors, and to facilitate a "safe" repatriation and family reunification. The Mexican official works with DHS agents to ensure the young girl's release from detention and repatriation back to Mexico. This contrasts with the image of the alleged smuggler, also a Mexican national, whom the official expresses little concern for, noting that he is "not interested" in what the Border Patrol does with his case, as if to suggest that he merits no protection, only punishment. Similar representations are evident in an illustrated pamphlet, *Guía del Migrante Mexicano* (Guide for Mexican Migrants), published by the Mexican government in 2004.[69] The Mexican Consulate circulated several million copies to warn migrants of the dangers of undocumented migration to the United States. Although the pamphlet generated much criticism in the United States as a tool for "aiding and encouraging" undocumented migration, in fact, it draws on a U.S. prosecutorial rhetoric and reproduces DHS enforcement priorities.[70] In its colorful illustrations, it represents migrant women and minors as victims, and smugglers as victimizers. The comic also instructs migrant workers to self-regulate their behaviors in the U.S. in order to prevent being classified as criminal aliens.

That Mexican government officials replicated DHS enforcement priorities was also evident in other cooperative enforcement actions. In matters of arrest, for instance, migrants I met in the shelters reported that INM officials at times criminally prosecuted non-Mexican nationals and indigenous Mexicans for failure to carry proper identity documents, even as they offered "protection" to those rescued from the desert or in need of medical assistance. In matters of detention and deportation, the Mexican Consulate indirectly assisted with repatriations, helping procure travel documents and increasingly screening Mexican nationals in jails and prisons for criminal alien removals, which fell under their mission of migrant protection.

Border agents depended on Mexican officials, then, to assist with voluntary returns and deportations of Mexican nationals. Mexican officials in turn leveraged this relationship to safeguard migrant rights. Through a careful negotiation of new enforcement priorities, they could at times influence border agents' enforcement actions such as releasing someone from detention (via repatriation) or seeking medical care.

Like Mexican officials, NGOs also advocate for migrant rights. Early forms of migrant advocacy focused primarily on labor issues, like challenging the dual wage system, poor working conditions, or deportation as a strike-breaking measure. But in a post–civil rights era, particularly in the context of criminal justice reforms for upholding a defendant's rights, migrant advocates drew on constitutional norms to challenge immigration enforcement practices such as search and seizure violations (racial profiling), denial of due process in deportation proceedings, unlawful detention, or cruel and unusual punishment (Border Patrol misconduct).

Migrant advocates in Southern Arizona have played a critical role in bringing national and international attention to the effects of U.S. immigration and border policies. They have applied political pressure on DHS and public officials to comply with certain due process rights and protections. They have publicly denounced racial profiling, Border Patrol misconduct, vigilantism, and, especially, migrant deaths. Their use of media, litigation, and other forms of advocacy and protest has served, in a way, to push back against the criminalization of unauthorized migration, by humanizing migrants through candlelight vigils where the names of deceased are read, providing humanitarian assistance to migrants in distress, and pushing for the prosecution of vigilantes and more enforcement oversight, for instance.

Advocating for migrant rights, on the other hand, often meant working directly with the Department of Homeland Security, even as advocates directly challenged immigration law enforcement. At times, relations were contentious, as when NGOs directly monitored and contested apprehension, detention, and deportation practices or other abuses of civil rights. Yet, there were also moments of cooperation.

In this enforcement terrain, some legal advocates found themselves in the difficult position of having to work within the framework of new criminal enforcement priorities. This is most evident in the efforts of legal advocates working directly with migrants in detention and deportation proceedings, for whom advocates provided services in the form of "know your rights" presentations, and legal representation within immigration courts.

Under the Legal Orientation Program (LOP), federally funded by the Department of Justice's Executive Office of Immigration Review (EOIR), three NGOs along the border provided rotating "know your rights" workshops for detained migrants that allowed them to identify cases to represent in immigration court.[71] As one advocate involved in the Legal Orientation Program explained,

> We got access to the detention centers in 1997–98, when the processing center came to be run more like a prison and received certification under the Bureau of Prisons. . . . We have about five hundred cases a year of Mexicans in detention and removal proceedings. Half of them are undocumented, the other half are legal residents. We try to get them relief, try to submit a cancellation of removal, accompany them to court, or just help them understand the whole process so that they can represent themselves.[72]

In fact, the vast majority of migrants ultimately represented themselves in court.[73] One national study of immigration courts found that the Tucson Sector had one of the highest removal caseloads and the lowest rates of legal representation. In the post IIRIRA-enforcement landscape that restructured deportation and constrained the discretion of immigration judges in order to make "criminal alien" removals easier and to free up prison beds, most migrants were increasingly removed through fast-track deportations that bypassed the immigration courts altogether, and limited migrants' access to local NGOs. The "know your rights" presentations, designed for detained migrants and those confined in jails and prisons, provided basic orientation on the detention and removal process, informed migrants of what to expect during their immigration hearing in detention, and gave an overview of the limited "choices" for relief available to them. They reviewed various types of criminal/aggravated felony charges and how those affect their options for relief, such as cancellation of removal, adjustment of status, asylum, or voluntary departure, for example.

During one "know your rights" presentation in a courtroom within an immigrant detention center, a legal advocate stood before a handful of detained migrant women from Central America. The security guard, a Latina, stood behind the presenter, also of Latin American ancestry.

"So is there any way for us to be able to stay?" asked a woman from Guatemala during the question-and-answer period.

"The only way you qualify," explained the presenter, "is if you have a close relative who can help you to adjust your status, or if you are claiming political asylum, but you said you were not afraid to go back to your country." The two Guatemalan women shook their heads.

"I was coming to the U.S. for a better future for my children," said one detainee, "and look where I ended up?" [Laughter.]

"But you did make it to the U.S.," said the presenter. "You are in the U.S."

"Yes, but I was tied up, I didn't enjoy it." [She puts her two hands together to simulate being handcuffed.]

"You should have asked them to untie you so you could enjoy the trip," said the Salvadoran woman next to her. [Laughter.]

"I was too scared . . . it was my first time."[74]

The detainee had crossed the border through the Sonoran desert and was caught and held at the Casa Grande Border Patrol Station. From there she was transferred to Tucson, from Tucson to Florence, and from Florence, she was eventually deported.

* * *

Because very few qualified for relief and most were deportable, the best that legal advocates could do, it seemed, was to facilitate a voluntary return in lieu of a deportation with harsher penalties and barriers to reentry. With few options to stay in the United States, they typically performed a role of speeding up a removal. Their tireless work enabled ICE and the Department of Homeland Security to "cut back on resources" and time spent detaining and removing migrants. According to a local ICE agent, "Before you would get a detainee that didn't understand or didn't want to. . . . [Under LOP] the attorneys tell them what is going to happen, so the judge isn't having to reset their hearings all the time."[75] For legal advocates, speeding up the deportation was a strategy for getting people out as quickly as possible "rather than having them sit in detention."

Of course, migrant advocates working directly with those in detention and removal proceedings perform important work that extends beyond the courtroom. Here I have focused on their direct role in helping detained migrants navigate the immigration system in order to illustrate the new terrain of immigration enforcement in which activists and NGOs must operate. Because of limited resources, legal advocates were forced to prioritize those individual cases most likely to win, such as those of unaccompanied minors; asylum seekers; domestic violence, torture, and trafficking survivors; or other crime victims willing to assist law enforcement as material witnesses in criminal cases.[76]

In line with DHS enforcement priorities, those cases most likely to qualify for relief were those of "vulnerable groups" without a criminal record. Migrant advocates were most effective when they positioned migrants as "victims" in order to access justice. They humanized migrants as rights-bearing individuals by highlighting their victimization. The Border Patrol and policy makers, in turn, responded to such victimization with more policing and punitive measures targeting smugglers, abusive spouses, and traffickers. In this new terrain, it seemed that migrant protection went hand in hand with greater criminalization and punishment, which has become an unchallenged vehicle through which to address migrant rights.

A New Enforcement Terrain

The federal mandate to target criminal aliens operates with tremendous legitimacy. It has become embedded in local political economies, and there has also been a standardization of criminal criteria across agencies that create an image of consensus. All agencies have begun to merge their intelligence and classificatory schemes to process people—not just immigrants—according to risk. This chapter examined how agents enforce the criminal alien mandate within a field or "network" involving a complex array of actors and relations, which informs the way agents enforce priorities and impose criminal versus undocumented status on the ground.

In 1972, Hansenfeld introduced a model to analyze organizations "whose explicit function . . . is to process and confer public statuses on people."[77] "People-processing organizations," as he called them, first assess attributes—the way a clinician or a judge might. They then make decisions about which course of action to pursue, and manage the new public status. "People processing," the theory goes, occurs within a network of exchange between the organization and other players in the field.

In their day-to-day work, border agents have been given tremendous discretion to classify behavior and then decide "who gets what, when, and how."[78] Such decisions occur within a network exchange between the Border Patrol and other players in the field. The field in which agents police the border includes not just *federal* mandates to classify criminals but also *local* relations between agents and others directly involved in immigration enforcement, as well as the political economy of U.S.-Mexico border communities.

On the U.S.-Mexico border, the Border Patrol's relationship to NGOs, the Mexican Consulate, the U.S. Attorney's Office, or the local police and sheriff's department, for instance, directly influences their decision to classify someone as a "UDA (undocumented alien)" or a criminal alien.

Enforcement priorities that target noncitizens with criminal convictions have complicated the ways in which agents confer public status on those they apprehend. Agents no longer simply confer citizenship status (e.g., citizen or alien; legal or illegal). They also confer criminal status and process citizens, legal permanent residents, alongside unauthorized migrants according to risk. As the following chapter shows, congressional mandates and agency directives, the Border Patrol's relations to other players in the field, and the political economy of border communities inform the ways in which agents confer public status on people as either "criminal" or "rights-bearing" individuals.

4

Victims and Culprits

Deportation as a Pipeline to Prison

At a migrant shelter in Nogales, Sonora, Mexico, about one hundred or so exhausted-looking women, men, and some very young boys are crammed into rows of tables for a hot meal.[1] A volunteer asks me to speak to some women sitting at the other end of the dining hall. They're crying. The two women wear U.S.-brand clothing; one of them carries a cell phone. They look pale and sleep-deprived. "*Nos agarraron* [They caught us]," one says, referring to the border agents who apprehended them. "*Me metieron a la cárcel por un mes* [They put me in prison]." She had been trying to cross for two months. One attempt had landed her in prison for a month. Her children are in the United States, and she's desperate to get back. She's trying again but has a criminal record now, which classifies her as a "criminal alien" and a high-priority target for criminal prosecution if she's caught again.

The other woman was deported from Utah.[2] Her husband and children followed her to Mexico, but the children, never having lived in Mexico, struggled to adjust. So her husband crossed back to the United States with their citizen children. They're waiting for her. The problem is that if she is caught violating her deportation order, she will be criminally prosecuted and imprisoned for reentry.

Another woman from Chiapas never made it to the United States. She was crossing for the first time when the Border Patrol apprehended her. Because she was a first-time crosser without a criminal record, the Border Patrol "voluntarily returned" her with no criminal penalty or bars to future migration. She's exhausted, but determined to go on.

From the shelter, I walk with other volunteers to the local bus depot, past the cemetery, where stranded migrants sleep. At this bus depot, Mexican officials offer discounted tickets back to the interior of Mexico. Humanitarian volunteers set up a card table outside to document abuses against migrants and help people telephone relatives and let them know they're safe. A migrant woman from the shelter is there and shares her intention to cross the border alone (without a guide). A U.S. volunteer looks concerned and explains to her in broken Spanish,

"*Es muy difícil, muy peligroso ir sola.*"

"I know [it's difficult and dangerous to go alone]," she says in broken English. "I lost for seven days."

Another volunteer, a retiree from the East Coast who's visiting for the first time, hands the young woman money, but she pulls her arms away.

"No, no," she says in English. "Thank you, but no. I don't want money."

The volunteer insists and places the money firmly in her hand.

"I sorry for coming to your country," she continues in English. "I don't do drugs. I no criminal. I work," she insists, as if to distance herself from criminal stigma by positioning herself as a worker, an economic migrant. Switching to Spanish, "*Yo voy hacer algo,*" she says with intense conviction. "*Un día yo voy a crear trabajos. Les prometo que voy crear trabajos* [One day I will create jobs. I promise to create jobs]."[3]

Visibly moved, the retiree opens her arms as if to welcome her to the United States, even though, at this moment, we are in Mexico. In that instance the U.S. volunteer, not the migrant, is the border crosser. The volunteer had not fully grasped that this woman's *home is the United States*. She learned English there. In fact, the reason she's so adamant about crossing is precisely because of the family and work obligations she left when she was forcibly expelled.

That several migrants at the shelter spoke English, wore U.S. corporate brands, or carried a cell phone is a testament to cross-border linkages between the United States and Mexico, or between the United States and Latin America, and to the historical presence of Mexicans and Latin American immigrants in the United States. Yet it is precisely these ties to the United States that criminal enforcement priorities punish. On the Arizona-Sonora border, migrants violating a deportation order (to get back to jobs, families, and their lives in the United States) were more likely to face criminal prosecution and incarceration. The first-time border crosser from Chiapas, by contrast, did not have a "criminal" record and bypassed criminal prosecution, imprisonment, and the criminal justice system altogether. At a border agent's discretion, she was processed through the civil immigration system, and not formally deported, but granted a "voluntary return," which allowed slightly more maneuverability and possibilities for future legal migration.

Proponents of border security argue that crime-centered approaches to immigration enforcement target high-priority criminal aliens for arrest, prosecution, and expulsion.[4] As this chapter shows, new enforcement priorities rooted in the Criminal Alien Program have transformed arrest and removal practices on the border to create the very population that it targets. During arrest, agents must now evaluate migrants according to criminal history alongside immigration status, classifying some as "criminal" and others as "crime victims," on the basis of criminal enforcement priorities from above and the complex local border context in which they operate. And while the Criminal Alien Program's initial purpose was to expel migrants from jails and prisons, deportation has in fact become one of the driving mechanisms by which immigrants are imprisoned and acquire a criminal record, thereby producing a criminal alien population.

"Illegal" and "Criminal" Tracks

In 2010, the Department of Homeland Security circulated a memo titled "Civil Immigration Enforcement: Priorities for Apprehension, Detention, and Removal of Aliens," instructing agents to direct agency resources, in the form of detention bed space and funding, toward the highest priorities.[5] It outlined DHS's enforcement priorities as follows.

Priority One includes "[a]liens who pose a danger to national security or a risk to public safety"; "Priority Two" includes new border crossers or "recent illegal entrants . . . who have recently violated immigration controls at the border, ports of entry, or through abuse of a visa"; and "Priority Three" includes "[a]liens who are subject to a final order of removal and abscond, fail to depart, or intentionally obstruct immigration controls."[6]

These official directives, building on earlier memos guiding enforcement action, provide some background to the patterned practices of enforcement I observed on the ground.[7] In their routine activities along the Arizona-Sonora borderlands, agents must distinguish between high-priority targets—criminal aliens—and the lower-priority, "noncriminal" population of border crossers and residents they encounter. The traditional, perhaps more familiar, mission has been apprehending authorized border crossers between ports of entry or investigating and enforcing immigration law. Now there exists an official mandate—backed by $18 billion in federal funding, technology, and critical partnerships with other agencies—to sort people on the basis of criminal history.

This has transformed the way agents process people. Traditionally, immigration enforcement on the border was largely an administrative process that moved from apprehension to removal, typically in the form of a voluntary return. One seventy-year-old ex-Bracero recounted what it was like to cross the border through Ambos Nogales in 1957.

"Back then the border was a fallen barbed wire fence. But you still had to be careful not to be seen by *la Migra* [Border Patrol]."

"Did you ever have any run-ins with the Border Patrol?" I asked.

"Sure. They caught me a few times."

"How was the treatment back then?"

"Well, the way I saw it is, if I talked back, they behaved badly. But if you didn't behave badly, they honestly treated you fine. They'd round us up. Take us to *el corralón* [pen or holding facility] until they had a bunch of us. Then they'd send us back. Some of us crossed again. Others went home. The decision was ours."

"Was *el corralón* run by immigration or the police? Was it a prison?"

"No, it was run by *Migración* . . . . [T]he police wouldn't bother us. It was *Migración* who caught us and sent us back. If you committed an act [criminal act], [the police] put you in jail. You paid [posted bail] and they'd let you go. But if you didn't do anything, [the police] wouldn't bother you. It was *Migración* who came out to the fields to look for us. Someone would shout '*Ay viene la Migra!*' and we'd run. If they caught us, they'd send us back to Mexico."

"But you were a Bracero. You had a labor contract. Wouldn't they let you go?"

"Yes, if you were a Bracero, you were legal. I'm talking about the times I crossed as an *alambrista* [referring to those who crossed without authorization through the *cerca de alambre*, or barbed wire fence]. If you crossed the Rio Bravo, you were a *mojado*. If you crossed through the wire fence, you were an *alambrista*."[8]

Another former Bracero recounted how they would desert or skip out on their labor contracts when working conditions were intolerable. Skipping out on a contract and becoming "illegal" was often the most effective way to resist the un-free labor practices for which the Bracero program became known.[9]

The ex-Bracero's account of crossing the Arizona-Sonora border in the postwar era captures a time when immigration and criminal enforcement fell within different arenas of law. The system in place now is one in which agents lean on both the immigration and criminal justice systems to regulate migration. Agents have considerably more discretion to process apprehended migrants through an immigration system that moves from apprehension to removal. Or they can push migrants into the criminal justice system, where the process moves from arrest to prosecution in federal criminal court to sentencing and incarceration in a federal prison back to mandatory immigrant detention, followed by a formal deportation.[10]

Like prosecutors in the criminal justice system, agents have always had some degree of discretion over whom to "stop, question, or arrest" and prosecute, detain, or deport, but so have immigration judges presiding over immigration hearings and making decisions about adjustment of status, release from detention, or deportation and other forms of relief.[11] As the authority of immigration judges narrowed, particularly under IIRIRA's passage in 1996, the decision-making authority of frontline officers expanded.[12] Jonathon Simon and others have documented similar changes in the criminal justice system whereby Congress pushed to overcome "judicial obstacles to enforcement" and "procedures advantageous to the defense." Similarly, in the immigration system, Congress took a prosecutorial approach to advancing the Criminal Alien Program and pushing new enforcement priorities by passing the 1996 IIRIRA, which constrained judicial review, and limiting procedural protections for immigrants with convictions.

Constraining judicial review and expanding frontline agents' authority doesn't mean that rights are absent, as there are constitutional norms that agents must uphold. But it is agents, as opposed to immigration judges, who now have considerably more discretion over the dispensation of rights and other forms of relief, which is not to be confused with benefits, such as adjustment of status. In other words, agents have more discretion to prosecute ("criminals") in the criminal justice system *and* to administer and grant access to basic forms of relief (to "crime victims") in the immigration system. Their day-to-day decisions are very much informed by their relations to other players in the field, such as NGOs or Mexican officials, for instance, but also by the complex reality they confront on the ground, one that congressional immigration debates seldom capture.

"Workers," Not "Criminals"

Integrated databases allow agents to assess the "attributes and situation" of migrants according to DHS enforcement priorities.[13] It allows them to track immigration history, such as unauthorized entry and prior removals as well as criminal history. The databases allow agents to rank migrants according to DHS enforcement priorities, but local reality also informs their perspectives and enforcement actions, at times in a different direction than perhaps Congress intended.

Enforcement priorities place undocumented border crossers or "recent illegal entrants" as a second-highest priority after "aliens who pose a danger to national security." Yet border agents didn't necessarily regard undocumented migrants as criminal, particularly veteran agents or those raised in border towns themselves, often attributing migration to economic rather than criminal forces. In fact, they distinguished between "illegal" and "criminal" aliens, in contrast to the tendency to conflate the two in popular discourse.

When making arrests, agents distinguished between those "coming over to work" and those "coming to commit crimes." Agents describe those coming to work as "docile," noting that "they won't look at you in the eyes"; they are afraid, disoriented, and they won't run. At other times, "you can just tell," they explain, "by looking at their shoes, their clothes and hands."

"Migrants are intimidated by us," explained one agent. "They come from countries where law enforcement is more authoritative. They don't look us in the eye. They look at our chest. Like I said, they're intimidated. The ones that talk back or try to run are smugglers because they don't want to get in trouble."[14] "They [migrants] don't always stop," explains another, "but when you're out there, they see the uniform and that's good. In Mexico, you're taught to respect authority. They do what you tell them."[15]

In describing their day-to-day work, agents also likened apprehended migrants to "crime victims," particularly when they encountered migrants lost in the desert, often already unconscious from severe dehydration "with blood running from their mouth and nose."[16] Recovering corpses is part of their daily work. Agents acknowledged the particular vulnerability of women. Even though women make up less than 20% of migrant apprehensions, their death rates from heat exposure are twice those of men.[17]

One agent acknowledged that the Border Patrol strategy indirectly victimized migrants by making them vulnerable to smugglers and putting them at risk when they cross through the desert. He stated that "to get across it used to cost between three hundred and five hundred, when I got here. Now you go to a smuggler and they charge fifteen hundred to two thousand a day. We [Border Patrol] made it more difficult for migrants, but we also made it more profitable for the smuggler. The one paying for it is the migrant."[18]

"You can't help feeling for them," said an agent about migrants. "You get family units carrying suitcases with everything they own. You can't help but feel sorry for them, but you have a job to do. You never get used to it. You always feel something. What they go through is sad and if you didn't have a job, you'd be doing the same thing. I know I would."[19] "We're dealing with people coming from Mexico and other countries," another agent explained. "When apprehending a family group, you see the faces on kids, fathers, very proud. They had to come to the U.S. I have a family and my worst nightmare is not being able to find a job or food. My nightmare is their reality."[20]

Because agents see migrants' complex vulnerabilities first-hand, they often expressed emotional ambiguity about their work. They emphasized their role in rescuing and coming to the aid of migrants in distress alongside descriptions of arresting families with "everything they own." Their complex views on migration shed some light on how they adapted criminal enforcement priorities to a cross-border context. They slotted migrants into high and low priorities based on varying (and gendered) degrees of vulnerability and risk. The traditional male migrant, "proud" father, worker, breadwinner earned a lower-risk, lower-priority ranking, as did some women, children, and elderly people, who fell into DHS's "vulnerable group" category and whom agents perceived to be more likely to be *at* risk than to be *a* risk.

Migrants, in turn, negotiated this new enforcement terrain by avoiding being labeled or perceived as "criminal." During arrest, for instance, they avoided a criminal label by positioning themselves as economic migrants—consciously or unconsciously distancing themselves from racial stereotypes of native-born African Americans and Latinas/os who turn to criminal acts instead of hard work. They do their part to communicate to agents, verbally and through body language and expression, that they are "workers," not "criminals." One Latino agent described how migrants often plead with agents for their release: "They tug at your heartstrings," he explains. "'Come on. Let me go. I want to work.' Or 'You're Mexican. Let us go.' And I tell them, 'You're coming here to work, right? If your boss asks you to do something, you do it or you get fired. It's not personal. I'm doing my job.'"[21]

Migrants convey to agents that they were "coming to work" by consenting to and not resisting arrest. They position themselves as undocumented workers rather than "criminal elements" who, according to Border Patrol agents, are more likely to resist arrest. Strategies used by migrants to quickly be "voluntarily returned" in order to try again were "don't run"; "get down on the ground immediately"; "don't try to stand up"; "don't look at them"; "don't speak."

To leverage agents' prosecutorial authority, migrants often had to "define themselves as victims," which deflects a criminal label.[22] A deportee from Arizona, for instance, describes an encounter with local vigilantes.

> I contracted a smuggler who tried to get me and seventeen other people across [the border] through Naco [near Douglas, Arizona]. We had been walking for four hours. Just before we arrived at the place where we would be picked up in cars, some men and women came out with video cameras even. They were armed, but they weren't *Migración*. They detained us for a while. "Sit down," they said, "and don't get up." They called *Migración* and turned us in. We asked the Border agents whether what they were doing was legal. And they said that's what they do, but in

reality it isn't legal and if they treated us badly, we could file a complaint with the Mexican Consulate. It was 2:00 or 3:00 in the morning and we said they hadn't treated us badly. What we wanted was for them [Border Patrol] to send us back to Mexico [to try again]. And yes, they sent us to Naco, Sonora. I signed a voluntary departure.[23]

Here the deportees questioned the legality of the vigilante arrest and reported the incident (as a crime) to the Border Patrol. The agent admitted that "what they do isn't legal" and invited them to file a complaint with the Mexican Consulate. They opted instead for a voluntary return, which the agent granted, and allowed them to return to Mexico in order to reattempt their crossing.

Similarly, a migrant from Chiapas, and human rights activist, also described his victimization by smugglers who sequestered him. "I contracted a *pollero* in Altar [Sonora], crossed through Sasabe, and made it to Phoenix," says the activist deportee from Chiapas.

I was on my way to Los Angeles, but the coyote wanted more money, so they kept us in Phoenix at gunpoint. There were forty of us to start with. Little by little as the families wired money under the smuggler's name, the group got smaller. I paid eight hundred dollars, and they wanted another six hundred dollars to get to LA. "I paid already," I said. They harassed a few of us. "We're human," we told them.

"You aren't human. You don't know God. God exists. We're human beings."

We didn't know what they would do to us. We tried to convince them to let us go, but they wouldn't. A group of us got to be friends. One of us broke a window and got out. The coyotes were angry and threatened us with guns for letting him get away. They were convinced he would snitch and bring in the law. They ran out and left us there. We just stood there.

"Why didn't you leave?" [another deportee asks in shock].

I don't know. We thought they were hiding and would kill us. They came back that night and drove us to the boss, to a nice house in Phoenix. He was so angry that we were there and told them to get rid of us. As we were leaving the house, we took off and ran as fast as we could. They never caught up to us. We ran toward a busy street to be picked up by the Border Patrol.[24]

Like the human rights activist from Chiapas, migrants often reported turning themselves in to the Border Patrol, particularly after a bad experience with a smuggler. In the West Desert roads, it's common to see migrants walking along roads in order to be picked up by the Border Patrol. This enables them to be processed quickly and, if resources permit, to try again. During an early morning drive near Sasabe, Arizona, for instance, I noticed three men with backpacks and gallons of water walking along the shoulder of the road. A U.S. Border Patrol vehicle was stationed a short distance from them. The border agent looked in their direction but made no move to apprehend them.[25] He didn't have to. They'd depleted their water supply. Their guide was gone. They were turning themselves in. In this case, the empty plastic jugs they carried and the way they walked, southbound, toward the vehicle signaled that they were "noncriminal" UDAs (undocumented aliens), as opposed to smugglers.

This noncriminal status allowed migrants to access very basic forms of relief and protection, which can be a matter of life and death during the border crossing.[26] Migrants perceived to be "workers," not "criminals," were less likely to report physical violence at the hands of border agents.[27] A group of migrants at a shelter described how consenting to traditional arrest rituals between agents and migrant workers and avoiding "behaving badly" mitigated the likelihood of escalated force during an arrest.

DEPORTEE FROM PHOENIX, ARIZONA: They catch you. They tell you they're *Migración*. One already knows [the routine]. Yes because they won't do anything to you.

DEPORTEE FROM TUCSON, ARIZONA: Well here [at the border] they will, if you make them chase you, if you want to run.

DEPORTEE FROM CALIFORNIA: If one behaves badly, they behave badly.

INTERVIEWER: What's behaving badly?

EVERYONE AT ONCE: "Running." "Getting angry at them." "One isn't supposed to get angry." "They grab you. Put you in their truck and send you back. That's it."

DEPORTEE FROM PHOENIX, ARIZONA: It's their job.

DEPORTEE FROM CALIFORNIA: Yes, it's their job.

DEPORTEE FROM PHOENIX: If you put yourself in their place, you'd do the same. If I work for immigration and I see five people, I detain them because that's my job. That's what they get paid for.

DEPORTEE FROM CALIFORNIA: Before there were many from *Migración* who spoke to you harshly. They'd mistreat you a little more. But they're less aggressive now.

INTERVIEWER: So have you ever been mistreated by a Border Patrol agent?

EVERYONE: No, no. By *Migración*? No.

Here migrants describe agents as "less aggressive" than in the past, when "they spoke more harshly" and mistreated migrants "a little more." By playing a traditional male migrant worker role and complying with their apprehension, migrants were able to stay below the radar of criminal enforcement actions. New border crossers or migrants without a criminal record reported surprisingly fewer violent incidents with the Border Patrol. One migrant standing next to his coyote described the Border Patrol in this way: "They're not all bad. There are some who are *buenas gentes* [good people]. They even joke sometimes." They laugh as one of the men recounts an exchange with an agent. "He noticed that I'd been caught before and said, 'You should find yourself another coyote because the one you have right now isn't very good.' Then he wished me luck on the next try."[28] "Not all agents are bad," a local Nogales resident explained to me. "Some are good—they talk to them [migrants] in a nice way. They joke with them. They tell them, 'You picked the wrong place to cross. . . . You know you're always gonna get caught here [Nogales]. You should have gone further out.'"[29]

Those without a criminal record were eligible for voluntary departure, which bypassed the criminal justice system. The voluntary departure system is based on the recognition that immigrants in removal proceedings have the right to a hearing. Under the voluntary departure system, a person signs a form waiving her or his right to a hearing and agrees to depart voluntarily.[30] A Border Patrol agent or an immigration judge under the Executive Office of Immigration Review can grant *voluntary departure* as a form of relief with less severe penalties and consequences than a formal deportation, which imposes bars on future migration. (Noncriminal) Mexican nationals who sign a voluntary departure form are typically "returned" to Mexico the same day.

Central American migrants (without a criminal record) were detained until they could come before an immigration judge and seek relief, with assistance from local NGOs who help navigate the complex legal system. Migrants without a criminal mark were eligible to be *released on their own recognizance*, a form of relief in which apprehended migrants admit to entering illegally and accept removal, after which they are paroled from detention while their hearing is pending. This enabled them to attend their final removal hearing in their cities of destination, where they might have better access to family and resources.

This long-standing form of relief for detained migrants made national headlines when Immigration and Customs Enforcement (ICE) publicly announced that it would use discretion to release "noncriminal" migrants from detention due to across-the-board federal cuts by Congress in 2012. In Arizona, ICE had released 342 detainees (out of two thousand people nationwide).[31] This is the first time I had ever seen ICE publicly distinguish between high-priority ("criminal") and lower-priority ("noncriminal") undocumented migrants—though I had certainly observed these distinctions in the field for some years. Neither politicians nor the press could handle the complexity of this distinction. Politicians railed at ICE for releasing "criminals" onto the streets. And reporters covering the story couldn't understand why, if people were noncriminal, they were being imprisoned or detained in the first place.[32] Political pressure led ICE to rearrest some of the detainees.

In addition to being able to access relief from detention in some cases, apprehended border crossers without a criminal record were also eligible, in rare cases, for *adjustment of status* through the family preference system, or for asylum in cases where the person cannot return because of a "well-founded fear of persecution."[33] In some cases, migrants also qualified for a U Visa, a form of relief of undocumented victims of crime who assist law enforcement with the investigation and prosecution of human smugglers, for instance.[34] They could also build stronger cases when filing complaints (against vigilantes or border agents) with the Mexican Consulate and NGOs, or when serving as plaintiffs in lawsuits.[35]

Most of these "rights" or forms of relief are by no means extensive and are more procedural than substantive, but they matter because they are one of criminal immigration enforcement's defining features. When implementing criminal enforcement priorities, agents had more discretion to prosecute some, while administering rights and forms of relief to others on the basis of criminal history. Those who are "illegal" but without a criminal mark, could *as undocumented migrants* access basic procedural rights that facilitate the border crossing. Those branded "criminal" were denied relief, barred from future legal migration, and faced with prison time and forced expulsion *as criminal aliens.*[36]

"Criminals", Not "Victims"

When apprehending a group, border agents order everyone to drop all of their belongings and sit on the ground until backup arrives. Agents assess criminal status according to demeanor, dress, behavior, and even body marks.[37] "In large groups, the scouts walk ahead. Migrants walk upright," an agent explains. "[Drug] smugglers are slouched over from carrying heavy backpacks. Regular migrants carry smaller backpacks. The [drug] smuggler will have raspberries on their shoulders or hemp from the burlap [sacks] on their shoulders."[38] Smugglers, I was told, usually "try to run because they have something to hide." They tend to be "better dressed and carry cell phones." "If I apprehend a group of five to ten, the smuggler, the guide, will run. The group doesn't know where to go. They'll listen . . . or we do what we have to do to gain control."[39]

An agent explains how the Border Patrol processes unauthorized border crossers after arrest. "If an agent catches people in the field, he brings them to another agent who transports them to the station. From there another agent will process them. . . . If a criminal alien is apprehended, an agent is called in to do a report."[40]

When processing apprehended migrants, agents photograph and scan all ten fingerprints, entering this and biographical information into the Automatic Biometric Identification System, established in 1994. They can now also automatically search the FBI's ten-print Integrated Automated Fingerprint Identification System (IAFIS) and Criminal Master File and the Department of Defense's Automated Biometric Identification System (ABIS). Within minutes, the integrated search enables agents to identify "recidivists" (i.e., multiple unauthorized entries) and "lookouts" (i.e., migrants with prior criminal records).

Yet even the most sophisticated and comprehensive advances in criminal alien tracking confirm what has already been well documented in research on immigrants and crime—that crime rates among immigrants are quite low. "With respect to criminality," a recent congressional report states,

> the proportion of people apprehended by the Border Patrol with previous convictions for major crimes hovered between 1.9% in 2005 and 2.5% in 2008 before falling to 0.9% in FY2011, the lowest level since USBP [U.S. Border Patrol] began matching records against IAFIS. . . . Fewer than 10,000 aliens with major criminal records were apprehended by the Border Patrol in FY2010 and FY2011 combined.[41]

Despite the low numbers of apprehended migrants convicted of *major* offenses, Border Patrol agents must follow through on agency directives. An ICE official explains, "There is a thirty-four-hundred-bed mandate. . . . [Agents] start with priority targets, then move to next priority. If we are only at twenty-eight hundred [bed space capacity] that day, we *must go to next level priority*. The president has proposed to cut the bed level. Congress has increased it every year" (emphasis added).[42]

The reality on the ground is that very few apprehended migrants actually qualify as high-priority targets—terrorist threats or high security risks.[43] Yet the bed space capacity requires that agents prosecute persons lower on the priority scale. This includes "aliens who are subject to a final order of removal" (i.e., those who violate deportation orders), which were in the past processed through a civil immigration system or administratively, through voluntary return.

Enforcement priorities stemming from the Criminal Alien Program, then, have transformed deportation from an expulsion mechanism to a vehicle for criminal prosecution and imprisonment, as shown in the following description of removal hearings.

Though the Justice Department's Executive Office for Immigration Review (EOIR) oversees the hearings, the courtroom is housed in an immigration detention facility managed by the DHS's Office of Enforcement and Removal under ICE. An agent escorts me to a courtroom where that day's removal hearings are being held.

The courtroom's silence breaks when an officer arrives with detainees dressed in navy blue uniforms and wearing wristbands.[44] One by one, they fill the benches, waiting nervously for their removal hearing to begin. Undocumented migrants do not have the right to a court-appointed attorney in immigration proceedings. EOIR has reported that as many as 84% of detained migrants lack representation during their immigration court hearings.[45]

At this particular hearing, not a single detainee has an attorney. The judge addresses the group directly: "You are citizens of another country. . . . You entered illegally. . . . You are on U.S. soil without an adequate visa." Invoking basic constitutional frameworks of "fairness," he says, "Each of you is deportable . . . but we still need to talk about relief," referring to the possibility that they might qualify for relief from deportation, such as political asylum or other forms of adjustment of status.

He calls the first detainee to the stand. Through a translator, the judge confirms his nationality, and the country he will be deported to. "Mexico," says the detainee.

"Do you have any fear of persecution if you go back to Mexico?"

"No."

"Do you have family legally in the U.S.?"

"No."

"Do you know what a voluntary departure is?" asks the judge.

"Sí."

"Would you like to apply?"

"Sí."

"Does the government oppose?" the judge asks the federal prosecutor, an attorney for DHS.

"Yes," the government attorney replies. The judge reschedules another hearing in a week in order to determine eligibility for voluntary departure. Confused that his response prompted another hearing that will prolong his time in detention, the detainee becomes visibly nervous and requests—through the translator—formal deportation instead.

"I didn't understand," he said. "I accept deportation." Within seconds, the judge issues an order of deportation and bars him from future entry for ten years.[46] Violating that deportation order, he warns, will result in criminal prosecution and imprisonment.

The entire hearing lasts minutes. The judge calls the next detainee and then another. One by one, each detainee anxiously follows the lead of the one before and asks for deportation. "Are you a citizen of Mexico?"

"*Sí.*"

"Do you have any fear of persecution?"

"No."

"Do you have legal family in the U.S.?"

"No."

"Do you know what a voluntary departure is?"

"*Sí.*"

"Do you want to apply?"

"No."

"Are you asking for deportation?"

"*Sí.*"

The next defendant is also a citizen of Mexico. He has no fear of persecution, but he does have legal family in the United States. After further question the judge declares, "They can't sponsor you. It has to be a mother or father. . . . Do you know what a voluntary departure is?"

"No," says the detainee. "I want deportation."

To the next detainee, the judge asks, "Are you a citizen of Mexico?"

"*Sí.*"

"Do you have any fear of persecution in Mexico?"

"No."

"Do you have any legal family in the U.S.?"

"*Sí.*"

"Have they sponsored you [to adjust your status]?"

"No."

"If deportation causes hardship to your mother or father you could qualify for cancellation of removal."

"I want deportation," the detainee says through a translator.

"Do you want voluntary departure or deportation?" the judge asks.

"Deportation," declares the detainee.

Like falling dominoes, every detainee asked to be deported. Their minimum-security blue uniforms signaled that they all qualified for voluntary departure, which has less stringent penalties and more possibilities for future migration, yet, without legal representation, no one seemed to understand the process enough to request it; they each asked to be deported.[47]

In other hearings involving Central American detainees, the judge issued a deportation at cost to the federal government, because detainees could not afford the airfare to "voluntarily return" to their home country. During one hearing, the judge called a Guatemalan national in a blue uniform to the bench. He didn't have a lawyer. Through a translator, the detainee admitted to crossing without a visa through Douglas, Arizona.

"Are you a U.S. citizen?"

"No."

"Do you have a visa?"

"No."

"Do you have any fear of persecution if you are deported to Guatemala?"

"No."

"Do you have legal family in the U.S.?"

"No."

"Do you have money to pay your trip back to Guatemala?"

"No."

The judge issued a formal deportation.

In another hearing, the judge called a citizen of El Salvador, also in blue uniform, to the bench. "Did you cross the border illegally through Douglas, Arizona?"

"Yes, I'm sorry."

"No need to apologize to me. I have the fortune of having been born here. Do you have the money to pay your trip to El Salvador?"

"No."

"This makes you deportable at the government's expense. Do you want to appeal or accept deportation?"

"I accept deportation."

The judge tries another detainee from El Salvador without legal representation. He admits to crossing without authorization through Douglas, Arizona. He does not qualify for political asylum. Nor does he have any legal family in the United States.

"Do you have money to pay your trip to El Salvador?"

"No."

"Then there's no relief available. You are deportable at the government's expense. You have the right to appeal or accept deportation." The detainee asks to appeal. "You don't qualify for relief [voluntary departure], if you can't pay. I see no good reason for you to be released [from detention] on bond [while he appeals his case]. The appeal could take ninety days or more. Your case is not complex. The law almost always deports you. You entered illegally. You don't qualify for relief, and are deportable." After each case, the judge warns detainees that should they violate the deportation order, they will most certainly be prosecuted and sentenced to prison.

"I was already working in Phoenix, but I got deported," shares a formerly incarcerated man from Honduras wearing a rosary around his neck. "I served time in Florence for coming back without papers. Is that a crime?" he asks, looking bewildered.[48]

Criminal prosecutions for reentry after deportation occurred through Operation Streamline. Since 2005, Streamline has charged undocumented border crossers with federal crimes of illegal entry and reentry in federal district courts.[49] In 2010 when I first began observing these hearings in courts in Tucson, of the total cases referred for prosecution, 51% were for illegal entry, and 42% were for reentry cases, that is, for those who had violated a prior deportation order and reentered the country without authorization. Now all cases are for reentry.[50]

The plea bargain, which most migrants accept, plays a crucial role in producing a population of "criminal aliens." When migrants plead guilty to illegal entry and reentry, they are essentially consenting to being classified as criminals. Under Operation Streamline, illegal entry is prosecuted as a petty misdemeanor offense, which can be punishable with up to six months of jail time. According to the Federal Bureau of Justice Statistics, 81% of all convicted immigrants received a prison sentence in 2010. The median prison sentence was twenty-four months in Arizona.[51]

Federal public defenders and other court-appointed attorneys advise migrants to accept the plea bargain in exchange for a lower sentence of time served. The reentry or "flip-flop" cases, as they are known, are considered felonies. When migrants are prosecuted for reentry, charges usually include both a felony for violating a prior deportation order and a petty misdemeanor for illegal entry. Here attorneys advise migrants to accept the plea bargain, which drops the felony so that migrants are only convicted of the misdemeanor.[52] What they often do not realize, however, is that accepting the plea bargain effectively marks them as criminals, a status that places them at greater risk the next time they attempt a border crossing.[53]

During one hearing I observed a migrant who rejected the guilty plea. The judge asked him, through a translator, if he pled guilty, and he absolutely declined. Everything came to a halt. His attorney stepped in on his behalf to explain to the judge that he did not speak English or Spanish but Mam, a Mayan dialect. The attorney pulled him aside and then brought him back before the judge. No Mam interpreter was provided. When asked a second time whether he accepted the guilty plea, he said, "*Sí.*" And his trial was over.[54] This little drama highlights the importance of the guilty plea in bringing this "criminal" migrant population into being. Without it—in order words, if everyone in that courtroom rejected the guilty plea bargain and asked for a trial—this federal prosecution program's legitimacy (and the classification it upholds) would probably unravel.

Others would be criminally prosecuted for violating a deportation order after a prior arrest or conviction, mostly for nonviolent offenses like traffic violations or disorderly conduct (bar fights).

A deportee from Seattle recounts his arrest for driving without a license. Undocumented migrants are ineligible for driver's licenses in many states throughout the United States.[55] "The police stopped me," he says. "They asked me for my license. They put me in jail for a week. Then they sent me to a prison that was much bigger for five days. They handcuffed our hands and stomach. They took us to Seattle. From there, they put us on a plane to San Diego. From San Diego they deported us to Tijuana." He eventually made it to Phoenix, where his own coyote repatriated him back to Mexico. "In prison, I met a man from Puebla. His brother-in-law helped us get to Phoenix [from Tijuana]. In the end they were charging me. They beat me because I couldn't pay. They sent me back to Mexico with the *riteros* because I couldn't pay the $1,350 they were charging me."[56] In this case, it was his smuggler that repatriated him, but his prior record would still trigger criminal penalties if he reentered.

Another deportee was from the same town in Mexico as my family. The police arrested him in San Francisco, California, after he'd been in a fight. They transferred him to Florence, Arizona, and deported him. He had no family in the United States. He'd been working as a day laborer for three years before his arrest. The man next to him was a formerly incarcerated deportee from Oakland, California, the Fruitvale district. The police arrested him after a bar fight. He'd been working as a day laborer for six years. After serving his sentence, he was transferred to Florence, Arizona, and deported, as a "criminal alien," to Nogales, Sonora.[57]

Criminal defendants are eligible for court-appointed attorneys, who at the time were less familiar with the immigration consequences of a criminal conviction and often advised migrants to accept a plea bargain. But the 1996 IIRIRA law made any conviction with a sentence of a year or more an aggravated felony.[58] When migrants pleaded guilty to misdemeanors like driving without a license or disorderly conduct, these offenses counted as aggravated felonies in the immigration system. Many migrants were legally classified as criminal aliens through this broad aggravated felony category that triggered their deportation.

Others are formally classified as criminal aliens when they "plead guilty to using false documents to gain employment," particularly after a workplace raid.[59] In the more high-profile Swift, New Bedford, and Postville raids that rounded up thousands, the vast majority of deportees had no prior criminal record but became criminal aliens through deportation and criminal prosecution for identity theft.[60]

Once they were classified as criminal aliens, migrants' access to basic forms of relief and protections was severely limited.[61] The criminal label increased the likelihood of violence during arrest. Migrants who step into the gray area of criminal suspects are often—to put it in the language of local residents—"treated like dogs." If they got tired and tried to stand up, "they were hit like animals." If they tried to run, "they were dragged by the hair, kicked, or insulted." Despite the numerous reports of human rights abuses on the border, agents don't randomly dispense violence. There is a legal logic to it.[62] A criminal mark justifies violence and a suspension of rights. The use of force during arrest creates criminal suspects. Referring to the litigations and complaints of Border Patrol misconduct, agents reported "making an example" of those who do not comply, typically through an escalation of force.[63]

Migrants classified as criminal aliens were also barred from accessing relief from deportation. Even though deportation is still considered a civil procedure, migrants classified as criminal aliens were expelled directly from prison, without ever coming before an immigration judge. The office of Enforcement and Removal Operations (ERO) under ICE oversees criminal alien removals. Through the Institutional Removal Program, immigrants within correctional facilities are identified for removal. ERO relies on video teleconferencing technology to carry out removal hearings in the prison even before they have served out their sentence.[64] Inmates are formally ordered removed even before their date of release. "We get an order via television," a supervisory agent explained, "so when someone is released they are also removed."[65]

ICE also uses various forms of fast-track deportations that bypass a proper trial, particularly for those classified as criminal aliens. A staff attorney at a legal advocacy NGO explained the new and multiple ways to formally deport someone, which represent a departure from traditional immigration hearings in which a judge issues a deportation order:

1. Administrative removal is a method of deportation in which ICE agents may determine the deportability of those with an aggravated felony conviction (which includes various types of misdemeanors).
2. Stipulated removal involves a plea bargain in which migrants sign a form declaring that they want to stipulate their deportation. The judge signs off.
3. Reinstatement of removal simply restores a prior deportation order and eliminates the need for migrants to come before a judge.
4. Expedited removal is a form of deportation for migrants apprehended at a port of entry or one hundred miles within the border who do not qualify for other forms of relief such as political asylum or voluntary return.[66]

Many of the fast-track methods are for those who do not qualify, because of a conviction or prior deportation order, for voluntary departure or other forms of relief. So whereas noncriminal migrants can access a traditional hearing and apply for voluntary departure, those marked as criminal are stripped of these rights. Such deportation practices were upheld in a 2006 Supreme Court case. The Supreme Court "reinforced the divide between those deportees who may still have procedural rights and those, essentially, who do not."[67]

Deportation is, at times, a final step in the tedious process of channeling migrants through the criminal justice system, but in many cases it is the beginning. It is the beginning of a process that, in many ways, acts as a pipeline to prison and transforms undocumented immigrants into criminal aliens. Most apprehensions, whether processed administratively (as civil offenses) or criminally, typically end in a removal or deportation, which bars migrants from admission to the United States for ten years and includes criminal penalties if they reenter and are arrested again.[68] Because of extensive ties to the United States, most migrants, even those barred from reentry and threatened with imprisonment, will cross again.[69] Violating a deportation order is classified as a felony and has become a direct path to prosecution, sentencing, and criminal branding.

Border crossers now confront an immigration system that confers criminal status alongside legal status. Deportation has become a pipeline to incarceration as more people get sentenced to prison for violating a deportation order. The restructured deportation system in particular is one of the chief mechanisms directly contributing to the rising rates of federal sentencing for immigration violations and creating a criminal alien population.

Criminalizing through Rights

I asked a supervisory agent from the Office of Enforcement and Removal (formerly Detention and Removal, or DRO) whether the rise in criminal alien removals meant that immigrants were committing more crimes. "There are not more criminals than before," he explained, while biting into a sandwich.

> We're just able to identify them a lot better. Before each [law enforcement] agency had its own database. We would then turn fingerprints over to the FBI. . . . Now city, federal agencies are integrating their information. If you get fingerprinted in San Diego or El Paso, it'll come back [in the database]. Of one hundred apprehensions, maybe one or two might

be criminal offenders . . . a shoplifter or sexual offender . . . but the majority come to have a better life, for better work.[70]

According to the agent, less than 2% of apprehended migrants have a prior criminal record. Higher crime rates among immigrants do not account for the rise in criminal alien apprehensions and removals. Surprisingly, he attributes the rise to the biometric *technological* capacity (through databases and risk metrics) to "identify" and track a criminal alien population.

Congress has given frontline agents more resources and wider discretion to process apprehended migrants through the immigration or criminal justice system. Although few apprehended migrants have prior criminal records, agents increasingly process migrants through the criminal justice system in order to fill quotas, meet benchmarks, and follow through on federal mandates that target criminal aliens. As one ICE official explained, "Prosecutorial discretion is a legal concept. It exists in a [legal] framework. We can't abdicate responsibility. . . . One line of reasoning is that if your budget is ten dollars, and if you only spend seven dollars, we should stop. . . . We [ICE] believe we are still required to spend [the remaining] three dollars."[71]

"Street-level bureaucrats" like social workers, teachers, or police officers, or in this case border guards, often use discretion to make the most of limited resources.[72] They typically have far too many cases and too few resources to handle them. Yet on the Arizona-Sonora border, it's the opposite. Agents have *too few cases of high-priority criminal aliens* and abundant federal resources for criminal alien tracking.

Funding for bed space and biometric technology has enabled an increase in the number of deportations. Yet formal deportation had never been the primary mechanism to expel someone from the country. Deportations at the government's expense were simply too costly and were vehemently contested early on by labor and civil liberties groups. Instead of formal deportations, immigration officials relied on a "voluntary departure complex," particularly when "returning" Mexican nationals to Mexico. In recent years, however, formal deportations have actually surpassed voluntary returns.

The rise in formal deportations matters because it increases the likelihood of criminal prosecution and imprisonment for immigration offenses. At the border, those most likely to be criminally prosecuted are those who violate a deportation order and are charged with reentry after deportation. And those more likely to violate a deportation order are those with a longer settlement history and ties to the United States. One judge acknowledged that many of those being charged for reentry are not first-time border crossers; they are not foreigners but reside in the United States; many speak English and have undeniable ties to the United States, even if these are not formally recognized.

At the border, deportation and criminal prosecution for reentry disproportionately target Mexicans. National figures confirm that most deportees, and those classified as criminal aliens, are Mexican.[73] Scholars have noted an unavoidable "correlation between rising deportations and the size of the Mexican foreign-born population in the U.S."[74]

A former DRO supervisor explained to me at the time that Mexican nationals were being detained increasingly after "coming out of jail and prison for reentry, alien smuggling, drugs. They're brought here after time served." After one hearing, I asked an immigration judge why so many Mexican nationals are in detention and deportation proceedings. The traditional practice has been to "voluntarily return" immediately after arrest. "Criminal aliens," he replied.

> They're brought from the county jails. Many have previous records for reentry [violating a deportation order]. We want to make sure they get formally deported so they won't come back. But they still have a right to a hearing. Most Mexican nationals don't belong here. It's too expensive. We can't afford to keep them here [in detention]. I don't care if they have a record; they still have a right to a hearing.[75]

Despite the overrepresentation of Mexicans and Central Americans in prosecution statistics and despite the fact that deportation is entangled with the history of fugitive slave laws and race-based immigration law,[76] border policing practices operate within what Naomi Murakawa refers to as a "proceduralist" and "rights-based" framework. Critics of criminalization argue that under this new blend of criminal and immigration enforcement, undocumented migrants, as noncitizens, have no rights.[77] On the border, agents do at times extend forms of relief and procedural protections to "noncriminal," rights-bearing migrants. Undocumented migrants without the stigma of a criminal conviction have some leverage and maneuverability. The noncriminal mark minimizes the threat of physical violence. "Noncriminal" migrants are less likely to be wrung through the criminal justice system and more likely to access very basic forms of relief that can facilitate the border crossing.

And because such procedural protections and forms of relief target migrants who are victimized by private citizens such as smugglers, vigilantes, or "border bandits," such practices also take attention away from federal border policies as a root cause of victimization. Moreover, this "proceduralist" framework permits excessive and legitimate forms of state violence against migrants classified as "criminal aliens." It also obscures historical racial violence embedded in U.S. border and domestic policing by making it appear fair, race neutral, and unbiased.

It is precisely these interplays of criminalization and rights, which punish some and grant relief and protection to others, that elicit migrants' consent and participation in implementing and normalizing new enforcement priorities. Migrants leveraged criminal/victim categories in order to access basic forms of relief and to mitigate the most punitive aspects of this new enforcement field. This masks the ways in which criminal enforcement priorities target those with longer settlement histories and ties to the United States, the very people whose deportation some Democrats seek to prevent and whom some Republicans push to make criminally ineligible for "amnesty," U.S. citizenship, and, ultimately, the right to vote in future elections.

5

The Citizen and the Criminal

The Overreach of Immigration Enforcement

In Douglas, Arizona, a Mexican American woman explains that she never visits Mexico anymore even though she has relatives there and lives only a few blocks from the international border.

"Why not?" I ask.

"'Cause of this," she says, raising her wrist to show a black clunky band around it. "I'm under house arrest." She tells of how she had been an informant for the Border Patrol's antismuggling operations. "I used to work for them. But I knew too much so they set me up."

"Who's they?" I ask.

"The Border Patrol. Sometimes I'd be out there," she continues, "in my car with my camera and they'd stop me. 'What are you doing out this late?' I'd tell them who I was working for and they'd let me go."

She reported on smuggling activity regularly until she witnessed Border Patrol agents involved in the very smuggling activities they were charged with policing.[1] "They work together," she explains, referring to border agents and smugglers. "They're not all like that. Some of them are though. . . . I saw agents letting people go and guiding them [migrants] to the holding houses. So they set me up."

She believes she was "set up" one day when an "illegal" came to her house asking for food and water. "I wasn't gonna to turn them away. And got arrested for smuggling."

Two hours have passed and she looks like she still has much more to say. It's dark, and I ask if I can come back to hear more of her stories. "I'm home all the time," she laughs, pointing to the police band on her wrist.[2]

There was something about this Mexican American woman's story that startled me. It was not the accounts of corruption. What disturbed me was her quasi-legal status and that border residents, mostly citizens and legal permanent residents, are being arrested, prosecuted, sentenced, and in some cases deported for immigration offenses.

That border policing inflicts collateral damage on Mexican and Native Americans living in the border region is not new or surprising. There is a long and violent history of Border Patrol agents targeting persons of Mexican ancestry and Native peoples regardless of citizenship status.[3] The forced expulsions of Mexicans in the thirties and fifties are woven into countless family histories. During Operation Wetback in 1954, when the United States expelled over one million Mexicans, immigration agents deported U.S.-born members of my own extended family. Even today various human rights reports and congressional hearings continue to document violations of the rights of citizens and legal permanent residents by Border Patrol agents.[4]

When I agreed to go door to door for a Border Patrol–community relations survey, I questioned why abuse documentation projects often focus on citizens and upright legal residents. Most people assume that border controls are there to protect the citizens' rights and to keep out "illegals." Protecting the rights of citizens and residents, in fact, is a major rationale for increasing border security. Highlighting the rights violations of the native born or morally upright serves as leverage to challenge the overall practices of immigration enforcement. But it also reinforces a citizen/noncitizen divide in matters of rights and equality.

Yet citizens' experiences with border policing are critical to understanding how criminalization works. The literature on racial profiling and immigration law enforcement suggests that agents racially target Latinas/os because they share the ethnicity of undocumented migrants.[5] This was one of the biggest critiques in debates about Arizona's Support Our Law Enforcement and Safe Neighborhoods Act (SB1070), signed into law on April 23, 2010. SB1070 required that state and local officers check a person's immigration status and make arrests without warrant where there is probable cause that the person is subject to removal from the United States.[6] Opponents argued that the "papers, please" section of the law, which the Supreme Court upheld, would subject Latina/o residents of Arizona to systematic discrimination. Supporters of the law dismissed these critiques. Governor Jan Brewer's public statement about SB1070 stressed, "There is no higher priority than protecting the citizens of Arizona" from crime and criminals.[7] Local police and sheriff's departments prepared civil rights training videos to preempt antidiscrimination litigation.[8]

What I witnessed in border communities, nearly a decade *before* the passage of SB1070, was more insidious than the overtly racial practices I had come to expect of border security. Residents of Douglas and Nogales, whose testimonies I helped document, were not pulled over explicitly on questions of race and alienage but on *criminal* grounds. In border communities, agents were not necessarily stopping Latina/o residents and asking for their papers, as they had done in the past. This still happens, but the more common practice is to target residents as suspected smugglers, and not just on the basis of their Mexican ancestry.

Moreover, federal border agents had become more directly involved in local crime control, as opposed to the more familiar scenario of local police and sheriff's deputies enforcing federal immigration law. In border towns like Nogales and Douglas, agents often prioritized "criminal networks" over "catching" individual migrants. "If all we did was catch people [undocumented migrants]," explained an agent, "we wouldn't fix the problem. We need to get the smuggling element out of here, to focus on them, make an example of them."[9]

Agents know better than anyone that migrant smuggling routes run through the West Desert, not border towns. Agents often explained that undocumented migrants in border towns are transient and don't stay because "[i]n border towns like Douglas, people [migrants] aren't coming here to work. There is no labor force. There are no jobs."[10] Yet the Border Patrol directly targeted border communities in their antismuggling operations.

This chapter documents what some scholars have described as "net-widening," resulting in border residents, who are mostly citizens, being prosecuted for immigration offenses. Most of the residents of the U.S.-Mexico border areas are not, in fact, immigrants.[11] Ninety-five percent of the residents of Nogales, Arizona, are of Mexican or Latin American ancestry. The majority are U.S. citizens. Others are legal permanent residents. In Douglas, Arizona, 82% of residents are Latina/o. Over 70% are U.S. citizens.[12]

In border towns, agents often stopped and searched residents whom they suspected to be involved in smuggling, the majority of whom were of Mexican descent. Most of those who are stopped are citizens and legal permanent residents. An agent explained that "50% of people there are pro–law enforcement. The other 50% are criminal elements against law enforcement. There's nothing else to make a living off of. Take the average-looking house and the people living there will be driving an Escalade. . . . [P]unishment for human smuggling is less severe than for drugs, unless you injure or kill someone."[13] Another agent noted that "[t]he unemployment rate is around 13%. There's no big industry. [Smuggling] is how a lot of families make ends meet. The majority are going to be nationals from Mexico, citizens here, and legal permanent residents."

Studies examining local law enforcement's growing role in immigration control document how noncitizens in the interior are brought into the criminal justice system through arrests and stops. At the border, this is precisely what criminal enforcement priorities (rooted in the Criminal Alien Program) allow agents to do to U.S. citizens. In prosecutorial approaches to migration, harsh punishment goes hand in hand with protecting victims' rights. National rhetoric portrays U.S. citizens as "victimized" by unauthorized migration. In border communities, residents get branded as the "perpetrators" and "criminals" not only through stops and arrests. Criminalizing processes go beyond this to actually brand residents as criminal through prosecution, sentencing, imprisonment, and even wrongful deportation.

Border Security and Domestic Policing

Every day, twenty-four hours a day, in the border towns of Nogales and Douglas, Arizona, Border Patrol vehicles patrol each street. Indeed, it is uncommon to walk for more than five minutes in either town without encountering a Border Patrol agent. Since Operation Safeguard, a high-profile Border Patrol operation launched in 1995, the number of agents in the Tucson Sector has more than doubled.[14] Many agents reside in the neighboring towns like Fort Huachuca or Tucson, but some agents live in the communities they patrol. When I began my fieldwork a decade ago, there were 2,200 agents. Today there are 4,200 for the entire sector, a 90% increase. In Douglas, Arizona, alone there were 550 agents; today that figure has almost doubled. With a population of 17,000, that number translates to approximately one agent for every 17 residents, which is lower than the average public school student-to-teacher ratio. Nogales, Arizona, has 20,000 inhabitants and over 700 agents.

Border security and human smuggling are now major sources of employment in places like Nogales and Douglas. Border agents acknowledged that people smuggling, like law enforcement, has become a major source of income in border towns because human smuggling had become more lucrative than drug smuggling. As one agent stated, "[I]t's big business now. It's bigger than drug smuggling. If a drug smuggler is caught, we get the drugs. They are confiscated. They won't get them back. If we apprehend a smuggler, we're talking about people. We send them back. The smuggler is there waiting for them to try to get them across."[15]

These are predominantly low-income border communities hit hard by global economic restructuring. Douglas, Arizona, was a smelting town for the Phelps Dodge Copper Mining Company. The mine has since closed. Nogales was once an agricultural produce distribution hub, when agriculture was still a dominant industry in the region. The *maquiladoras* (assembly plants) in the Mexican free trade zones of Agua Prieta and Nogales, Sonora, have also declined as manufacturing contracts have moved overseas. The poverty rate in Douglas is 31% higher than the national average.[16] In Nogales it's 23% higher.[17] The per capita income is fourteen thousand dollars in Nogales and thirteen thousand dollars in Douglas. On the Mexican side, the figures for poverty rates and income are even starker.

Border security is ubiquitous now, but this was not always the case. In fact, for most of their history, social and cultural life in these border towns has been organized around international commerce and cross-cultural exchange. The official ports of entry, constructed in the 1960s, were designed for this purpose—to facilitate economic and cultural exchange rather than for security.[18] Historian Geraldo Cadava notes that in the postwar years, political support for cross-border economic development overshadowed concerns about marijuana busts, prostitution, and black markets. Even today, the local economies of Nogales and Douglas still depend on sales tax from Mexican shoppers. Many Korean-owned discount shops line the business districts of Nogales and Douglas, selling all sorts of colorful plastic products manufactured in China for a mostly Mexican clientele. And the economies of Nogales and Agua Prieta, Sonora, depend on U.S. visitors who cross the border to buy sex, alcohol, affordable medicines, and other cheap goods and services.[19]

These cross-border ties are still vital to the region's identity. Residents recall the days before the wall went up and more Border Patrol agents came in, when they crossed the border informally through a hole in the fence. "When I was twelve or thirteen, I crossed with my cousins," recounts one resident. "It was like a game, you know, since we were from Nogales. They'd keep us for about four hours, and then let us go. They didn't take our fingerprints. They didn't photograph us. They just made us sign a paper [voluntary return] and let us go."[20] Residents liken their interactions with Border Patrol agents to a "game" played on a national stage, but with different meaning for locals with an understanding of the historic cross-border linkages in the borderlands.

Another native of Nogales, Sonora, explains how after the buildup those interactions no longer felt like a "game" but instead felt like "criminal persecution."

> Back then we'd cross for an infinite number of reasons. We'd cross through the hole in the fence to play basketball. We'd cross to make payments on something my mother had purchased on layaway. We'd cross to buy bread and milk. You'd look around and if the Border Patrol wasn't around, pum, you'd jump the fence and run to the store. Back then when the Border Patrol caught you they'd take you right back to the border crossing and return you to Mexico. And it was like a game, not the criminal persecution that exists today. Not a state of war.[21]

The border security buildup began gradually and then accelerated. Border Patrol operations in El Paso (1993) and San Diego (1994) shifted human smuggling routes to Southern Arizona.[22] In 1995, the Border Patrol launched Operation Safeguard to intercept the traffic on the Arizona-Sonora border. Safeguard provided the staffing and resources to multiply the number of agents, to construct border fencing in Nogales, Douglas, and the neighboring town of Naco, Arizona, and to strengthen "criminal alien removal" efforts.[23]

By 1998, Arizona had become the busiest crossing point along the entire border. In Douglas alone, Border Patrol agents were apprehending an average of three thousand people a day. Residents describe the endless sound of helicopters flying overhead, of Border Patrol agents chasing migrants through their homes, or of migrants running over their lawns and hiding on their property. As one local put it, "It was like a war zone here. Forty to sixty people running through at one time and the helicopters flying all night and shining the lights through here and they'd [Border Patrol] be chasing them like rabbits."[24] The former mayor of Douglas recounted that

> [t]he *indocumentados* would come through town until they put all this Border Patrol down here. . . . [Y]ou could see them walking through the town with their backpacks in groups of ten to fifty. They were all over town. They would walk up the alleys, walk up the streets. . . . [I]t was quite an impact. . . . When the Border Patrol came in here in force and they knew they had to stop it . . . the immediate strategy was to keep them out of town and push them into the desert on the east and west, and they did that and they did it effectively.[25]

Under the old strategy, a typical workday for Border Patrol agents involved "trying to catch as many illegals as they could during a shift." Now, border agents explained to me, they focus on preventing entry by "targeting an area" or "bringing an area under control."[26] To do this, the Border Patrol implemented a three-tiered policing strategy. Forward deployment is the first tier; it stations Border Patrol vehicles along the border facing Mexico. Second-tier enforcement involves agents patrolling the streets of border towns and outlying dirt roads and providing backup to the agents in tier one. Tier three includes managing checkpoints on the major highways.

This strategy pushed migrant flows out further, away from Arizona border towns to remote areas of the desert. With fewer migrants crossing through border towns, agents admitted that forward-facing deployment along the border wall could get "boring," especially during daytime shifts. Border Patrol agents did what anyone being asked to stare at a wall for extended periods of time would do—they occasionally fell asleep. A local street vendor describes watching agents sleeping as marijuana packs fly over the border wall. "I have cart that I push along the line [border]. Every day I see something new. Someone whistles and next thing you know a pack this big [arms outstretched] of marijuana gets thrown over the fence. It happens all the time. One time one hit us on the head, right *m'ija*?" She nods to her teenage daughter and they smile at each other. "I even want to start carrying a basket to catch some of it. Then I'll really be rich," she laughs. "The Border Patrol doesn't do anything. Nothing. They're just asleep in their trucks a lot of the time."

Her neighbor nods and adds, "Yes, they just fall asleep and in the summer, when they're in that nice air conditioning, there's nothing that's gonna get them out to chase after nobody."[27]

Despite the drastic reduction of migrant traffic through border towns, Border Patrol agents remained there. And as the number of migrant apprehensions declined in those towns, border agents came to play a greater role in local crime control, mostly antismuggling operations. By 2005, a decade after launching Operation Safeguard, the Border Patrol officially revised its national border security strategy to include, along with deterring illegal immigration, fighting terrorism and smuggling and "reducing crime in border communities."[28] According to one agent, "Rural areas don't have twenty-four-hour police and sheriffs on duty." He continued to explain that

[a]fter midnight, officers and deputies are on call. When they get calls, they call us for burglaries, domestic violence, or disturbances. We work with the local sheriff and police. We have general arrest authority but don't enforce local laws. We are expected to intervene. If I see a guy beating his girlfriend, I'll stop and intervene. If I'm getting coffee somewhere and I see someone shoplifting, I intervene. If there's a traffic accident, we'll be the first on the scene.[29]

This aim differs from enforcement practices in the U.S. interior, where local police have come to play a greater role in immigration law enforcement. In border communities, it's the opposite—immigration agents are directly involved in local crime control.

Generating Consent

Residents have pushed back against this onslaught of hyperpolicing, but most vigorously against the construction of the border wall, in part because it disrupts generations of cross-border cultural, political, and economic ties. Proposals to build a border wall in Nogales, Douglas, and Naco near Bisbee surfaced in 1993. Business and political leaders vehemently opposed it, fearing that the wall would negatively impact cross-border consumption, on which local economies so heavily depend. The City Council of Douglas voted it down unanimously. Nogales, Arizona, while split over the issue, voted against it in a referendum. Public officials in Naco, Arizona, also opposed it. The proposals eventually won support when presented as a form of crime control. By 1994, the Army Corps of Engineers began to install segments of a corrugated metal wall in Naco, Arizona, made of excess landing strips left over from the first war on Iraq. Shortly after its construction, smugglers used welding torches to burn a hole through it. Sections of the wall were eventually destroyed in a flood, but it was promptly replaced as a security measure. In Nogales, the County Board of Supervisors rejected the negative results of the referendum, and a border wall was built there a year later. In Douglas, officials eventually settled on a wrought iron fence, not as an anti-immigration initiative, but as a form of crime control. The fence looks less like rusted corrugated metal strips of excess military landing mats and more like prison bars. According to one official,

> They tore the old fence down, which had gaping holes in it. They were going to put landing mats as they did in Nogales and Naco. . . . They were going to ugly up the border. We dealt with head of the Border Patrol and convinced them to put up the aesthetically pleasing fence we have down there now, five miles east of town, three miles west.[30]

The Border Patrol's public relations office shifted public perceptions of the wall by adjusting its messaging to fit local conditions. It carefully avoided framing the project as anti-immigration, as anti-Mexico, or as a barrier to cross-border exchange in a region whose economic existence depends on it. The Border Patrol spearheaded a youth explorers program, organized donation drives, invited the participation of residents in antismuggling operations, and recruited community leaders for its citizens advisory council.[31]

Its local public relations campaigns moved away from the racial language so prevalent in national public discourses and drew on the apparently "race-neutral" language of "safety," "security," and "crime control."[32] At that time the Mexican economy was in a state of crisis and border communities felt its impact intensely because, as a native of Nogales, Sonora, explains, "One lives on what Mexicans buy." During the Mexican economic crisis of the mid-1990s, the value of the Mexican peso plummeted, while the value of the dollar shot up. She adds that "[p]eople stopped buying and many people lost their jobs. Businesses closed that had been around for fifty or sixty years. Prices shot way up, unemployment rose, and crime went up. I don't believe it's a crime to steal when you're hungry. And this is what happened. People began to steal. There was more crime."[33]

Residents expressed feelings about the economic insecurity they experienced as social anxiety about migration.[34] On the Mexican side, the *maquila* boom in the seventies and eighties stimulated massive internal Mexican migration to the border region. Agua Prieta's population grew to around 150,000.[35] The population of Nogales, Sonora, is approximately 200,000.[36] Many residents from Nogales and Agua Prieta blamed migrants for the crime. On the U.S. side, border towns experienced white flight after the mines closed. Seasonal Mexican migrants settled permanently as citizens, or as legal permanent residents who were able to adjust their immigration status when legal channels to do so still existed. Border Patrol operations in other places also pushed new waves of migrants from "the South" to cross clandestinely through Arizona border communities. U.S. border residents came to associate crime, mostly property theft, with waves of newcomers.

The Border Patrol played on people's fears and insecurities by framing border security as local crime control, which diffused local opposition to their operations. By the time I interviewed residents, almost a decade after the border buildup, the Border Patrol had won support for border security as a form of crime control, with no public discussion of how locals—mostly Latina/o citizens and legal permanent residents— would also become its targets.

Federal immigration agents' involvement in local crime control complicated relations between Border Patrol agents and local residents, who for generations had crossed the border daily—with a border crossing card or through holes in the fence—to shop or visit relatives and return to Mexico by day's end. On the Mexican side, border security disrupted traditional cross-border flows and provoked violent clashes between agents and border residents in Mexico. "I actually had a passport," recalled one native of Nogales, Sonora:

but my sister didn't so I'd put the document in my shoe and cross with her. It was becoming harder to cross. We had to cross through the arroyo, through tunnels.[37] It was completely dark under there. We'd go through a ton of puddles and we were afraid.

Another time I crossed [through a tunnel] with my brother. We set off a motion sensor and they [Border Patrol] sent someone to pick us up. My brother was really afraid and pleaded, "Man, man, just basketball. Friends *alla* [in Nogales, Arizona]."

The agent had a *cara de pocos amigos* [an unfriendly face] and told him, "Shut up. And don't call me man."

I got mad and said to my brother, "He doesn't want to be called a man, so call him a woman then." The agent got pretty angry and was about to hit me. "Go ahead," I said. "Hit me, and I'll sue you. I have your name and your plate number." He left us alone after that. He detained us for five hours. They interrogated me and accused me of carrying drugs. I talked to the supervisor and said, "Look, in all the time I've been stopped, I was never treated so badly," and he said, "OK, I'll talk to him."[38]

The border wall made it much harder for locals to go back and forth and also increased injuries—mostly sprains and bone fractures from the failed attempts of local youth to scale the wall in order to shop or visit friends and relatives. According to locals, people began to respond with violence, and it was common to see new Border Patrol vehicles with smashed-in windows or scrapes and gashes across passenger doors. The Border Patrol also reported a rise in "rocking" incidents in which local youth fling rocks and debris at Border Patrol agents stationed along the wall. In rock-throwing incidents, border agents have retaliated by shooting and killing local residents. During an alleged rock-throwing incident in 2012, a Border Patrol agent shot a sixteen-year-old Nogales, Sonora, resident in the back eleven times. Mexican officials reported that the teenager carried only a cell phone.[39]

On the U.S. side, locals also grappled with the heightened security. A Douglas resident living with her elderly mother recalls how every night they'd get groups of twenty to thirty migrants running through their yard at once. "We've never had any problems with them ['illegals']," she says, "but my mother worries that they might do something. . . . You just never know." She recounts an incident when a Border Patrol agent arrested someone in her yard.

> He'd been lost [in the desert] for four days and was very weak. My mother offered him some water, but the agent wouldn't let her give it to him. It's our property, you know? We never used to have these problems until they put up the fence and the lights. It seems like the Border Patrol brought the problem to the area. The more they try to do, the worse it gets.[40]

Mounting resentment and fear mixed with support for crime control. Local residents took pride in living in border towns with some of lowest crime rates in the country. They reported feeling safer and often credited the Border Patrol with bringing security and safety to the area and stamping out crime. "Love them. They come right away," says a fifty-something-year-old Douglas resident.

> Someone tried to break in once and I called Border Patrol. . . . [T]hey came within minutes. . . . Three or four years ago we used to get a lot of migrant traffic. Not so much anymore. I feel sorry for people crossing. . . . [T]he coyotes are to blame. The problems began when they started making money. . . . Ten years ago we didn't have to lock our doors. Now you can't do that—too many foreigners from down south. Agua Prieta has also changed. It's not safe anymore.[41]

Another thirty-nine-year-old Douglas resident agreed that "[t]he presence and the lights and walls help I guess." She manages a dollar store in town and works sixteen-hour shifts daily. She's never personally had any problems with crime, but hears stories about assaults and car theft. "I've never had any problems with the Border Patrol because like I said, I'm always working." I ask her if she knows how to contact the Border Patrol if she ever needs to file a complaint.

"Yes," she replies. "It's 911."

"911?" I ask.

"*Sí*, 9-1-1."

"You mean you call the police?"

"No, the Border Patrol, 911 connects you with the Border Patrol," she says matter-of-factly.[42]

Suspected Smugglers

The homes along International Boulevard in Nogales, Arizona, face the corrugated metal border wall. Nogales is set on hills, and many of the wooden frame houses are up high. You have to climb a flight of rusty metal stairs to get to them. "Beware of dog" signs hang from almost every gate. The sun is bright and the pedestrian traffic, mostly shoppers from Mexico, gives it a lively feel. The first home, an old adobe structure covered in overgrown vines, is completely abandoned. The alley next to it leads to a courtyard and other homes—small shacks with metal doors. A Border Patrol agent on a bicycle follows me as I walk along. He calls out to me in Spanish, but I ignore him. He calls out in English. "Where are you going?" he asks.

"Doing a survey," I respond.

His tone changes from one of suspicion to one of concern. "That's one of the biggest dope houses in Nogales, so I wondered why you were going in there," motioning that I should keep moving.[43]

I was questioned a lot when walking along the streets of Nogales and Douglas, Arizona, and when driving back from Agua Prieta with my then six-month-old in tow. When I met with the Mexican consul, he recounted the number of cases of Mexican American women charged with smuggling children through the ports of entry.[44] Like the border residents, I fit the profile of a human smuggler.

Border communities boast of some of the lowest crime rates in the country. Among immigration crimes, smuggling constitutes only a very small percentage, yet considerable energy went to antismuggling operations under the mandate of targeting criminal aliens. In pursuing smugglers, agents inadvertently targeted border residents, many of whom were U.S. citizens and legal permanent residents with a long history of settlement in the borderlands.

Border agents interrogated, arrested, and confiscated the property of border residents with alarming regularity. The interrogations and arrests were not based on whether targets were perceived as non-citizens but on whether or not they were criminals. In other words, agents arrested, prosecuted, incarcerated, and even deported residents for immigration *crimes*, specifically on suspicion of smuggling. "They hang out at the restaurants and grocery stores to see what people are buying," explains one forty-two-year-old native Douglas resident. His partner finishes his sentence. "If they catch you buying a lot of food," she said, "they think you are a smuggler."[45]

"It's gotten to a point where you can't even help someone because then they think you are a smuggler," explained a schoolteacher from Douglas. She is hesitant to talk to me at first. We chat about gourds, which she grows in her garden, that make good bird feeders. We chat about housecleaning and she apologizes for the mess even though her house is tidy.

> The woman next door had pigs so she built a pen out in back. Well, the smugglers would hide people out there and she got punished for it. We had to get dogs for the back because we don't want anyone back there. They'll take you to jail. Take your house, your car, and your papers. The other day, a woman came to my door and asked if I could give her some water. She had a baby bottle so I filled it and she drank it and she asked me for more. She asked me to fill it like four times. I felt bad for her and asked her where the baby was. She said she left the baby hiding with someone else. I filled up a gallon for her and a Border Patrol passed by and picked her up. He started yelling at me that I couldn't do that and I said to him, "If someone comes to my house and asks me for water I will give it. I don't work for the Border Patrol. That's your job."[46]

In one home, a forty-four-year-old woman invites me in but hesitates to speak. She doesn't make eye contact and looks down. I share some of my visits from the migrant shelters and some of the other stories I've heard, and this puts her at ease. She recounts an incident in which she loaned her car to a relative to go to Agua Prieta. "When he was coming back over, they [Border Patrol] stopped him. They saw it wasn't his car and found my papers [documents] in the glove compartment." The agents impounded her car, confiscated the documents, and sent an agent to her home to apprehend and deport her.

I told them I was legal, but they told me I had to leave. They wouldn't give me back my papers or my car. They said I had to take a voluntary departure and leave. I was going to until a friend told me to talk to a lawyer. I got my car and my papers back but I still had to pay the lawyer four hundred dollars.[47]

Walking through the neighborhoods along the border wall in Douglas, I notice a woman in a Border Patrol uniform walk into a house across the street. Border Patrol agents live alongside suspected smugglers and sometimes are even members of the same family. Everyone seems to be watching everyone else.

I visit the home of a resident who reports that the Border Patrol accused his neighbor of smuggling, confiscated his car, and threatened him with deportation.

He was driving his pick-up and some migrants asked him for a ride. He was talking to them, telling them that he couldn't and an agent passed by and stopped them all. The agents made the migrants climb onto his truck and accused him of being a coyote. My friend told the agent that he wasn't doing anything wrong, but the agent threatened him. The agent told him, "You can go to court and tell a judge, but they will only take away your papers." The agent took his car and the migrants and left him stranded there.[48]

In more extreme cases, some female residents confided to having been cavity searched for drugs. Others spoke of beatings or shootings by Border Patrol agents.[49] A Douglas resident told me that her relative had been shot by an agent and "the family two houses down, their son was killed." She later confessed that her husband had warned her against saying too much.

That was four or five years ago. She's eighteen now. You know how kids are. She and her brothers set their tents back there and were playing camp. At about three o'clock in the morning she heard dogs and got scared. She was running back home with her backpack and a Border Patrol shot her in the knee from behind. She doesn't remember anything but the heat on her leg. She passed out. The Border Patrol said she was carrying drugs in her backpack, but all she had were clothes. Her family complained, but they didn't get anything—nothing. ACCESS [state insurance plan for children] paid for her medical treatment. She's had four surgeries. She's married now and doesn't qualify for the insurance and she still needs another surgery to replace her knee. The other kid was twenty-one when he was shot. They accused him of stealing. They [Border Patrol] shot him five times. They [the victim's family] didn't get anything either.[50]

It's deathly hot, the border only one block away. I see a Border Patrol truck parked along the wrought iron border fence in Douglas. I keep walking and notice a Latino Border Patrol agent in uniform walk into a house on one of the side streets. I arrive at the home of a thirty-five-year-old Mexican woman, who lets me interview her while she bathes her six-month-old baby in the kitchen sink. Two other children are playing, and a young teenage girl comes in and walks through the house. She's on probation and isn't allowed to leave Douglas.[51]

In border towns, agents often prosecute residents for immigration crimes like smuggling. Like most law enforcement agents, they prioritize cases most likely to be prosecuted. And at the border, human smuggling now has a much higher prosecution rate than drug possession. Because of harsh federal and state antismuggling laws, prosecutors are more likely to convict human smugglers.[52] One law enforcement official explained that because of the backlogs in the criminal justice system, federal prosecutors often dismiss many cases of border residents charged with low-level drug offenses.[53] Since human smuggling has a much higher prosecution rate, border agents (and law enforcement) prioritize human smugglers, the majority of whom are U.S. citizens of various backgrounds.

In fact, many smuggling cases are now prosecuted at the state level, particular since Arizona's enactment of a harsh state-level antismuggling law in 2005. Since then, state and county-level prosecutions for alien smuggling now exceed federally prosecuted cases. Before the passage of Arizona's 2005 smuggling law, the federal district court handled a quarter of all smuggling cases nationwide—most of which involved U.S. citizens and some of which involved cases of Border Patrol agents indicted for smuggling. Since 2006, Maricopa County handles the largest number of smuggling cases, most of which apply the smuggling statute more loosely to include migrants in conspiracy to self-smuggle. Many of these prosecutions target low-level smugglers and, significantly, those of federal agents indicted on smuggling charges.[54]

Over the course of my fieldwork, I encountered numerous residents who were formal citizens but had been criminally prosecuted and charged with immigration violations, most having been accused of being low-level employees of human smuggling organizations. The Federal Bureau of Justice Statistics reported that in 2010, 50% of those charged with alien smuggling offenses were U.S. citizens, as the following account from a Douglas resident illustrates.[55]

> In January [2002] a friend of mine came across two migrant women and their children. They looked hungry so he picked them up and took them to get food. A Border Patrol [sic] stopped him. They put him in jail, accusing him of being a coyote. How could he possibly be a coyote if they were sitting in full view? All the seats were there. It's not like he had taken the seats out and was hiding them in the back the way coyotes do. He was in jail for three months for that.[56]

Often residents recount how their relatives lost their legal residency status and were deported after serving time for human smuggling.

> My brother served time and got deported after five years to Nogales, Sonora. The judge told him he couldn't come back. But he had never lived in Sonora. He's lived here his whole life. They deported him *en la madrugada* [at dawn], and he was terrified. He stayed in a hotel for a week and didn't come out, because he was afraid. After a while he got a fake Social Security and green card and just went back and forth for eight years until he got pulled over with some friends who didn't have papers. His friends got out of the car and started running. He told them not to run, but they did and so they took him *como traficante de ilegales* [as a smuggler]. Now they are going to give him ten years. And my concern is that that is too long. I'm not saying he shouldn't be punished, but they should just deport him. Why do they have to send him to prison again and for so long?[57]

That respondent's brother was a legal permanent resident, but I also learned of the deportation of U.S. citizens. I first heard of such cases during a visit to the immigration court within the detention facility in Florence, Arizona. An attorney with the Florence Immigration and Refugee Rights' Legal Orientation Program mentioned that she had just testified in Congress about the dozens of cases involving citizens in deportation proceedings. Jacqueline Stevens has written about this at greater length, citing over eighty cases in Arizona alone.[58] These are mostly people who have been incarcerated for drug offenses and who, for various reasons, are unable to prove their citizenship. They are misclassified as criminal aliens and put in removal proceedings, without the opportunity to come before an immigration judge.

Through the State Criminal Alien Assistance Program, which reimburses state and local law enforcement agencies for costs associated with noncitizen offenders, local jails and prisons typically refer cases to ICE for deportation directly from prison, in what are known as expedited removals.[59] Busloads of deported prisoners are dropped off regularly in Nogales, Sonora. "You can tell they're prisoners, too," a local resident explains,

> because they still have the prison clothes, light blue shirt, dark blue pants. They all carry a little cardboard box with their things. They drop them off *en la madrugada*. It's very disorienting to be dropped off at two in the morning. Everything is closed.
>
> They're not from Nogales [Sonora] or have never lived in Mexico and they're terrified. The prison gives them each a check for fifty dollars. Where are they going to cash a check at one, two, or three in the morning? The taxis are all there waiting for them; they know they are from the prison. They drive them all the way to God knows where to cash their checks—all because they drop them off at that hour. Why can't they drop them off at a decent hour? Someone should tell them that it doesn't make sense to drop them off at that hour.[60]

Search-and-seizure practices, criminal prosecution and incarceration, and deportation reclassify native-born and legal permanent residents as "criminals," less deserving of the rights of citizenship. In the legal literature, citizens are guaranteed rights under criminal and immigration law enforcement. Yet criminal history appears to trump legal status. In the United States criminal stigma has lasting effects. These include family separation, as well as barriers to employment, voting, public housing, and financial aid for higher education, and, in the case of legal permanent residents—deportation.[61] Like the undocumented migrants whom border agents pursue, citizen border residents with criminal convictions experience actual constraints on their physical and social mobility.

Though I've likened these effects on convicted citizens to imposition of noncitizen status, the residents I met don't necessarily see it this way. They are not quick to define their situation as a negation of their citizenship and rights. Nor do they regard their systemic mistreatment as a form of racial profiling. "It's not discrimination. It's how we perceive it. Sometimes we use discrimination as an excuse to be *victims*," explained a woman from Nogales.[62] Many do not see the Border Patrol enforcement actions as motivated by race. "It's not like when I was a kid or when my father was kid," explained a thirty-year-old Douglas resident. "They'd say things like 'Are you wet?' 'Are you a wetback?' 'Hey Beaner.' They're more PC [politically correct]. Now they just ask a bunch of unnecessary questions about where you've been and where you're going."[63]

Residents did not necessarily perceive their negative experiences with border security as rights violations or constraints on their citizenship, and yet they often expressed consciousness about rights and their entitlement as citizens or legal permanent residents. Collectively, they made use of legal channels formally available to them by, for example, filing complaints about misconduct; making phone calls to various officials to complain about the noise level of helicopters; joining the Border Patrol's citizens' advisory council; initiating lawsuits; or circulating petitions, as some did when a local vigilante handcuffed two migrants to a bench outside a local Wal-Mart.

Residents also resorted to more subtle forms of contestation, such as being noncompliant, talking back, or even using humor. Residents' accounts of mistreatment almost always included stories about Border Patrol follies. For instance: a Border Patrol agent stops a pizza delivery driver and asks what's in the box; a Border Patrol agent runs after a group of local kids (U.S. citizens) who amuse themselves by pretending to be undocumented and making the agents chase them; Border Patrol agents use civilians as human shields between themselves and migrants "because they're scared"; Border Patrol agents fall asleep in vehicles while packs of marijuana get flung over the border wall.

Challenging border-policing practices that disproportionately target Latina/o residents is difficult. It is not easy to name and confront shame, mistreatment, and fear produced by activities carried out in the name of safety, security, or crime reduction. Understandably, rather than questioning the roots of criminalization or the criminal classifications that mark them, residents blamed the criminality of smugglers, even as they themselves have become the primary suspects.

"Do you want to know what I think should be done to them [smugglers]?" a seventy-four-year-old Douglas resident asked.

"What?" I replied.

"They should be stripped down until they are completely naked. And they [authorities] should grab a wet whip and give them lashings." I laughed nervously, glancing at a Bible on her coffee table. She said, "You think I'm kidding, don't you?"[64]

Outside a Nogales resident's home, a middle-aged woman draws my attention to parked vans that shuttle residents between Nogales and Tucson and Phoenix and says she hates them. "They transport them [migrants]. They wanted to park their trucks in my neighbor's lot across the street and he said no. I don't want anything to do with it. I don't want to get involved in that [smuggling]. They bring people then leave them to die. They harm them in the desert. Yes," she continues, "we are all accomplices, we are all accomplices." She repeats this several times.[65]

Punishing Activists

As residents, local activists both challenge border agent misconduct and maintain regular, cooperative communication with the Border Patrol in matters of migrant deaths, vigilante assaults, and detention and deportation. Through an established Legal Orientation Program, DHS allows certain NGOs to offer pro bono legal services and to conduct "know your rights" presentations for detained migrants. Other groups known locally as the "Samaritans" negotiated an agreement with the Border Patrol to provide humanitarian assistance to migrants in distress by placing water stations in the desert or by administering first aid under Arizona's Good Samaritan laws, which protect from liability anyone who renders care in an emergency situation.[66]

While border agents and NGOs shared a common goal of "reducing migrant fatalities," the Border Patrol has drawn on prosecutorial rhetoric in order to arrest activists on smuggling charges. In an early case on October 19, 1976, ten Border Patrol agents and one Tucson police officer raided and charged members of the Manzo Area Council with alien smuggling and document fraud.[67] Manzo was a Tucson-based War on Poverty Program focused on social services. During the mid-1970s, it shifted its focus more to immigrant legal advocacy, in response to raids and sweeps in the Tucson area. The Border Patrol confiscated eight hundred files containing information about the immigration status of Manzo's clients. A few weeks later, the Border Patrol arrested and deported 150–200 former Manzo clients. It also charged its executive director, Margo Cowan, along with three volunteers, with transporting aliens and aiding them in eluding inspection, entering false statements, perjury, and conspiracy to smuggle. They faced prison sentences totaling seventy-seven years and ninety-eight thousand dollars in fines. Manzo organized press conferences challenging the classification of its clients as "illegal." Cowan defended her organization, stating that "most of our clients have never been to a deportation hearing, nor have they had their status defined. They find themselves without documents, but they do not find themselves in an illegal status, technically speaking. This is at the heart of our defense. Furthermore," she added, "20% of our clients are U.S.-born but can't prove it. Some of them are forced to live in Sonora, Mexico, until they can prove their U.S. citizenship. We are saying that people are not here illegally until they have been adjudicated in some kind of hearing or court of law."[68] As part of the campaign, former clients of Manzo filed a class action lawsuit against the Border Patrol, on grounds of "illegal search and seizure, illegal questioning of clients, and improper deportation procedures." Mobilizations against the prosecution of the "Manzo 4" pressured the U.S. Attorney's Office to eventually drop the charges.[69]

During the Sanctuary movement, the former INS investigated and charged activists on human smuggling charges. At the time, several churches declared themselves public sanctuaries, operating as an "underground railroad" that brought refugees across the border through Nogales, transported refugees to other parts of the United States, provided social services, and helped with asylum applications. After several years of covert government investigations, fourteen members were indicted, eleven were prosecuted, and eight were eventually convicted on conspiracy and smuggling charges in 1986.[70]

At the time of my fieldwork, the Border Patrol arrested and prosecuted two twenty-four-year-old humanitarian workers, Shanti Sellz and Daniel Strauss, on smuggling charges.[71] On July 9, 2005, they had been out in the desert doing relief work when they encountered three seriously ill migrants who had drunk contaminated water from a cattle tank. They were driving them to a medical station in Tucson.[72] The defendants faced up to ten years and thousands of dollars in fines because smuggling is a felony. Local activists mobilized under the slogan, "humanitarian aid is never a crime." After a long, grueling year, prosecutors dropped the charges against them.[73] By distancing rescuers from "real" criminals (i.e., smugglers), the slogan inadvertently and implicitly draws on a prosecutorial framework that interprets humanitarian assistance as legitimate work supporting victims' rights and opposing migrant victimization.

As these cases show, the Border Patrol also targets white, middle-class activists as suspected smugglers. The justification is that crime-centered approaches to immigration enforcement treat everyone equally. One local white resident and activist shared his own experiences of being pulled over several times. He was once pulled over when he was driving with his Mexican wife, and another time for giving some church members from Agua Prieta, Sonora, a ride to Douglas, Arizona. And he was pulled over yet again for picking up some strangers on the side of the road. "I'm from [the South] and these kinda things don't happen [to people like me] there. When I get stopped I just think that's the way things are here. They [Border Patrol] know who I am," he says calmly. He has a friend who is an agent who told him the Border Patrol had a file on him. "I'm always watching my back. I think I've been taking the situation here for granted."[74]

Prosecuting Patriots

The drive into Douglas is peaceful and scenic, except for the handmade anti-immigrant billboards that line the barbed wire fences along Davis Road. I notice a middle-aged white man with a stout frame dressed in military fatigues and carrying a rifle over his shoulder as he walks along the edge of the road. Up the road there are four other men, also dressed in fatigues and also armed.[75] On the outskirts of Southern Arizona border towns, some residents engage in vigilante activity along the border, in which individuals and armed militia groups take the law into their own hands by intercepting migrant routes on public and private lands. Here I do not focus on high-profile groups like Ranch Rescue or American Border Patrol, since their leadership is not from Arizona, nor is much of their funding. Anti-immigrant groups like the Federation for American Immigration Reform fund them externally.[76] Arizona has its own homegrown vigilantism in which private citizens mimic Border Patrol arrests.

At its core, vigilantism is a form of what the sociologist Emile Durkheim calls "moral outrage" directed at those who offend the "common consciousness."[77] Early expressions of vigilantism targeted "outlaws" and violators of social law. Later forms of vigilantism, which emerged after the U.S. Civil War, targeted groups (i.e., racial minorities, labor radicals, civil liberties advocates) who challenged race and class hierarchies.[78] Arizona vigilantism certainly expresses aspects of earlier forms. Vigilantism in Arizona is a reaction to and directly challenges the extension of social citizenship and rights to racial minorities in the post–civil rights era. Following passage of the 1965 Immigration Law and again with passage of the Immigration Reform and Control Act in 1986, many families legalized their immigration status. Many of the seasonal migrants whom ranchers and growers once depended on so heavily are now permanently settled residents. Like much of the country, Arizona is experiencing major changes in its ethno-racial composition. Vigilantism expresses the ambivalence and anxiety of dominant groups in one of the fastest-growing states in the country.

And yet vigilantism in Arizona has adapted to a post–civil rights enforcement terrain. This post-1960s vigilantism entails "cooperation with police" and parallels law enforcement.[79] Indeed, what I observed in Southern Arizona is that vigilantism draws on both crime control and "color-blind constitutionalism" for legitimacy.[80] Like the Border Patrol, local vigilantes draw on a message of crime control and security. In news interviews they frame their work as "restoring the rule of law." Chris Simcox, the founder of the Minuteman Project, describes its work as "operating within the law to support the enforcement of the law."[81] The common justification is that their vigilante actions are citizen's arrests, in which the vigilante serves as the patriotic citizen and migrants are the alleged criminals.

But local vigilantes also draw on a (victims') rights rhetoric. They affirm their right to make citizen's arrests, their right to bear arms, and their right to defend private property. They are also forced (by law) to recognize, albeit reluctantly, some basic constitutional protections to which migrants are entitled.[82] Local vigilantes, particularly the Minuteman Project, made conscious efforts to avoid being labeled as a hate group and recruited African American and Latina/o supporters.[83] The Minuteman Project website states that "the Minuteman Project has no affiliation nor will we accept assistance from separatist, racist or supremacist groups."[84] Local vigilantes like Simcox have referred to themselves as the "White Martin Luther Kings" and have compared the Minuteman Project to the civil rights movement.[85]

Yet even as they draw on a language of rights and crime control to justify their actions, local vigilantes, too, have also on occasion been criminally charged.

When I was out in the field, the local paper covered an incident in which a twenty-four-year-old army reservist, Patrick Haab, held seven undocumented migrants at gunpoint at a rest stop on Interstate 8 and then called the Border Patrol. Impersonating a Border Patrol agent, he ordered the migrants to squat and threatened to shoot them. When the Border Patrol arrived, they apprehended and processed the migrants. They also arrested Haab, a U.S. citizen, for aggravated assault with a deadly weapon, which outraged anti-immigrant groups.

Although the U.S. Attorney's Office tried to justify Haab's actions as a citizen's arrest, the argument did not hold up in court because in Arizona citizens can only make arrests for a felony. Unlawful entry is a petty misdemeanor. Law professor Ingrid Eagly has written about this case in her study of immigration prosecution in Arizona.[86] What interests me about the case is how prosecutorial approaches to migration can extend to citizens, in this case for detaining migrants at gunpoint. In this case, Haab was the perpetrator and migrants were the crime victims. In fact, since they had no prior record, the migrants were processed administratively and never criminally charged for illegal entry.

That year, Arizona had just passed a law that made smuggling a felony. The county attorney's office drew on that law to make the case that the migrants were in a conspiracy to "smuggle themselves."[87] The seven migrants were never actually prosecuted, but the threat of prosecution was enough to alter their status from that of crime victims to that of criminals and to make a case that Haab's holding them at gunpoint was a citizen's arrest rather than a state crime. On April 28, 2005, criminal charges against Haab were dropped. Because criminal status was displaced onto the men he assaulted, Haab walked away with his status as a noncriminal patriot intact.

In a similar case, local activists drew on prosecutorial rhetoric to criminally charge a local vigilante and rancher, Roger Barnett. In the 1990s, Barnett and his brothers made international news for apprehending migrants and turning them over to the U.S. Border Patrol. Roger Barnett credits himself with apprehending over fourteen thousand undocumented immigrants using techniques borrowed from the U.S. Border Patrol.[88] He founded the Arizona Ranchers Alliance in 1999 and the Shadow Border Patrol in 2000 and is a member of a local group, Concerned Citizens of Cochise County, which was founded in 1999.

Between 1999 and 2002, when I began my fieldwork, the Mexican Consulate had documented forty-three cases of armed U.S. citizens forcibly apprehending undocumented migrants in Cochise County, many of which involved Roger Barnett and his brother.

- April 4, 1999: Roger Barnett and others, all of them armed, apprehended twenty-seven people near Interstate 80.
- October 10, 1999: Roger and Donald Barnett, accompanied by Larry Vance from Ranch Rescue and a television crew, apprehended twenty-one immigrants. Barnett threatened the group with his rifle.
- November 20, 1999: Roger Barnett and his wife apprehended twenty-seven persons at gunpoint.
- February 13, 2000: Roger Barnett apprehended eighteen undocumented immigrants at gunpoint near Interstate 80, and photographed them before turning them over to the Border Patrol.
- February 25, 2000: the Barnett brothers apprehended twenty-three Mexican nationals at gunpoint. This time they threatened them with dogs.
- April 9, 2000: Roger Barnett intercepted two vehicles transporting

sixteen migrants on Interstate 80. Barnett ordered the vehicles to pull over, demanded the keys to the vehicles, insulted the group, and then photographed them before calling the Border Patrol.

- August 16, 2000: Roger Barnett apprehended undocumented migrants on Interstate 80. The apprehension occurred before an ABC television crew. Barnett ordered the group, in Spanish, to sit on the ground while the reporters interviewed him, after which he called the Border Patrol.[89]

On October 30, 2004, Barnett and his brother Donald stopped four members of a Mexican American family from Douglas, including two children ages nine and eleven, and their eleven-year-old friend. The family was on public land leased to Barnett for cattle grazing. Barnett yelled racial obscenities, pointed an AR-15 assault rifle at one of the children, and threatened to kill them all.[90] The Cochise County prosecutor declined to file charges against Barnett, arguing that "no jury in Cochise County will ever convict Roger Barnett."[91] The family filed a civil lawsuit and won $98,750 in damages for false imprisonment and emotional distress. Despite attempts to prosecute Barnett, he walked away without a criminal conviction and with his status as noncriminal citizen intact.

In an earlier high-profile case, local civil rights activists pressed for criminal charges against two local vigilantes.[92] On August 18, 1976, Patrick and Thomas Hanigan, sons of a local rancher just outside Douglas, Arizona, forced three Mexican migrants into their truck, drove them out to a field, hung them from a tree, burned their feet, then told them to run back to Mexico while they fired shots at them. The county prosecutor declined to file charges on grounds that the migrants trespassed on the Hanigans' private property. It took political pressure from immigrant-rights and civil rights groups to bring the Hanigans to trial. In 1976, an all-white jury acquitted Thomas and Patrick on all counts of assault, kidnapping, and robbery. In 1980, after intense political pressure from civil rights groups, federal prosecutors reopened the case, on appeal, and failed to convict the Hanigan brothers. During the third and final trial in 1981, federal prosecutors acquitted Thomas Hanigan but convicted Patrick Hanigan on all three counts. Thomas Hanigan was convicted of smuggling 574 pounds of marijuana a few weeks later.[93]

These high-profile cases illustrate a particular interplay of rights discourses and crime control. They also convey the ways in which local vigilantes have distanced themselves from overt racial discourses. In these cases, local vigilantes affirm their "rights" as citizen victims to engage in violent attacks and kidnapping, by conferring criminal status on those they assault—as trespassers on private property or as smugglers.[94] Migrant and civil rights advocates, in turn, also get pulled into crime-control frameworks by mobilizing to prosecute vigilantes in order to protect rights.

The Overreach of Enforcement Priorities

The criminal alien mandate, which prioritizes criminal arrest and prosecution for immigration offenses alongside criminal deportation, has transformed border policing. Federal immigration agents not only arrest and expel criminal aliens; they are also involved in local crime control. Though the escalation aroused tensions between agents and border residents, the Border Patrol diffused this with the promise of "public safety." According to an agent, "When the Border Patrol experienced a growth spurt," referring to the massive escalation of policing under Safeguard,

> there was some resentment. There were only forty agents in 1995; that's an average of four to five people a shift. Now there are over four hundred. But now, if we were to pull back, resentment would be strong. The chief of police would have to deploy [more officers] and expand the police force. They wouldn't want us to leave. Some do. But we have no plans to downsize.[95]

This blend of immigration control and domestic policing extends its reach beyond undocumented migrants and targets the very citizens it is supposed to protect. Agents stopped, searched, interrogated, and arrested border residents on suspicion of smuggling with alarming regularity, often for giving water to distressed migrants or having someone who might be undocumented in their vehicles. Border residents often do not have the economic and political capital to challenge the charges brought against them. For those citizens who cannot or do not fight their case, a criminal mark justifies violence, constraints on mobility, constraints on the right to vote, access to public housing and other social safety net services, and an overall stigmatized social status.

Citizen activists charged with human smuggling were able to deflect criminal status by highlighting the victimization of the migrants they aided and the humanitarian nature of their advocacy work. They also drew on financial resources and social capital to challenge their cases and were never officially branded as criminal. Vigilantes used their connections to law enforcement, prosecutors, and anti-immigrant advocates to contest criminal charges, partly by deflecting criminality onto those they assaulted and portraying themselves as citizen victims. These subtle actions normalize a prosecutorial rhetoric that reinforces the personhood of "crime victims" and the second-class citizenship of those stigmatized as criminal.

Prosecutorial approaches that uphold rights and aggressively punish differ from the traditional ways that agents enforced immigration law. Historically, the Border Patrol overtly targeted persons of Mexican ancestry through violent means, without regard for rights or the Constitution. Because crime control engulfs everyone—even White citizens who are not the typical suspects—the racial underpinnings of immigration law enforcement are less visible. This captures the way a 150-year history of racial and exclusionary violence on the U.S.-Mexico border can be retold and normalized as part of the inevitable cost of security and crime control.

Enacted on the ground, on a daily basis, such enforcement actions extend the collateral consequences of a conviction to an immigration and border context. The lasting stigma of a conviction, in this case an immigration conviction, justifies a negation of personhood and rights for those with a criminal record, regardless of citizenship. The diffusion of DHS enforcement priorities, rooted in the Criminal Alien Program, institutionalizes a linkage between citizenship and criminal history, whereby the citizen becomes the antithesis to the criminal.

6

A New Enforcement Terrain

Criminal Justice Reforms and Border Security

On October 10, 2013, immigrant-rights activists shut down Operation Streamline hearings in the federal courthouse in Tucson, Arizona. In an act of civil disobedience, twelve activists chained themselves to the wheels of buses that would have transported apprehended migrants to the courthouse for criminal prosecution hearings under Streamline. Another six linked themselves to the vehicle entrance of the federal building in order to block buses from entering. The hearings had to be canceled that day for the first time since 2008, when Streamline began in Arizona.[1]

Only months before, nine undocumented antideportation activists took part in a protest at the Arizona-Sonora border, where they turned themselves in to the Department of Homeland Security (DHS) and petitioned for humanitarian parole, a form of relief from deportation. All had grown up in the United States. Two had been deported. The others were living in cities throughout the United States. In an act of civil disobedience, they crossed the border into Mexico without a visa or authorization to reenter the United States. There they joined other deported activists and turned themselves in at the U.S. Port of Entry in Nogales, Arizona. Once they were in DHS custody, agents at the port of entry transferred them to a detention center in Florence, Arizona, while their cases went under review. In detention, they staged a hunger strike to call international attention to U.S. detention and deportation policies.[2] Referring explicitly to the Department of Homeland Security's enforcement "priorities" that guide prosecutorial discretion, one activist explained the protest in this way: "The idea we're trying to make about immigration is that there's no reason to detain them. They're not high priority, they're not a flight risk, in fact they're actually fighting to stay in the country."[3] They petitioned their cases on grounds that they were not high-risk priorities for the DHS. Letters of support came in from all over the country. An attorney and founding member of the Manzo Area Council and long-time Arizona and border-rights activist, Margo Cowan, successfully represented their case. They leveraged their "noncriminal" status, which made them eligible for humanitarian parole. They were released from detention in August 2013.[4]

Other protests and actions followed suit, including one by thirty deported long-term residents of the United States who presented themselves at the port of entry in El Paso, Texas. Other undocumented long-term resident activists have engaged in civil disobedience outside detention centers around the country, often chaining themselves to buses loaded with deportees. The protests last for hours, as police officers figure out how to cut through the homemade tubes encasing the chains that link the activists to one another in order to arrest them. The protests depart from the tactics of the mainstream immigrant-rights movement, which traditionally works through the legislative channels of Congress. These grassroots activists have directly pressured the Obama administration to use its executive authority to halt deportations and criminal prosecutions, most of which stem from violations of deportation orders.

These mobilizations give visibility to aspects of border security that are mostly hidden from public view—detention centers, prisons, and courtrooms, for instance. Through the use of their bodies, which are generally rendered invisible by the legal system, undocumented activists expose new enforcement priorities and practices that are at once punitive and "humanitarian." They reenact—on a national stage and in public view—criminal arrests when local police take them into custody for civil disobedience. By openly and collectively presenting themselves at U.S. ports of entry after being deported, they have turned individual deportation and detention cases into public issues. Their actions have also exposed the "humanitarian" elements within enforcement, particularly when they draw on prosecutorial discretion and leverage their status as "noncriminal," lower-priority enforcement targets to successfully challenge their deportations and those of loved ones.

In its own way this book gives visibility to such unprecedented "prosecutorial" approaches to managing migration. Jonathon Simon describes this prosecutorial model as one that inflicts punishment and upholds "victims'" rights.[5] Extended to the immigration system, this approach leans on prosecutorial discretion to both aggressively punish and protect.

Prosecutorial discretion in the immigration system has a long history but operates differently than in the past. For one thing, enforcement priorities were not centered on criminal history as they are today. And in early struggles over prosecutorial discretion, antideportation activists opposed giving more discretion to the former INS and immigration agents, in particular, fearing that expanding the discretion of immigration agents would serve as a strike-breaking measure against radical immigrant labor organizing. They pushed instead to expand the immigration courts, legal representation in deportation proceedings, and due process rights.[6]

The current prosecutorial approach has expanded border agents' discretion, while constraining judicial review in the immigration system.[7] Immigration judges have less discretion today to review immigration cases and to administer relief. It is frontline agents who now have more authority to administer rights and to punish. And they increasingly do so on the basis of criminal status. They have considerable discretion to sort people according to criminal history and to administer punishment and "rights" on the basis of criminal status.

However, agents do not just implement enforcement priorities from above. Their enforcement actions (and their ability to carry out the federal criminal alien mandate) are very much shaped by their *relationships* to other players in the field.[8] This allows them to carry out or implement a federal criminal alien mandate, albeit in ways that make policy on the ground. As Michael Lipsky's theory of street-level bureaucrats attests, front line agents *make* policy through their everyday, routine actions. In the case of border agents, their relationship to other players informs how they forge enforcement priorities and criminal alien categories.

The cross-border context in which border agents operate on the ground sheds some light on why agents recognize the rights-bearing status of some, while branding others as criminal—and why the prosecutorial turn in immigration isn't exclusively punitive. Prosecutorial approaches to migration look different on the border than in a national arena. In national immigration debates, this prosecutorial rhetoric positions unauthorized immigrants as "criminal" "lawbreakers" and American (typically white, but not exclusively) citizens as "victims." Yet on the border, these distinctions are not so stark. Those directly involved in immigration enforcement—border agents, local law enforcement, Mexican officials, NGOs, for instance—wrestle with whether immigrants are criminals or rights-bearing individuals. In such a complex geography marked by cross-border exchange, some unauthorized "workers" may be classified as "victims" (e.g., of smugglers, "*bajadores*," border agents, vigilantes, the desert climate, and U.S. border and immigration policies), while some, including U.S. citizen residents in border communities, are classified as "criminal" and prosecuted for immigration offenses like smuggling.

Political elites invested in cross-border trade, Mexican officials, and some NGOs and activists pressure DHS and border agents to uphold migrant rights or to not obstruct cross-border flows on which national and local economies depend. And at other moments, the same players comply with calls for more crime control, "order," and "security." On the surface, political pressure on border agents to operate within a constitutional framework, or to adhere to legality, seems in conflict with calls for order, security, and safety.[9] But on the border, adhering to legality while meting out harsh punishment to ensure "order" are complementary goals. Both facilitate the global movement of (undocumented, subordinated) workers and (unfettered) capital.

It is precisely this interplay of "rights" for some, punishment for others that generates the consensus necessary for enforcement priorities to thrive. By appropriating and deploying a particular kind of "rights" for "deserving" noncriminals, border agents appeased Mexican government officials on whom they rely for intelligence, economic elites who depend on cross-border consumption, and human- and civil-rights advocates and NGOs with access to media connections, legal resources, and political capital. When agents simultaneously punish (through detention and incarceration), they placate anti-immigrant groups demanding that the federal government "do something about immigration," conservative politicians in Phoenix whose constituents also feel threatened by the changing demographics of Arizona, ranchers who no longer employ migrant labor but resent the migrant traffic through their leased lands, and, frankly, politicians who are eager to secure a steady stream of congressional funding for border security, particularly detention beds.

These underlying power dynamics are not immediately visible. This is how criminalization takes hold, not forcefully, but subtly, stealthily, and with the compliance of all involved, including those it targets.

Political consensus masks how, below the surface, new enforcement priorities bring about new forms of criminalization that differ from illegalization. There is a tendency in popular and scholarly discourse to conflate the two. This makes sense, in a way, if one defines criminalization as processes that turn certain conduct or groups of people into crime and criminals. Scholars have convincingly argued that criminalization happens well before a conviction, during a stop or arrest when certain groups are presumed guilty well before any formal conviction.[10] As recent police shootings of unarmed Black youth throughout the United States attest, it is racial status, particularly for Black and brown youth, that is the "felony."[11] This definition of criminalization certainly applies to racial profiling practices in the immigration context, wherein immigrants of color, particularly Mexicans on the border, are assumed to be "illegal" and are profiled on the basis of their ethnicity.[12] They are "criminalized" by historic immigration enforcement practices that link Mexicans to illegality.[13]

More recent scholarship on criminalization, however, expands the concept to show how criminalization—the act of being branded criminal—imposes a legal and caste-like stigma that lasts well *beyond* the punishment.[14] In its expanded conceptualization, the criminal stigma that criminalization imposes illuminates what is distinct about new enforcement priorities. Enforcement priorities impose a criminal stigma that differs from illegal status.

Under the current prosecutorial approach to immigration enforcement, at least as I observed it on the ground, illegal and criminal status are not the same. Illegal status can be shed through legalization and assimilationist paths to formal citizenship. Criminal stigma cannot, partly because, in the United States, it is rooted in a historical association between Blackness and criminality.[15] In this new enforcement terrain, illegalization affords basic procedural protections to "noncriminal" border crossers that facilitate their migration as undocumented migrants. Criminalization, on the other hand, amounts to the branding of a caste-like criminal stigma that can be applied within and across borders to citizens and noncitizens alike. Citizens who are criminally branded for immigration offenses experience legal constraints on their rights.

In this shifting enforcement context, agents do not just stop and arrest people because they have "reasonable suspicion" that they are violating *immigration* law. Agents stop and search border residents on *criminal* grounds, often as suspected smugglers. This means that agents are increasingly sorting and processing people according to *criminal* rather than *legal* status.

Criminal status, then, complicates traditional hierarchies of legal status (e.g., citizen, legal permanent resident, unauthorized immigrant).[16] On the border, violating immigration law is not automatically classified as criminal. It becomes so through the criminal prosecution. Apprehended migrants without a criminal record are considered undocumented aliens. Their "noncriminal" status as "victims" or "workers" allows them to be processed through a civil or administrative track in the immigration system. Those branded as criminal aliens occupy a different social position and are funneled through the criminal justice system. They experience a suspension of rights, undergo constraints on mobility, and are subjected to legitimate forms of exclusionary violence, as the rise in Border Patrol shootings shows. In many of these cases, agents are never indicted because they position themselves as "victims" acting in self-defense or generally justify their actions on criminal grounds, much as in cases of police shootings of unarmed Black men.

These new enforcement priorities matter, because they aren't going away. On the contrary, recent criminal justice reforms suggest that they are being refined and entrenched. Proposals to relax drug sentencing for "nonviolent" offenders (e.g., victims of the drug war) and to mitigate the collateral consequences of a conviction simultaneously pledge to focus resources "on serious cases" and to draw new boundaries around those considered to be the "worst" kind of offenders. The prosecutorial logic is the same, but redraws the boundaries of who its enforcement targets will be (e.g., "gang members," "terrorists"). This implements reforms and eliminates some disparity in sentencing, while also justifying extreme forms of punishment for its new targets, such as banishment, indefinite detention, and torture.[17]

Similarly, in the immigration system, the Department of Homeland Security introduced a new Priority Enforcement Program in 2015, instructing agents to use prosecutorial discretion in deciding "whom to stop, question, and arrest; whom to detain or release; . . . and whether to grant deferred action, parole, or a stay of removal instead of pursuing removal in a case."[18] The guidelines channel resources toward the DHS's highest enforcement priorities. Priority One now includes aliens suspected of terrorism; aliens apprehended at the border; aliens not younger than sixteen involved in a "criminal street gang"; and aliens convicted of an "aggravated felony" as defined by the 1996 IIRIRA. Priority Two includes aliens with multiple misdemeanors, excluding minor traffic violations, and those apprehended "anywhere in the United States" who enter or reenter unlawfully. Priority Three includes aliens who violate final orders of removal. The memo also instructs agents to apply enforcement priorities to "aliens subject to mandatory detention by law."[19]

Like earlier memos on prosecutorial discretion, the guidelines also outline humanitarian considerations, particularly in cases where apprehended migrants "qualify for asylum or other forms of relief"; or where there are other "compelling and exceptional factors that clearly indicate the alien is not a threat to national security, border security, or public safety and should not therefore be an enforcement priority." Agents are required to consider factors such as

> extenuating circumstances involving the offense of conviction; extended length of time since the offense of conviction; length of time in the United States; military service; family or community ties in the United States; status as a victim, witness or plaintiff in civil or criminal proceedings; or compelling humanitarian factors such as poor health, age, pregnancy, a young child, or a seriously ill relative.

In mandatory detention cases, agents are directed to avoid filling beds with "aliens who are known to be suffering from serious physical or mental illness, who are disabled, elderly, pregnant, or nursing, who demonstrate that they are primary caretakers of children or an infirm person, or whose detention is otherwise not in the public interest."[20]

Similarly to recent reductions in the prison population, the Migration Policy Institute estimates that deportations of "noncriminal," settled, unauthorized immigrants residing in the interior are likely to fall under the new program, while deportations *on the border* are likely to increase. More research is needed on how agents will implement the new program on the border. According to estimates, less than 3% of unauthorized migrants will fall within the highest priority and approximately 13% fall *within* one of the three priorities.[21] Yet agents still have tremendous discretion to pursue enforcement actions against those "who fall outside" enforcement priorities. The new program assumes that border crossers do not have ties to the United States and does not consider the impact of criminal enforcement priorities on settled immigrants and border residents residing in punitive states like Arizona.

Not only are enforcement priorities not going away, then. These enforcement priorities—designed initially to expel noncitizens from U.S. prisons and jail under CAP—are also being exported throughout the world. In a public forum on border security, former chief of the Border Patrol and former chief Border Patrol agent for the Tucson Sector discussed the importance of regional partnerships with Mexico and Canada in going after the most serious criminals.[22] Drawing on riskmetrics and biometric technologies, regional partnerships would create a global category of criminal outcasts (e.g., "organized criminal gangs" or suspected terrorists).[23]

There is evidence that U.S. criminal enforcement priorities are being diffused globally to justify indefinite detention, torture, and the use of drones. As activist and philosopher Rebecca Gordon notes in her book *Mainstreaming Torture*, such classifications form the basis of what she calls the U.S. torture regime. It targets those branded as criminal in U.S. jails and prisons. And it extends throughout globally dispersed CIA black sites or secret prisons outside U.S. territories.[24] Criminal enforcement priorities incorporate the criminal justice system's punitive, castelike stigma, rooted in an association between Blackness and criminality; combines this with the immigration system's sovereign power to arrest and deport, rooted in Chinese exclusion and Mexican subordination; and exports them abroad to justify torture and indefinite detention in the war on terror.[25]

DHS's enforcement priorities and the transformation of immigration enforcement has implications for advocates and academics. In the immigrant-rights movement, two core issues are legalization and border enforcement. For decades now, immigration debates have been deeply divided on questions of legalization and have shown surprising bipartisan consensus on prosecutorial approaches to immigration enforcement. Under the Obama administration, enforcement-only approaches were no different from Republican-backed proposals in their support for measures that (1) give more authority to front-line Border Patrol, police, and sheriff's deputies than to immigration judges trained in immigration law; (2) favor formal deportation over the traditional practice of voluntary departure; (3) prosecute immigrants in criminal rather than immigration courts; and (4) impose a criminal stigma that blocks rather than facilitates possibilities for legal migration, adjustment of status, and citizenship. This bipartisan consensus puts mainstream pro-immigrant factions of the national immigration debate in a position to concede to immigration reform bills that criminalize some while legalizing the status of others.[26]

For advocates, it no longer seems viable to just push for legalization since enforcement priorities and criminal prosecution for immigration offenses make people ineligible through criminal branding.[27] But what if the mainstream movement put "mass criminalization" at the center of its analysis and directly challenged criminal enforcement priorities? There is an implicit antiracist critique in this approach because it directly challenges the anti-Black roots of criminal branding. It takes up the plight of those who have been stigmatized as criminal, as well as those on their way to becoming criminalized, which, until recently, the immigrant-rights movement has avoided.

This becomes particularly important as immigration transforms the United States into a "majority-minority" country. Will criminal enforcement priorities in the immigration system reproduce U.S. racial hierarchies? And will new generations of immigrant-rights activists challenge them?[28]

Reframing the movement in this way also opens up possibilities for stronger alliances with communities who have felt and fought mass incarceration for decades, as well as Arab American, Muslim immigrant communities that have also been targeted on criminal grounds, particularly since 9/11. Challenging criminal enforcement priorities in the immigration system also means rethinking the traditional citizenship/noncitizenship divide and understanding how criminal status transcends citizenship and place of birth. As the experiences of residents in heavily policed communities along the border show, prosecutorial approaches to border security and migration management target everyone, not just noncitizens.

For academics, particularly those concerned with borders and migration, this means rethinking the logic and function of border controls beyond territorial control and keeping out foreigners. The entire framework for thinking about migration control has shifted. Prosecutorial approaches to managing migration have merged migration control with domestic policing to target people with longer settlement histories, including U.S. citizens.

Border scholars have begun to investigate how the U.S. Border Patrol provides training, funding, and technology to countries in Central America and Mexico particularly to target "organized criminal gangs" or suspected terrorists, while, I would add, providing some protection for crime victims (of trafficking, for instance) in the form of humanitarian assistance. This is shifting traditional approaches to managing migration. Migration control is no longer just about keeping out foreigners but has merged with crime control to target enforcement priorities within and beyond borders.

As academics, we must also interrogate further historical linkages between the immigration system and the criminal justice system. The Criminal Alien Program (CAP), as told through the story of the detention bed mandate, is one such linkage. At its inception, CAP initially had little to do with keeping out or punishing immigrants per se. Rather, it emerged from the crisis of prison overcrowding in the 1980s, when Reagan launched the War on Drugs and the prison population exploded. The prison bed shortage that emerged from the passage of the 1984 Comprehensive Crime Control Act ignited a commitment to expel noncitizens from prisons and jails in order to make room for the native-born Black and Latina/o youth who would fill them. Criminal deportations were a difficult undertaking because most of those in prison for drug convictions were shielded from deportation due to their legal permanent residency status and relation to U.S. citizen children and spouses.

To purge long-term "noncitizen" residents from prisons required revamping the detention and deportation system. This is precisely what the 1996 Illegal Immigration Reform and Immigrant Responsibility Act

(IIRIRA) did. Known for retroactive deportations of noncitizens with criminal convictions and for mandatory detention provisions, the 1996 law created an immigrant detention bed shortage. That bed space shortage led to measures to criminally prosecute and deport immigrants directly from prisons. Criminal prosecution allowed for the bypassing of immigration courts and detention, and for curtailing forms of relief from deportation, including the possibility of detention parole. Bipartisan funding for biometric technologies and detention beds, which agents must fill, provided the necessary infrastructure to carry out a criminal alien mandate that ultimately transformed immigration and border enforcement to what it is today.

What is particularly striking about the political origins of the Criminal Alien Program is how the criminal stigma that prosecutorial approaches to migration impose is rooted in anti-Black criminalization. In this way, the criminal status that border agents now have the authority to confer in an immigration context is directly linked to historical struggles over African American citizenship from slavery and Reconstruction to the Jim Crow and the civil rights eras. Michelle Alexander makes this connection clear when she refers to mass incarceration, and the lasting stigma of a conviction, as "the new Jim Crow." The durability of criminal stigma is a distinct feature of U.S. republicanism, in part because of a deep-seated association of Blackness with criminality.[29]

The punitive turn in immigration enforcement is very much a part of this history, but it also stems from related struggles over citizenship and civil rights in the immigration system. It isn't coincidental that the emergence of the criminal alien mandate injects criminal classifications (and its lasting stigma) into the immigration system at precisely the time when the former Immigration and Naturalization Service feels mounting pressure to comply with constitutional norms in a post–civil rights era. Nor is it surprising that, by its logic if not by design, the criminal alien mandate targets post-1965 immigrants of color, long-term residents, at a time when immigrants and minorities were drawing on civil- and human-rights norms to challenge immigration enforcement practices. It is in a post-1965 context, a time when formally excluded groups—"immigrants," "Latinas/os," "minorities"—are transforming the demographic and political landscape of Arizona and the country, that the immigration system increasingly leans on criminal processes through what critical race theorists refer to as "color-blind constitution-alism."[30] This is a period in which the legitimacy of overt racial grounds for exclusion and expulsion lost some legitimacy, and new, "race-neutral" criminal criteria (e.g., criminal aliens) gained prominence.

As scholars, then, we must also consider the implications of new enforcement priorities for how we think about race and citizenship. As this book shows, the punitive turn in immigration enforcement is not entirely about "enforcement with consequences" that discourages undocumented migration or disincentivizes border crossers. Instead, it aggressively targets and disrupts the settlement of those already living in the country, those who dare to claim rights, and those who are transforming the demographic and political landscape of the United States, many of whom are not "foreigners." The punitive turn, the entry of immigrants into the criminal justice system, the mass deportations, and the rising rates of incarceration for immigration offenses, are ultimately based in post–civil rights challenges to the racially imbued edifice of citizenship and the legacy of unresolved struggles over the coexistence of slavery and democracy.

NOTES

INTRODUCTION

1 "Operation Safeguard: The Administration's FY1995 Immigration Initiative for Arizona," Vertical File, Border Patrol (INS), Programs and Activities, Operation Safeguard, USCIS Library, Department of Homeland Security, Washington, DC.

2 Ibid.

3 "Post–civil rights" refers to the period after the civil rights movement, otherwise known as the era of mass incarceration.

4 During the Great Depression, an estimated one million people of Mexican descent were expelled from the United States through raids, deportation, and repatriation. Despite the association of immigration with crime, these were largely civil or administrative removals or self-repatriations. See Balderrama and Rodríguez, *Decade of Betrayal*; Abraham Hoffman, *Unwanted Mexican Americans in the Great Depression: Repatriation Pressures, 1929–1939* (Tucson: University of Arizona Press, 1974).

5 Author interview with her father.

6 U.S. Immigration and Customs Enforcement, "Immigration Enforcement: Criminal Alien Program: Overview." https://www.ice.gov/criminal-alien-program.

7 U.S. Sentencing Commission, *2012 Sourcebook*.

8 Lopez and Light, "A Rising Share."

9 Light, Lopez, and Gonzales-Barrera, "The Rise of Federal Immigration Crimes."

10 Lipsky, *Street-level Bureaucracy*.

11 For an account of this campaign, one of the first to bring together immigrant-rights and criminal-justice groups, see Zoe Hammer's "Community, Identity, and Political Struggle: Challenging Immigrant Prisons in Arizona," in *Beyond Walls and Cages: Prisons, Borders, and Global Crisis*, edited by Jenna M. Loyd, Matt Mitchelson, and Andrew Burridge (Athens: University of Georgia Press, 2012).

12 Local NGOs and churches facilitated my entry into the migrant shelters in Sonora, the detention centers, and other public spaces. Through my connections to social justice organizations, local NGOs took me in and generously shared their U.S. and Mexican contacts. I was admittedly nervous about conducting fieldwork on both sides of the border, concerned that my U.S. citizenship would fail to fully protect me as a woman of color. The NGOs, more specifically the people who staffed them, offered the sense of protection and legitimacy necessary to conduct the fieldwork safely in both Mexican and U.S. border cities, and for this I am ever grateful.

13 I struggled initially to find a respectful and appropriate approach to those meetings; in the end, what worked best was a focus group/discussion format. It seemed more beneficial to everyone involved to listen to one another's experiences in order to exchange information, build networks, and "turn personal troubles into public issues," to put it in the words of C. Wright Mills. Those meetings went well, in part, because we were in Mexico, where most of the people were, technically, citizens.

14 Smugglers, also important players in the field, provided a more nuanced perspective on the role of smuggling in local economies that differed from their common portrayal as ruthless criminals.

15 Both Mexican and U.S. immigration agents also took me on "ride-alongs" on the Mexican and U.S. sides of the border, and provided me with arrest and removal statistics for the Arizona-Sonora border.

16 Tom Beal, "Florence: A Prison Town, Sure, but Arizona in Miniature, Too," *Arizona Daily Star*, November 27, 2011.

17 Please note that although this book focuses on the Arizona-Sonora border, the research conducted was a comparative study of the Tucson and El Paso Border Patrol Sectors.

18 Among its controversial provisions, SB 1070 made unauthorized entry a state-level misdemeanor crime. It also required state and local law enforcement to check immigration status when making stops or arrests. It included measures to criminalize those sheltering and harboring unauthorized immigrants. The Supreme Court struck down all but the most controversial "Papers Please" provision allowing local law enforcement to check immigration status.

19 Maria Jimenez, "Law Enforcement and Violence against Women of Color," panel presentation at the Color of Violence Conference, University of California–Santa Cruz, April 28, 2000.

20 Hasenfeld, "People-Processing Organizations."

21 For an earlier exemplary ethnography of immigration law see Coutin, *Legalizing Moves*.

22 U.S. Customs and Border Protection, *2012–2016 Border Patrol Strategic Plan: Mission; Protect America* (Washington, DC: U.S. Customs and Border Protection, 2012), p. 9. https://www.cbp.gov/sites/default/files/documents/bp_strategic_plan.pdf.

23 Chacón, "Unsecured Borders."

24 Rosenblum, *Border Security*.

25 Stumpf, "The Crimmigration Crisis"; Miller, "Citizenship and Severity."

26 Critical criminologists have defined criminalization as the processes that transform certain acts and groups of people into crime and criminals. My conceptualization draws from more recent studies that highlight the ways in which a "large web of laws, rules, policies, and customs" confers criminal status—a stigmatized and denigrated social status functioning similarly to racial

caste. See Alexander, *The New Jim Crow*; Rios, *Punished*; Wacquant, "Race as Civic Felony"; Goffman, *On the Run*.

27 Coutin, *Legalizing Moves*.

28 See Coutin, "Contesting Criminality."

29 Alexander, *The New Jim Crow*.

30 Muhammad, *The Condemnation of Blackness*.

31 Biggers, *State out of the Union*.

32 Simon, "'Prosecutor-in-chief': Executive Authority since the War on Crime," in *Governing through Crime*.

33 Miller, "Citizenship and Severity," p. 4.

CHAPTER 1. THE POST–CIVIL RIGHTS BORDERLAND

1 Fieldnotes, July 16, 2010.

2 Lydgate, "Assembly-Line Justice."

3 Under immigration law, noncitizens are not entitled to a court-appointed attorney. See Eagly and Shafer, "A National Study of Access to Counsel in Immigration Court."

4 Eagly, "Prosecuting Immigration"; Harwood, "Arrests without Warrant."

5 INS fell under the Department of Justice from 1940 until 2003, when it was reorganized under the Department of Homeland Security.

6 Kanstroom, "Deportation, Social Control, and Punishment."

7 Miller, "Blurring the Boundaries"; Legomsky, "New Path of Immigration Law."

8 Legomsky, "New Path of Immigration Law."

9 Due process refers to the safeguarding of the legal rights of an individual, as stated in the Constitution. The Fifth Amendment to the Constitution states that "no person shall be deprived of life, liberty, property or due process of law." The Fourteenth Amendment states, "nor shall any state deprive any person of life, liberty, or property without due process of law." There is a general distinction between *procedural* and *substantive* due process. Procedural due process ensures that the rights of an individual are upheld in the *procedures* through which the government deprives one of life, liberty, and property. Substantive due process refers to the *substance* of laws and limits the government's power to enact laws that fundamentally affect one's rights to life, liberty, and property. See Chemerinsky and Levenson, *Criminal Procedure*; Aleinikoff and Motomura, *Immigration and Citizenship*; Motomura, "The Curious Evolution of Immigration Law."

10 Savage and Goode, "Two Powerful Signals"; Clear and Frost, *The Punishment Imperative*; Jacobson, "Reversing the Punitive Turn."

11 Fox Butterfield, "With Cash Tight, States Reassess Long Prison Terms"; Greenhouse, "Crack Cocaine Limbo"; Margulies, "Coming Out of the Turn."

12 Motivans, "Immigration Offenders"; Lopez and Light, "A Rising Share."

13 U.S. Department of Homeland Security, *2011 Yearbook of Immigration Statistics*.

14 See U.S. Sentencing Commission, *2012 Sourcebook*.

15 Under the Chinese Exclusion Acts and the Immigration Act of 1924, for instance, race and national origins were used as criteria for admissions and exclusion. See Ngai, *Impossible Subjects*; Nevins, *Operation Gatekeeper*; Hernandez, *Migra!*; Salyer, *Laws as Harsh as Tigers*; Hing, *Defining America*; Johnson, *Huddled Masses Myth*.

16 Here I draw on David Garland and Jonathon Simon's conceptualization of crime victims as citizen subjects. See Garland, *Culture of Control*; Simon, *Governing through Crime*.

17 The 1996 Illegal Immigration Reform and Immigrant Responsibility Act (IIRIRA), for instance, greatly expanded the category of aggravated felony to include non-violent misdemeanors and immigration violations, thereby growing the population of "criminal aliens." See Medina, "Criminalization of Immigration Law"; Morawetz, "Understanding the Impact of the 1996 Deportation Laws"; Morawetz, "Rethinking Retroactive Deportation"; Kanstroom, "Deportation, Social Control, and Punishment."

18 Eagly, "Local Immigration Prosecution"; Dowling and Inda, *Governing Immigration through Crime*.

19 I refer to these as instrumentalist perspectives—that is, those concerned with law and policy's effects and effectiveness.

20 Meissner et al., *Immigration Enforcement in the United States*; Lopez and Light, "A Rising Share"; Rosenblum, *Border Security*.

21 Scheingold, The Politics of Law and Order; Spelman, "What Recent Studies Do (and Don't) Tell Us about Imprisonment and Crime"; Tonrey and Petersilia, "American Prisons"; Kovandzic and Vieretis, "The Effect of County-level Prison Population on Crime Rates"; Gainsborough and Mauer, "Diminishing Returns"; Hagan, *Who Are the Criminals?*

22 Kubrin, Martinez, and Zatz, *Punishing Immigrants*; Martinez and Valenzuela, *Immigration and Crime*.

23 I refer to these as constitutive explanations, which give primacy to the symbolic dimensions of law and policy. See Garland, *Culture of Control*; Young, *The Exclusive Society*; Garland, *Punishment and Modern Society*.

24 Feeley and Simon, "The New Penology."

25 Simon, "Refugees in a Carceral Age."

26 Simon, *Governing through Crime*; Miller, "Citizenship and Severity"; Dowling and Inda, *Governing Immigration through Crime*.

27 Koulish, "Entering the Risk Society"; Harcourt, *Against Prediction*; Warner, "The Social Construction of the Criminal Alien."

28 Welch, "Panic, Risk, Control"; Petintseva, "Social Control and Justice."

29 D'Appollonia, *Frontiers of Fear*; Huysmans, *The Politics of Insecurity*; Bigo and Guild, *Controlling Frontiers*; Ibrahim, "The Securitization of Migration"; Bigo, "Security and Immigration"; Ceyhan and Tsoukala, "The Securitization of Migration in Western Societies"; Faist, "'Extension du domaine de la lutte.'"

30 I refer to these as structural explanations that focus on the *material* conditions resulting in *discourses* about crime and security or punitive laws and policies.

Here I highlight studies attuned to the intersections among culture, economy, and society—that is, analyses that consider the *symbolic* and *material* dimensions of social life. Of course, some studies focus exclusively on material or economic factors, such as those linking punishment to changes in the economy, arguing that punitive measures like criminal deportations are more prevalent in times of economic decline. See King, Massoglia, and Uggen, "Employment and Exile"; Melossi, "Punishment and Social Action." Other structural perspectives consider how race and gender shape enforcement practices and outcomes. See, for instance, Golash-Boza, "Racism and the Consequences of Immigration Policy"; Golash-Boza and Hondagneu-Sotelo, "Latino Men and the Deportation Crisis."

31 See Wacquant, *Punishing the Poor*; Andreas, *Border Games*. Peter Andreas's work on the intensification of U.S.-Mexico border policing in the 1990s also draws important connections between liberalization of economies through free trade agreements and criminalization.

32 Wacquant, "Crafting the Neoliberal State: Workfare, Prisonfare, and Social Insecurity," p. 209. See also "Theoretical Coda: A Sketch of the Neoliberal State," in Wacquant, *Punishing the Poor*.

33 Wacquant, "Theoretical Coda" (*supra* note 32).

34 Dowling and Inda, *Governing Immigration through Crime*; Rosas, *Barrio Libre*; Cacho, *Social Death*.

35 See Beckett, *Making Crime Pay*; Western, *Punishment and Inequality*; Simon, *Governing through Crime*; Flamm, *Law and Order*; Weaver, "Frontlash"; Alexander, *The New Jim Crow*.

36 Beckett, *Making Crime Pay*.

37 Simon, *Governing through Crime*.

38 Weaver, "Frontlash."

39 Alexander, *The New Jim Crow*.

40 Murakawa, *The First Civil Right*.

41 Richie, *Arrested Justice*.

42 Stumpf, "The Crimmigration Crisis."

43 Cacho, *Social Death*.

44 Some migration scholars have considered how the rights revolution imposed constraints on the state, including the ability to criminally deport immigrants. See Hollifield, Hunt, and Tichenor, "The Liberal Paradox"; Schuck, "Removing Criminal Aliens"; Hollifield, *Immigrants, Markets, and States*; Hollifield, Martin, and Orrenius, *Controlling Immigration*.

45 See Stumpf, "The Crimmigration Crisis"; Legomsky, "The New Path of Immigration Law"; Chacón, "Unsecured Borders"; Chacón, "Managing Migration through Crime"; Kanstroom, "Deportation, Social Control, and Punishment."

46 Beckett, *Making Crime Pay*; Simon, *Governing through Crime*; Weaver, "Frontlash."

47 For exemplary models of this blended approach in the area of border studies see Hernandez, *Migra!*—which chronicles early-twentieth-century political strug-

gles over U.S.-Mexico border enforcement, culminating in what she calls "the Mexicanization of the legal/illegal divide." Joseph Nevins's *Operation Gatekeeper* analyzes the "illegalization" of immigrants through territorial and symbolic construction of the U.S.-Mexico border.

48 Meeks, *Border Citizens*, pp. 28–29.

49 According to historian Catherine Benton-Cohen, Chinese workers were completely excluded, while Blacks occupied a higher social status than Mexicans. See Benton-Cohen, *Borderline Americans*.

50 Heyman, *Life and Labor on the Border*.

51 For a thorough account of the 1917 Bisbee strike and deportation, see Cohen, *Borderline Americans*.

52 Berg, "Manufacturing in Arizona," p. 142.

53 Kukino, "Arizona's Growing Service Sector."

54 Shermer, *Sunbelt Capitalism*, p. 32.

55 Shermer, *Sunbelt Capitalism*.

56 Shermer, *Barry Goldwater*.

57 Shermer "Drafting a Movement"; Larkin, "Southwestern Strategy."

58 Mathew Whitaker, *Race Works*; Meeks, *Border Citizens*.

59 Lynch, *Sunbelt Justice*, p. 114.

60 Ibid., p. 94.

61 Ibid., p. 51.

62 Ibid.

63 Ibid., p. 95.

64 Ibid., p. 96.

65 Nadelhoff, *Benchmarks*; Davis and Russell, *Arizona's Traditional Economy*.

66 Cadava, *Standing on Common Ground*, p. 178.

67 See U.S. Census Bureau, Small Area Income and Poverty Estimates (SAIPE), "Percent of Total Population in Poverty: 2002," https://www.census.gov/did/www/saipe/data/statecounty/maps/iy2002/Tot_Pct_Poor2002.pdfProgram; and "Small Area Income and Poverty Estimate (SAIPE), All Ages in Poverty, 2002—Arizona," December 2004, http://sasweb.ssd.census.gov/cgi-bin/broker.

68 Author interview, Douglas, AZ, January 13, 2003.

69 Andreas, *Border Games*.

70 Author interview, Bisbee, AZ, January 24, 2003.

71 Author interview, Douglas, AZ, January 13, 2003.

72 This characterization runs counter to the portrayal of such border towns depicted by public officials. In economic development brochures, the economic base is said to be government and tourism from Mexico. Because economic impact studies are produced to attract investment, they highlight a bilingual labor force, low crime rate, and affordable cost of living rather than dependence on immigration, smuggling, and law enforcement. Actual figures on the underground economy are not readily available, although there are some estimates on the size of the narcotics and smuggling industry. This characterization of South Arizona/North-

east Sonoran economies is based on observations of the types of businesses, such as transportation, lodging, and other services associated with migration and the smuggling industry.

73 Author interview, Douglas, AZ, January 13, 2003.

74 Author interview, Douglas, AZ, February 26, 2004.

75 Lorey, *United States–Mexico Border Statistics.*

76 Cadava, *Standing on Common Ground*, p. 177.

77 Shermer, *Sunbelt Capitalism*, p. 45.

78 Brown and Patten, "Latinos in the 2014 Election: Arizona"; Foley, "Latino Vote Could Tip the Scales for Democrats in Arizona"; Hart, *Arizona's Emerging Latino Vote.*

79 Biggers, "The Arizonification of America."

80 McGirr, *Suburban Warriors*; Shermer, *Sunbelt Capitalism.*

81 Shermer, *Sunbelt Capitalism*, pp. 292–301.

82 "Watergate Scandal Key Players," *Washington Post*, June 5, 2012, http://www.washingtonpost.com/politics/watergate-scandal-key-players/2012/06/05/gJQA-kn1jLV_gallery.html.

83 Shermer, *Sunbelt Capitalism.*

84 Cadava, *Standing on Common Ground.*

85 Shermer, *Barry Goldwater.*

86 Cadava, *Standing on Common Ground.*

87 Perla and Coutin, "Legacies and Origins," pp. 73–91.

88 Author interview, March 15, 2005.

89 The key role that the Manzo Area Council played and the involvement of the Mexican community in general have often been omitted from scholarly accounts of the Sanctuary movement. As one former Manzo member pointed out, "There is a widespread assumption that Mexicans did not support Salvadorans and that is not true. Many of the safe houses were in our neighborhoods. Mexican churches in Nogales and Tucson were also involved." Author interview, March 15, 2005.

90 Cadava, *Standing on Common Ground*, p. 206.

91 Shahani and Greene, "Local Democracy on ICE."

92 "Operation Safeguard: The Administration's FY1995 Immigration Initiative for Arizona," Vertical File, Border Patrol (INS), Programs and Activities, Operation Safeguard, USCIS library, Department of Homeland Security, Washington, DC.

93 Author interview, Nogales, AZ, February 11, 2003.

94 Hammer-Tomizuka and Allen, "Hate or Heroism."

95 Fieldnotes, Douglas, AZ, October 30, 2001.

96 Hammer-Tomizuka and Allen, "Hate or Heroism."

97 Formerly called the Mesilla Organizing Project, a direct reference to the Gadsden Purchase when the United States acquired the territory of Arizona from Mexico.

98 Shahani and Greene, "Local Democracy on ICE," p. 7.

99 Ibid., p. 11.

100 Ibid., p. 12.

101 Ibid., p. 8.
102 Liptak, "Blocking Parts of Arizona Law."

CHAPTER 2. BEDS AND BIOMETRICS

1 Fieldnotes, October 8, 2013.
2 "#Not1More Campaign Holds National Convergence," in #1More Timeline: Key Events. Retrieved from http://www.notonemoredeportation.com/the-history-of-the-not1more-campaign/.
3 Shear, "Obama."
4 Conversation with former deputy general counsel, Department of Homeland Security, Northwestern Law School, October 25, 2013, Chicago, Illinois.
5 Motomura, "Prosecutorial Discretion in Context"; Martin, "A Defense of Immigration-Enforcement Discretion."
6 Between the 1880s and the world wars, laws targeted paupers, lunatics, idiots, prostitutes, Chinese, Japanese, Southern and Eastern European immigrants, and radicals. See Salyer, *Laws as Harsh as Tigers*; Hing, *Defining America*; Johnson, *Huddled Masses Myth*.
7 Legal challenges to the Chinese Exclusion Acts of 1882 offer important insights as to why the Immigration Service insisted that immigration enforcement was a civil, not a criminal matter. The Supreme Court ruling in the Fong Yue Ting case, for instance, asserted that a deportation proceeding

> is in no proper sense a trial and sentence for a crime of offense. The order of deportation is not a punishment for a crime. It is not a banishment. . . . It is but a method of enforcing the return to his own country of an alien. . . . [H]e has not therefore been deprived of his life, liberty or property without due process of law and the provisions of the constitution, securing the right of trial by jury, and prohibiting unreasonable searches and seizures, and cruel and unusual punishment have no application.

See discussion of *Fong Yue Ting v. United States* in Aleinikoff, Martin, and Motomura, *Immigration and Citizenship*.
8 Laws in 1875 barred prostitutes and felons from admission. In 1891 Congress imposed restrictions for crimes of moral turpitude. See Salyer, *Laws as Harsh as Tigers*; Kanstroom, *Deportation Nation*; Johnson, *Huddled Masses Myth*.
9 U.S. Immigration and Naturalization Service, "Time Limitations for Deportation," Lecture No. 16 (Washington, DC: U.S. Department of Labor, Immigration and Naturalization Service, May 21, 1934), U.S. Citizenship and Immigration Services Historical Library, Washington, DC. See also Ngai, *Impossible Subjects*.
10 Referring to the former Immigration Service's detention policy, the INS commissioner wrote in the 1920 annual report that

> "[w]hile regulation and exclusion, and therefore detention, are necessary in respect of immigration, it should be understood by all who participate in administering these laws that they are not intended to be penalizing. . . . Accordingly, every reasonable effort is made by the department, within the

limits of appropriations, to minimize all the necessary hardships of their detention and to abolish all that are not necessary." This quotation from the first annual report of the Department of Labor expresses the policy of the Department regarding immigrant detention.

See U.S. Department of Labor, *Annual Report of the Commissioner General of Immigration to the Secretary of Labor* (Washington, DC: U.S. Department of Labor, 1920), U.S. Citizenship and Immigration Services Historical Library, Washington, DC.

11 See Hernandez, *Migra!* p. 2.This period also marked the end of a major wave of European migration to the United States and the beginnings of Mexican migration to the Southwest, and the Great Migration of African Americans from the rural South to cities throughout the Northeast, the Midwest, and the West.

12 Murolo and Chitty, *From the Folks Who Brought You the Weekend*; Montgomery, "The 'New Unionism' and the Transformation of Workers' Consciousness in America, 1909–02," in *Workers' Control in America.*

13 In Bisbee, Arizona, for example, sheriff's deputies and militia groups violently deported hundreds of mostly Mexican and Eastern European strikers in 1917. And there were others in Arizona and throughout the country. See Benton-Cohen, *Borderline Americans.*

14 American Civil Liberties Union, *Report upon the Illegal Practices of the United States Department of Justice*, 1920. American Civil Liberties Union Records, Subgroup 2, Printed Materials Series, 1920–1995, Princeton University Library, Princeton, New Jersey.

15 See United States, Wickersham Commission, *Report on Crime and the Foreign Born for the National Commission on Law Observance and Enforcement*, no. 10 (Washington, DC: Government Printing Office, 1931), p. 4. Cited in Frances Fisher Kane, "The Challenges of the Wickersham Deportations Report," *Journal of Criminal Law and Criminology* 23.4 (1932): 575. http://scholarlycommons.law.northwestern.edu/cgi/viewcontent.cgi?article=2323&context=jclc. See the Wickersham Commission's two-volume *Report on the Causes of Crime.*

16 See "Deportation Policy and the Making and Unmaking of Illegal Aliens," in Ngai, *Impossible Subjects.*

17 U.S. House of Representatives, "Deportation of Aliens: Minority Report," Rept. 2418, Part 2, 70th Cong., 2nd sess. (February 12, 1929), p. 3.

18 Ibid.

19 Ibid.

20 *An Act making it a felony with penalty for Certain aliens to enter the United States of America under Certain Conditions in Violation of Law*, S.5094, PL-70–1018, 70th Cong., 2nd sess. (March 4, 1929).

21 Herman I. Branse, "Criminal Prosecutions under the Immigration and Naturalization Laws," *INS Monthly Review* 4.12 (July 1947), U.S. Citizenship and Immigration Services Historical Library, Washington, DC.

22 United States Senate Committee on Immigration, "Deportation of Criminals, Preservation of Family Units, Permit Non-criminal Aliens to Legalize Their Status: Hearing on S. 2969, a bill to authorize deportation of criminals, to guard from the separation from their families of the non-criminal classes," 74th Cong., 2nd sess. (February 24, 1936).

23 For a discussion of how the Immigration Service administered relief from deportation differently for European and non-European migrants, particularly Mexicans, see "Deportation Policy and the Making and Unmaking of Illegal Aliens," in Ngai, *Impossible Subjects.*

24 D. W. MacCormack, "Continuance of the Lecture Course of Study for the Immigration and Naturalization Service," Lecture No. 21 (Washington, DC: U.S. Department of Labor, Immigration and Naturalization Service, November 5, 1934), U.S. Citizenship and Immigration Services Historical Library, Washington, DC.

25 United States Senate Committee on Immigration, "Deportation of Criminals" (*supra* note 22), p. 18.

26 U.S. Immigration and Naturalization Service, "Immigration Border Patrol," Lecture No. 7 (Washington, DC: U.S. Department of Labor, Immigration and Naturalization Service, March 19, 1934), p. 11, U.S. Citizenship and Immigration Services Historical Library, Washington, DC.

27 United States Senate Committee on Immigration, "Deportation of Criminals" (*supra* note 22), pp. 76–77.

28 United States Senate Committee on Immigration, "Deportation of Criminals" (*supra* note 22), p. 79.

29 Hugh Carter, "The Deported Criminal Alien," *INS Monthly Review* 7.4 (circa 1947), Record Group 85, National Archives, Washington, DC. Also housed at the U.S. Citizenship and Immigration Services Historical Library, Washington, DC.

30 Muhammad, *Condemnation of Blackness*, p. 139.

31 Hernandez, *Migra!*

32 Calavita, *Inside the State.*

33 U.S. Immigration and Naturalization Service, "Immigration Border Patrol" (*supra* note 26), p. 11.

34 U.S. Department of Labor, *Annual Report of the Commissioner General of Immigration* (Washington, DC: U.S. Department of Labor, 1927), U.S. Citizenship and Immigration Services Historical Library, Washington, DC.

35 The 1940 Alien Registration Act (Smith Act), for instance, gave discretionary relief to migrants of "good moral character," and imposed criminal penalties for advocating "the overthrow of the US government. See Blanse, "Criminal Prosecutions;" Ngai, *Impossible Subjects.*

36 Cole, *Enemy Aliens.*

37 United States, Wickersham Commission, *Report on Lawlessness in Law Enforcement: Report to the National Commission on Law Observance and Enforcement,* No. 11 (Washington, DC: U.S. Government Printing Office, June 26, 1931).

38 American Civil Liberties Union, *Report upon Illegal Practices* (*supra* note 14).

39 *Powell v. Arizona*, 287 U.S. 45 (1932). In this famous case, nine Black men were charged with raping two white women on a train. In this landmark case the Supreme Court overturned the convictions on grounds that they violated constitutional rights to counsel, a fair trial, and due process. See Chemerinsky and Levenson, *Criminal Procedure*.

40 Samuel Walker, "Guide to the Microfilm Edition of Records of the Wickersham Commission on Law Enforcement and Observance: Part 1, Records of the Committee on Official Lawlessness" (Bethesda, MD: University Publications of America, 1965), p. 10. http://www.lexisnexis.com/documents/academic/upa_ cis/1965_WickershamCommPt1.pdf.

41 United States, Wickersham Commission, *Report on the Enforcement of the Deportation Laws of the United States: Report to the National Commission on Law Observance and Enforcement*, No. 5 (Washington, DC: Government Printing Office, May 27, 1931).

42 For early landmark cases on criminal justice reforms see *Brown v. Mississippi* (excludes evidence in court extracted through police violence and forced confessions) and *Powell v. Alabama* (criminal defendants have the right to be represented by a lawyer). See Chemerinsky and Levenson, *Criminal Procedure*.

43 Vialet, "Brief History of U.S. Immigration Policy."

44 Durand and Massey, *Beyond Smoke and Mirrors*.

45 United States Immigration and Naturalization Service, "Budget Amendment, Additional Investigator Personnel," in *Authorization and Budget Request for the Congress, FY 1970*, vol. 1, U.S. Citizenship and Immigration Services Historical Library, Washington, DC, p. 20.

46 United States Immigration and Naturalization Service, "Programs for the Reduction of Crime," in *Authorization and Budget Request for the Congress, FY 1972*, vol. 1a, U.S. Citizenship and Immigration Services Historical Library, Washington, DC, p. 2.

47 Beckett, *Making Crime Pay*.

48 Lyndon B. Johnson, "Statement by the President upon Signing the Omnibus Crime Control and Safe Streets Act of 1968," June 19, 1968, http://www.presidency. ucsb.edu/ws/?pid=28939.

49 Beckett, *Making Crime Pay*. See also United States Immigration and Naturalization Service, "Letter to Robert P. Mayo, Director, Bureau of the Budget, 13 October 1969," in *Authorization and Budget Request for the Congress, FY 1971*, vol. 4, U.S. Citizenship and Immigration Services Historical Library, Washington, DC.

50 Simon, *Governing through Crime*.

51 In FY 1970, one begins to see numerous references to "crime fighting" and "anticrime" initiatives in budget requests before Congress. Before this, references to crime are associated with "subversives," "radicals," or "moral turpitude" cases. See United States Immigration and Naturalization Service, *Authorization and Budget Request for the Congress, FY 1970*, vol. 1 (*supra* note 45).

52 "Department of Justice: United States Immigration and Naturalization Service, Fiscal Year 1970, Budget Amendment," p. 17 in United States Immigration and Naturalization Service, *Authorization and Budget Request for the Congress, FY 1970*, vol. 1 (*supra* note 45).

53 "Statement for Use at the Hearing before the House Appropriation Subcommittee: Budget Estimates, Fiscal Year 1972," p. 17 in United States Immigration and Naturalization Service, *Authorization and Budget Request for the Congress, FY 1972*, vol. 1a (*supra* note 46).

54 "Address by Leonard Chapman, Commissioner, Immigration and Naturalization Service, before the Open Forum Panel, Department of State, Thursday, November 5, 1975, Washington, DC," p. 2, Collection of Addresses, Testimony, Speeches, etc./Leonard Fielding Chapman, Jr., 1973–1977, U.S. Citizenship and Immigration Services Historical Library, Washington, DC.

55 "Statement for Use at the Hearing before the House Appropriation Subcommittee: Budget Estimates, Fiscal Year 1966," p. 36 in United States Immigration and Naturalization Service, *Authorization and Budget Request for the Congress, FY 1966*, USCIS History Library, Washington, DC.

56 Samuel Walker, *Popular Justice*, pp. 185–89; Phillip Hirschkop and M. A. Milleman, "The Unconstitutionality of Prison Life," *Virginia Law Review* 55 (1969): 795–835.

57 Before Congress, the INS commissioner explained that "included in the Service Lookout Book are the names of persons excluded or deported on criminal, immoral, narcotic, subversive, or alien smuggling grounds." In "Program for the Reduction of Crime (Narrative), exhibit 48," p. 1 in United States Immigration and Naturalization Service, *Authorization and Budget Request for the Congress, FY 1976*, USCIS History Library, U.S. Citizenship and Immigration Services, Washington, DC.

58 "Department of Justice: Immigration and Naturalization Service, Report of Field Operations, Investigating Aliens' Status, Force and Workload," p. 27.77 in United States Immigration and Naturalization Service, *Authorization and Budget Request for the Congress, FY 1968*, USCIS History Library, U.S. Citizenship and Immigration Services, Washington, DC.

59 "Department of Justice: Immigration and Naturalization Service, Programs for the Reduction of Crime (Narrative)," p. 7 in United States Immigration and Naturalization Service, *Authorization and Budget Request for the Congress, FY 1971*, vol. 1, USCIS History Library, U.S. Citizenship and Immigration Services, Washington, DC.

60 The 1946 Administrative Procedures Act included the right to appeal federal decisions in federal court. Congress finally extended this right to INS decisions in 1961. See Law, *The Immigration Battle*, p. 25.

61 "INS Budget Request Authorization Statement, Detention and Deportation Narrative," p. 10 in United States Immigration and Naturalization Service, *Authorization and Budget Request for the Congress, FY 1976*, vol. 1976–1980, USCIS Historical Library, Washington, DC.

62 Broyles and Haynes, *Desert Duty*, p. 114.

63 "Address by Leonard Chapman" (*supra* note 54), pp. 6–7.

64 See Israel, "Criminal Procedure, the Berger Court, and the Legacy of the Warren Court"; Gutman, "The Criminal Gets the Breaks"; "The Rights of the Guilty"; Kamisar, "When the Cops Were Not 'Handcuffed.'"

65 U.S. Commission on Civil Rights, *The Tarnished Golden Door.*

66 Johnson and Trujillo, *Immigration Law and the US-Mexico Border*; Johnson, *The Huddled Masses Myth.*

67 "Chapter Two: Jurisdiction," p. 2-2 in U.S. Immigration and Naturalization Service, *Border Patrol Handbook, 1971*, USCIS Historical Library, Washington DC. See also "Chapter 6: Improper Actions and Their Consequences," pp. 29–35 in U.S. Immigration and Naturalization Service, *The Law of Search and Seizure for Immigration Officers*, USCIS Historical Library, Washington, DC; "Powers and Responsibilities of Immigration Officers," by Charles Gordon, General Counsel of INS, published in *American Bar Association Journal* 1973, appendix 2-B in *INS Investigator's Handbook*, 1980, USCIS Historical Library; and "Guidelines to Constitutional Stop and Frisk, Prepared by the Criminal Division, DOJ, 1972," appendix 17-B in *Border Patrol Handbook, 1985*, USCIS Historical Library. See also reports on legal challenges to raids or area control operations in the INS communique "Open Line: Keeping You Informed," *INS Communique*, vol. 1–4, 1974–1977, USCIS Historical Library, Washington DC.

68 "Chapter Five: Civil Rights in Law Enforcement," p. 5-1 in U.S. Immigration and Naturalization Service, *Border Patrol Handbook, 1971*, USCIS Historical Library, Washington, DC.

69 Wildes, "The Operations Instructions," p. 101.

70 Criminal history—referring mostly to "immoral" conduct and "subversive activities"—was the fifth and last criterion after (1) advanced or tender age; (2) number of years present in the United States; (3) physical or mental conditions requiring treatment in the United States; and (4) family situation—the effect of expulsion. See Leon Wildes, "The Nonpriority Program of the Immigration and Naturalization Service."

71 Wildes, "The Operations Instructions," p. 101.

72 By 1971, even preventive detention had been constricted by Congress. See Cole, *Enemy Aliens.*

73 The commissioner also stated that "[t]hough detention and expulsion activities continue to rise, no additional positions are being sought in this budget." See Budget Amendment, Detention and Deportation, p. 45 in U. S. Immigration and Naturalization Service, *Authorization and Budget, FY 1970*, vol. 1 (*supra* note 45). The focus of budget requests was not on detention and deportation but on "major increases in Border Patrol personnel and equipment." See "Budget Amendment, Border Patrol," p. 50 in U.S. Immigration and Naturalization Service, *Authorization and Budget, FY 1970*, vol. 1 (*supra* note 45).

74 See "Chapter 5: Illegal Detentions" and "Chapter Four: Handling of Persons in Custody," in *Border Patrol Handbook, 1971* (*supra* note 67).

75 Office of the General Counsel, "Legal Consideration on the Treatment of Family Members Who Are Not Eligible for Legalization Decision Memo 8715," May 29, 1987. On file with the author.

76 Clear and Frost, *The Punishment Imperative.*

77 Alexander, *The New Jim Crow*; Beckett, *Making Crime Pay.*

78 Subcommittee on Commerce, Justice, State, and the Judiciary Appropriations, Committee on Appropriations, House of Representatives, "Departments of Commerce, Justice, and State, the Judiciary, and Related Agencies Appropriations for 1984, Part 6: Department of Justice," HRG-1983-HAP-0023, March 16–18, 21–22, 1983, p. 426.

79 Subcommittee on Courts, Civil Liberties, and the Administration of Justice, Committee on the Judiciary, House of Representatives, "Federal Prison Policy," HRG-1987-HJH-0039, March 5, 1987.

80 Alejandro Portes, *City on the Edge.*

81 American Civil Liberties Union, "Detention of Undocumented Aliens: Actions by the INS Prior to the Adoption of the Immigration Reform and Control Act of 1986" (Washington, DC: ACLU, October 1990).

82 Ibid.

83 Simon, "Refugees in a Carceral Age."

84 Table 2: INS Spending for Detention, in American Civil Liberties Union, "Detention of Undocumented Aliens" (*supra* note 81), p. 7.

85 American Civil Liberties Union, "Detention of Undocumented Aliens" (*supra* note 81), p. 33.

86 American Civil Liberties Union, "Detention of Undocumented Aliens" (*supra* note 81), p. 36.

87 Welch, *Detained.*

88 American Civil Liberties Union, "Detention of Undocumented Aliens" (*supra* note 81), p. 22.

89 Subcommittee on Commerce, Justice, State, and the Judiciary Appropriations, Committee on Appropriations, House of Representatives, "Departments of Commerce, Justice, and State, the Judiciary, and Related Agencies Appropriations for 1988, Part 4: Department of Justice," HRG-1987-HAP-0011, March 5, 11–13, 16–17, 1987, p. 138.

90 In 1983, the Department of Justice also created the Executive Office of Immigration Review (EOIR), which includes the Office of the Chief Immigration Judge, which oversees all of the immigration courts in the United States, and the Board of Immigration Appeals, which is the highest tribunal dedicated to immigration. See Subcommittee on Immigration and Claims, Committee on the Judiciary, House of Representatives, "INS and the Executive Office for Immigration Review," HRG-2001-HJH-0037, May 15, 2001.

91 Many of those involved habeas corpus petitions challenging the detention of Cuban, Salvadoran and Haitian asylum seekers. Among the most high-profile case in the eighties were *Orantes-Hernandez v. Smith* (injunction challenging

procedure in Salvadoran asylum cases); *Hotel and Restaurant Employees Union v. Smith*; *Ortega v. Rowe*; *Fernandez-Roque v. Smith*. See Subcommittee on Commerce, Justice, State, and the Judiciary Appropriations, Committee on Appropriations, House of Representatives, "Departments of Commerce, Justice, and State, the Judiciary, and Related Agencies Appropriations for 1985, Part 8: Department of Justice," HRG-1984-HAP-0053, April 3–6, 10, 1984, pp. 893–95.

92 Subcommittee on Courts, Civil Liberties, and the Administration of Justice, "Federal Prison Policy" (*supra* note 78), p. 3.

93 See "INS budget justification to enforce the McKay Amendment," in Subcommittee on Commerce, Justice, State, and the Judiciary Appropriations, "Departments of Commerce, Justice, and State, the Judiciary, and Related Agencies Appropriations for 1988, Part 4: Department of Justice" (*supra* note 89), p. 1631.

94 Subcommittee on Commerce, Justice, State, and the Judiciary Appropriations, "Departments of Commerce, Justice, and State, the Judiciary, and Related Agencies Appropriations for 1988, Part 4: Department of Justice" (*supra* note 89), p. 1411.

95 Subcommittee on Commerce, Justice, State, and the Judiciary Appropriations, "Departments of Commerce, Justice, and State, the Judiciary, and Related Agencies Appropriations for 1988, Part 4: Department of Justice" (*supra* note 89), pp. 1252–53.

96 U.S. Immigration and Naturalization Service, "Criminal Alien Program (CAP): Procedures Manual" (Office of the General Counsel, Immigration and Naturalization Service, May 1, 1988), USCIS Historical Library, Washington, DC, p. 3.

97 Ibid., p. 4.

98 Ibid., p. 23.

99 Ibid., p. 13.

100 Beckett, *Making Crime Pay*.

101 Vialet, "Brief History of United States Immigration Policy."

102 Subcommittee on Commerce, Justice, State, and the Judiciary Appropriations, "Departments of Commerce, Justice, and State, the Judiciary, and Related Agencies Appropriations for 1988, Part 4: Department of Justice" (*supra* note 89), p. 139.

103 Martin, "A Defense of Immigration-Enforcement Discretion."

104 Welch, *Detained,* p 73.

105 Committee on the Judiciary, House of Representatives, House and Senate Reports, *Illegal Immigration Reform and Immigrant Responsibility Act of 1996*, HR 104–828, 14382 HR 828, September 24, 1996.

106 Newton, *Illegal, Alien, or Immigrant*; Chavez, *Covering Immigration*; Tichenor, *Dividing Lines*.

107 Weaver, "Frontlash."

108 Subcommittee on Commerce, Justice, State, and the Judiciary Appropriations, Committee on Appropriations, House of Representatives, "Departments of Commerce, Justice, and State, the Judiciary, and Related Agencies Appropriations for

1998, Part 6: The Judiciary; Department of State," HRG-1997-HAP-0070, February 26, March 4–6, 12–13, 19, April 9–10, 15, 1997, p. 1039.

109 Ibid., p. 1021.

110 Ibid., p. 1040.

111 Ibid., p. 1057.

112 Ibid., p.1052.

113 Ibid., pp. 1109–10.

114 Conversation with former INS commissioner, Washington DC, March 2014.

115 Rep. Lamar Smith, "Guidelines for Use of Prosecutorial Discretion in Removal Proceedings," letter to Janet Reno, Attorney General, and INS Commissioner Doris Meissner, November 4, 1999, *Interpreter Releases* 76 (December 3, 1999): 1730.

116 Meissner, "Exercising Prosecutorial Discretion Memo," p. 1.

117 Ibid., p. 2.

118 Ibid., p. 9.

119 Cole, *Enemy Aliens.*

120 *Zadvydas v. Davis*, No. 99-7791. Argued February 21, 2001. Decided June 28, 2001.

121 Cole, *Enemy Aliens*, p. 25.

122 Margulies, *Guantanamo.*

123 Subcommittee on Immigration and Claims, Committee on the Judiciary, House of Representatives, "INS and the Executive Office for Immigration Review," HRG-2001-HJH-0037, May 15, 2001.

124 Redburn, Reuter, and Majmundar, *Budgeting for Immigration Enforcement.*

125 Harwood, *In Liberty's Shadow.*

126 Redburn, Reuter, and Majmundar, *Budgeting for Immigration Enforcement.*

127 Janice Kephart-Roberts, "Memorandum for the Record: Interview of INS Commissioner, October 1993–November 2000," November 25, 2003. National Archives, http://media.nara.gov/9-11/MFR/t-0148-911MFR-00720.pdf.

128 Dunn, *The Militarization of the U.S.-Mexico Border.*

129 Blas Núñez-Neto, Alison Siskin, and Jennifer Lake, "Border Security Backgrounder, Memorandum to the House Committee on International Relations, Subcommittee on International Terrorism and Non Proliferation" (Washington, DC: Congressional Research Service, June 28, 2006).

130 "Speech of Hon. Sheila Jackson of Texas," *9/11 Recommendations Implementation Act*, House of Representatives, 108th Congress, 2nd sess., vol. 150, no. 130, October 11, 2004, p. 1956.

131 Smith, "Program Streamlining Immigration Enforcement."

132 Alison Siskin, *Immigration-Related Detention: Current Legislative Issues* (Washington, DC: Congressional Research Service, September 8, 2004).

133 Select Committee on Intelligence, House of Representatives, *Intelligence Reform and Terrorism Prevention Act of 2004*, HR 108–796 (December 7, 2004). See also *Public Law 108–458* [S. 2845], 108th Congress, Stat. 3638, December 17, 2004, p. 118.

134 Pallares and Flores-Gonzalez, *Marcha.*

135 Subcommittee on Homeland Security, Committee on Appropriations, House of Representatives, "U.S. Representative Harold Rogers (R-KY) Holds a Hearing on Fiscal Year 2007 Appropriations for the Secure Border Initiative, Immigration and Customs Enforcement of Customs and Border Protection," 109th Congress, April 6, 2006.

136 Ibid., p. 20.

137 Ibid., p. 17.

138 Ibid., p. 19.

139 Committee on Appropriations, Senate, "Department of Homeland Security Appropriations Bill, 2008," SR 110–84 (June 18, 2007), p. 5.

140 Ibid., p. 46.

141 Committee on Appropriations, Senate, "Department of Homeland Security Appropriations Bill, 2010," SR 111–31, 111th Cong. 1st sess. (June 18, 2009), p. 49.

142 Alison Siskin and Chad C. Haddal, *Immigration-Related Detention: Current Legislative Issues* (Washington, DC: Congressional Research Service, January 27, 2010), p. 14.

143 Jennifer E. Lake and William L. Painter, *Homeland Security Department: FY 2012 Appropriations* (Washington, DC: Congressional Research Service, September 2, 2011), pp. 30–31. See also Immigration and Customs Enforcement, Department of Homeland Security, "Secretary Napolitano and ICE Assistant Secretary Morton Announce Immigration Detention Reform Initiatives," press release, October 6, 2009. https://www.dhs.gov/news/2009/10/06/new-immigration-detention-reform-initiatives-announced

144 Morton, "Civil Immigration Enforcement."

145 Committee on the Judiciary, House of Representatives, *Keep Our Communities Safe Act of 2011*, 112th Congress 255 (October 18, 2011).

146 Lake and Painter, "Homeland Security Department" (*supra* note 143), pp. 30–31.

147 Committee on Appropriations, House of Representatives, "Department of Homeland Security Appropriations Bill, 2013," 112th Congress 492 (May 23, 2012), p. 4.

148 Ibid., p. 5.

149 Ibid., p. 201.

150 *Consolidated and Further Continuing Appropriations Act, 2013*, HR 933, bill summary: https://beta.congress.gov/bill/113th-congress/house-bill/933.

151 *Department of Homeland Security Appropriations Act, 2014*, HR 2217, bill summary: https://beta.congress.gov/bill/113th-congress/house-bill/2217.

152 National Immigration Justice Center, "Immigration Detention Bed Quota Timeline," March 2014. http://immigrantjustice.org/sites/immigrantjustice.org/files/Immigration_Detention_Bed_Quota_Timeline_2014_03.pdf.

153 *Accountability in Immigration Detention Act of 2014*, HR 4620, bill summary: https://beta.congress.gov/bill/113th-congress/house-bill/4620/cosponsors.

154 Murakawa, *The First Civil Right*.

155 Waslin, "The Impact of Immigration Enforcement Outsourcing on ICE Priorities."

CHAPTER 3. PROTECTORS AND PROSECUTORS

1 Fieldnotes, October 2, 2002.

2 For important accounts of the role of nonstate actors in domestic policing and migration control, see Victor Rios, "The Coupling of Criminal Justice and Community Institutions," in *Punished*; and Gaya Lahav, "The Rise of Nonstate Actors in Migration Regulation," in Foner, Rumbaut, and Gold, *Immigration Research for a New Century*.

3 Simon, *Governing through Crime*.

4 Murakawa, *The First Civil Right*.

5 Simon, *Governing through Crime*, p. 108.

6 Doty, *Law into Their Own Hands*; Biggers, *State out of the Union*.

7 Author interview, February 3, 2003.

8 Ibid.

9 This differs from immigrant arrest practices by law enforcement in other counties away from the border, such as Maricopa County or Pima County. In 2013, the well-known sheriff of Maricopa County, Joe Arpio, was found guilty of racial profiling. See Schwartz, "Judge Orders Sheriff Joe Arpaio."

10 See Heyman, "U.S. Immigration Officers of Mexican Ancestry"; Heyman, "Putting Power in the Anthropology of Bureaucracy."

11 Author interview, February 3, 2003.

12 Author interview, January 30, 2003.

13 Author interview, January 14, 2003.

14 Rubio-Goldsmith, McCormack, and Martinez, "The Funnel Effect"; Nevins, *Dying to Live*.

15 Miller, *Border Patrol Nation*.

16 This account focuses on Nogales and Douglas and does not cover the impact on the Tohono O'odham Nation, although there are parallels. See "Unfinished Business in Indian Country" in Miller, *Border Patrol Nation*.

17 Author interview, January 14, 2003.

18 Ibid.

19 Ibid.

20 For an excellent ethnographic account of this period see Rosas, *Barrio Libre*.

21 Author interview, February 3, 2003.

22 Author interview, February 11, 2003.

23 Salant et al., *Illegal Immigrants in U.S./Mexico Border Counties*; Salant, *Illegal Immigrants in Arizona's Border Counties*; Salant, *Border Impact*; Salant, *Fighting the Drug Wars*.

24 Author interview, January 14, 2003.

25 National Conference of State Legislatures, "State Criminal Alien Assistance Program," April 13, 2013. http://www.ncsl.org/research/immigration/state-criminal-alien-assistance-program.aspx.

26 Bureau of Justice Assistance, U.S. Department of Justice, "State Criminal Alien Assistance Program (SCAAP) Guidelines," 2015. https://www.bja.gov/Funding/15SCAAP_Guidelines.pdf.

27 On DHS funding for the Tohono O'odham Nation's tribal police, see Miller, "Unfinished Business in Indian Country," in *Border Patrol Nation*. See also "Border Security: Partnership Agreements and Enhanced Oversight Could Strengthen Coordination of Efforts on Indian Reservations" (Washington, DC: Government Accountability Office, April 2013).

28 Hammer-Tomizuka, "Prison Expansion in Arizona, 1993–2002," in *Criminal Alienation*.

29 Associated Press, "Santa Cruz County Readies Newer, Bigger Jail."

30 "Agenda: Discussion and Possible Direction regarding Cochise County Jail Expansion/Remodel (Bisbee)," Board of Supervisors, July 8, 2014. http://agenda.cochise.az.gov/agenda_publish.cfm?id=&mt=WKS&get_month=7&get_year=2014&dsp=agm&seq=1860&rev=0&ag=711&ln=30518&nseq=0&nrev=0&pseq=&prev=#ReturnTo30518.

31 Eagly, "Local Immigration Prosecution."

32 Swedlund, "Deputies Tied Body of Crosser to Hood."

33 Official statements from INS officials identified three main courses of action when processing migrants for illegal entry—"Voluntary Departure," "Voluntary Return," and NTAs or Notices to Appear before an Immigration Judge. Criminal Prosecution is never mentioned as a main course of action, even as agents are required to conduct thorough background checks. See "Processing Persons Arrested for Illegal Entry into the United States between Ports of Entry," Statement of Michael Pearson, Executive Associate Commissioner, Field Operations, INS, Before the Committee on Governmental Affairs, Permanent Subcommittee on Investigations, November 13, 2001. On file with the author.

34 Rosenblum, *Border Security*.

35 Author interview, January 4, 2004.

36 Smith, "Program Streamlining Immigration Enforcement," p. 27.

37 Smith, "Technology Speeds Judicial Process."

38 Sunnucks, "Arizona Budget Deficit Labeled Country's Worst."

39 TRAC Immigration, "Federal Prosecutors along Southwest Border Overwhelmed by Soaring Arizona Drug Cases," Transactional Records Access Clearinghouse: Immigration, Syracuse University, April 19, 2010. http://trac.syr.edu/immigration/reports/230/.

40 TRAC Immigration, "FY 2009 Federal Prosecutions Sharply Higher: Surge Driven by Steep Jump in Immigration Filings," Transactional Records Access Clearinghouse: Immigration, Syracuse University, December 21, 2009. http://trac.syr.edu/tracreports/crim/223/.

41 Ibid.

42 "Federal Prosecutors along Southwest Border Overwhelmed" (*supra* note 39).

43 Giblin, "Hiring Freeze Puts Squeeze on Federal Prosecutors in Arizona." See also "Federal Courts Hit Hard by Increased Law Enforcement on Border: Defendants Charged in the Border District Courts and Courts Affected," *Third Branch*, July 2008. http://www.uscourts.gov/news/TheThirdBranch/08–07–01/Federal_Courts_Hit_Hard_by_Increased_Law_Enforcement_on_Border.aspx.

44 "Federal Courts Hit Hard" (*supra* note 43).

45 Fieldnotes, March 23, 2011.

46 Fieldnotes, January 11, 2013.

47 Fieldnotes, July 21, 2010.

48 Fieldnotes, January 9, 2013.

49 The U.S. Court of Appeals for the Ninth Circuit has ruled that guilty pleas obtained during en masse hearings under Operation Streamline violate Rule 11 of the Federal Rules of Criminal Procedure. See U.S. Court of Appeals for the Ninth Circuit, *United States v. Arqueta-Ramos*, September 20, 2013. See also Kerwin and McCabe, "Arrested on Entry."

50 Kerwin and McCabe, "Arrested on Entry."

51 "Hear from the Judges: Presiding Judge, Federal District Court, District of Arizona," in Robbins, "Border Patrol Program."

52 Author interview, January 9, 2013.

53 Internal memo, November 22, 2005, on file with the author.

54 Ibid.

55 Fieldnotes, January 2013.

56 "Federal Courts Hit Hard" (*supra* note 43).

57 "Hear from the Judges: Presiding Judge, Federal District Court, Del Rio, Texas Division," in Robbins, "Border Patrol Program."

58 Gonzales, *Mexican Consuls and Labor Organizing*; Hernandez, *Migra!*

59 Balderrama and Rodriguez, *A Decade of Betrayal*.

60 Calavita, *Inside the State*.

61 Gonzales, *Mexican Consuls and Labor Organizing*.

62 Nevins and Aizeki, *Dying to Live*.

63 Author interview, February 19, 2003.

64 U.S. Border Patrol: Tucson Sector, News Release: "Border Patrol Renews Highly Successful Campaign to Discourage Desert Crossings," April 19, 1995, Vertical File, Border Patrol, Programs and Activities, Arizona, USCIS Historical Library, Washington, DC.

65 Author interview, November 12, 2001.

66 Ibid.

67 Fieldnotes, Sasabe, Sonora, February 27, 2003.

68 Alba and Castillo, *New Approaches to Migration Management*; Diaz and Kuhner, *Women Migrants in Transit and Detention in Mexico*.

69 Luntz, "Guía del Migrante Mexicano."

70 For an example of anti-immigrant outrage over the Mexican Consulate's "Guide for Mexican Migrants," see Mac Donald, "Mexico's Undiplomatic Diplomats."

71 Siulc et al., *Legal Orientation Program Evaluation.*

72 Author interview, August 24, 2004.

73 Eagly and Shafer's study found that "detained migrants represented themselves 86% of the time. In Arizona, where immigration courts have some of the highest caseloads, only .002% of detained migrants had legal representation. Mexicans had the lowest rates of legal representation in court." See Eagly and Shafer, "A National Study."

74 Fieldnotes, October 25, 2004.

75 Author interview, November 5, 2004. See also Subcommittee on Immigration, Committee on the Judiciary, U.S. Senate, "INS Oversight and Reform: Detention." 105th Congress, September 16, 1998.

76 Lakhani, "From Problems of Living to Problems of Law"; Lakhani, "Producing Immigrant Victims' 'Right' to Legal Status and the Management of Legal Uncertainty"; Menjívar and Salcido, "Gendered Paths to Legal Status."

77 Hansenfeld, "People-Processing Organizations."

78 Ibid.

CHAPTER 4. VICTIMS AND CULPRITS

1 There are currently three migrant shelters in Nogales, Sonora. See Isacson and Meyer, *Beyond the Border Buildup.*

2 Migration flows through the Arizona-Sonora border once were mostly regional. Seasonal migrants crossed the border to labor in the mines, fields, or cattle ranches, then would return to Mexico. The restructuring of economies and escalation of policing transformed migratory flows. Border crossers are mostly long-distance migrants from new sending regions in southern Mexico, El Salvador, Guatemala, and Honduras. And unlike earlier waves of migrants, many of those passing through the shelter are deportees with extensive ties to the United States. Many have lived and worked in the United States for most of their lives. Many have lost their legal permanent residency status and have been deported from places like Chicago, Seattle, and San Francisco. Or they were deported after being arrested by the police in new gateway cities in places like South Carolina, Alabama, and Georgia. Many more have parents, children, spouses, and other relatives in the United States.

3 Fieldnotes, Nogales, AZ, January 8, 2013.

4 For discussion of the Obama administration's policy of prosecutorial discretion and law enforcement priorities, see Memorandum from John Morton, Assistant Secretary, U.S. Immigration and Customs Enforcement, on civil immigration enforcement, June 17, 2011. http://www.ice.gov/doclib/secure-communities/pdf/prosecutorial-discretion-memo.pdf.

5 These guidelines were revised in 2014 but were not yet in effect when I conducted fieldwork. I address the new Priority Enforcement Program in the book's conclusion. See Jeh Charles Johnson, "Policies for the Apprehension, Detention, and Removal of Undocumented Immigrants," November 20, 2014, U.S. Department of

Homeland Security. http://www.dhs.gov/sites/default/files/publications/14_1120_memo_prosecutorial_discretion.pdf.

6 Morton, "Civil Immigration Enforcement"; Morton, "Exercising Prosecutorial Discretion."

7 Zatz and Rodriguez, "Limits of Discretion."

8 Author interview with former Bracero, "Caravan of Ex-Braceros," Chicago, IL, September 8, 2013.

9 For a discussion of "skips" see Calavita, *Inside the State*.

10 Ingrid Eagly provides a thorough account of how migrants are processed through the immigration and criminal justice system in the interior, as opposed to the border. See Eagly, "Criminal Justice for Noncitizens."

11 See Kanstroom, "Discretion, Jurisdiction Stripping, and Retroactivity, 1965–2006," in *Deportation Nation*; Motomura, "Prosecutorial Discretion in Context."

12 Simon, *Governing through Crime*, p. 35.

13 Hansenfeld, "People-Processing Organizations."

14 Author interview, January 20, 2003.

15 Author interview, January 5, 2004.

16 Guerette, *Migrant Death*, p. 113.

17 Ibid.

18 Author interview, circa January 14, 2004.

19 Author interview, January 5, 2004.

20 Author interview, February 20, 2003.

21 Author interview, January 5, 2004.

22 Simon, *Governing through Crime*, p. 75.

23 Fieldnotes, Agua Prieta, Sonora, December 24, 2003.

24 The Border Patrol never caught up to them. They worked in Phoenix to save enough to buy a truck, and then decided to go to Colorado. The Border Patrol apprehended them at a traffic checkpoint and confiscated the truck and deported them. Fieldnotes, Agua Prieta, Sonora, February 20, 2003.

25 Fieldnotes, January 16, 2004.

26 On the rights of noncitizens see Bosniak, "Membership and the Difference That Alienage Makes"; Schuck, "The Transformation of Immigration Law."

27 Migrants were more likely to report abuses by smugglers, *bajadores*, and vigilantes than by Border Patrol agents.

28 Fieldnotes, Altar, Sonora, February 6, 2003.

29 Fieldnotes, Nogales, AZ, October 17, 2003.

30 Heyman, "Putting Power in the Anthropology of Bureaucracy."

31 Trevizo, "ICE Says Most Released in Arizona Weren't Criminals."

32 Semple, "Immigrants Released Ahead of Automatic Budget Cuts."

33 The language derives from the Refugee Act of 1980, which brought the United States in line with international human rights law concerning the status of refugees.

34 For an overview of the U visa see Farb, "The U Visa Unveiled"; and Hanson, "The U-Visa: Immigration Law's Best Kept Secret."

35 See, for instance, Pollack, "2 Illegal Immigrants."

36 To clarify this, I would argue that despite the tendency to conflate illegality and criminality, these have become two different social standings. Police and the media conflate the two, but Border Patrol and ICE distinguish between noncriminal undocumented aliens and criminal aliens. I think of "illegal" status as part of the process of becoming formally criminalized. This is a very different social position from that occupied by those who are branded as criminal aliens through criminal prosecution, incarceration, and deportation.

37 For a discussion of criminal alien arrest by police or local law enforcement see Eagly, "Criminal Justice for Noncitizens."

38 Author interview, January 9, 2002.

39 Author interview, January 5, 2004.

40 Author interview, January 4, 2004.

41 Rosenblum, *Border Security*, p. 29.

42 Q & A with former deputy general counsel, Department of Homeland Security, Northwestern Law School, October 25, 2013, Chicago, Illinois.

43 Rosenblum, *Border Security*.

44 The office of Enforcement and Removal Operations (ERO) under ICE, formerly Detention and Removal (DRO), manages local detention facilities and accepts detainees from the Border Patrol and local, county, and federal correctional facilities. ERO classifies detainees into three categories: low, medium, and high. Detention uniforms are color coded according to each category: blue is assigned to detainees with misdemeanor charges or immigration violations; orange uniforms are assigned to nonviolent criminal aliens; and red is for detainees with more serious criminal charges.

45 See Siulc et al., "Improving Efficiency."

46 Formal deportation is different from a voluntary return, in that it includes bars to future legal migration and further criminal penalties, ranging from two to twenty years, for those who violate the deportation order.

47 I spoke with an immigration attorney after the hearings and described what I observed. "Very sad," she said, "but very common. They don't know the difference between a voluntary departure and deportation. So they do what everyone else is doing. . . . They qualify for voluntary departure. They just don't know what it is." Fieldnotes, Service Processing [Detention] Center, El Paso, Texas, October 25, 2004.

48 Fieldnotes, Nogales, Sonora, October 4, 2002.

49 Lydgate, *Assembly-line Justice*.

50 Telephone interview with federal public defender, District of Arizona, March 29, 2013.

51 See Motivans, "Immigration Offenders," pp. 29–30.

52 Ibid.

53 In *Padilla v. Kentucky*, the Supreme Court ruled that criminal defense lawyers must inform their clients about how "deportation is an integral part—indeed,

sometimes the most important part—of the penalty that may be imposed on noncitizen defendants who plead guilty to specified crimes."

54 Fieldnotes, Tucson, AZ, July 16, 2010.
55 Waslin, "Driving While Immigrant."
56 Fieldnotes, Agua Prieta, Sonora, December 24, 2003.
57 Fieldnotes, Nogales, Sonora, November 8, 2002.
58 Morawetz, "Understanding the Impact of the 1996 Deportation Laws."
59 Kanstroom, *Aftermath*.
60 See Camayd-Freixas, "Interpreting after the Largest ICE Raid in U.S. History"; Human Rights Watch, "Forced Apart"; Capps et al., "Paying the Price."
61 See Eagly, "Criminal Justice for Noncitizens"; Chacón, "Whose Community Shield"; Demleitner, "Misguided Prevention"; Hing, "Providing a Second Chance"; Miller, "Citizenship and Severity"; Schuck, "Removing Criminal Aliens."
62 Border agents do not dispense violence randomly but within a legal constitutional framework. They sort and distinguish between illegal and criminal status. Non-citizens with criminal status face a clear suspension of rights and are often subject to force. Undocumented border crossers without a criminal mark can claim basic procedural protections and are less likely to experience violence by border agents. One could also argue that the Border Patrol "subcontracts" the more extra-legal forms of violence to vigilantes and smugglers.
63 Ortega, "Border Killings"; PBS, "Border Patrol Series Prompts OIG Investigation."
64 Eagly, "Remote Adjudication in Immigration."
65 Author interview, November 5, 2004.
66 Author interview with attorney, Florence, Arizona, July 2010. See also Johnson and Trujillo, *Immigration Law*; and Kanstroom, *Aftermath*.
67 Kanstroom, *Aftermath*, p. 66.
68 See Motomura, "The Discretion That Matters," p. 1834.
69 See Cornelius, "Impacts of Border Enforcement."
70 Author interview, November 5, 2004.
71 Conversation with former deputy general counsel, Department of Homeland Security, Northwestern Law School, October 25, 2013, Chicago, Illinois.
72 Lipsky, "Street-level Bureaucracy."
73 See Golash-Boza, "Racism and the Consequences of U.S. Immigration Policy"; and Golash-Boza and Hondagneu-Sotelo, "Latino Immigrant Men."
74 Kanstroom, *Aftermath*, pp. 31–32.
75 Fieldnotes, El Paso, TX, October 25, 2004.
76 See Kanstroom, *Deportation Nation*; and Ngai, *Impossible Subjects*.
77 Kubrin, Martinez, and Zatz, *Punishing Immigrants*; Kanstroom, *Aftermath*; De Genova and Puetz, *Deportation Regime*; Dunn, *Blockading the Border*; and Brotherton and Kretsedemas, *Keeping Out the Other*.

CHAPTER 5. THE CITIZEN AND THE CRIMINAL

1 Lucas, "144 Border Agents Charged with Alien, Drug Smuggling."

2 Fieldnotes, Douglas, AZ, October 3, 2002.

3 For a history of policing and expulsion of Mexicans from the United States, see Hernandez, *Migra!*; García, *Operation Wetback*; Balderrama and Rodríguez, *Decade of Betrayal.*

4 See American Civil Liberties Union (ACLU) Statement on "Human Rights Violations on the United States–Mexico Border," submitted to Office of the United Nations High Commissioner for Human Rights, 67th Session of the United Nations General Assembly, October 25, 2012; Amnesty International, *In Hostile Terrain*; No More Deaths Coalition, *A Culture of Cruelty.*

5 See Johnson, "The Intersection of Race and Class"; Romero, "Racial Profiling"; Chacón, "Border Exceptionalism."

6 Among its most controversial provisions are those that make failing to carry registration papers, performing unauthorized labor, and transporting unauthorized persons a state crime.

7 "Statement by Governor Jan Brewer," State of Arizona, Office of the Governor, April 23, 2010.

8 Fieldnotes, July 2010. See also "Declaration of Tony Estrada, Santa Cruz County Sherriff," U.S. District Court for the District of Arizona, *U.S. v. the State of Arizona*, June 28, 2010; Associated Press, "Arizona Immigration Law SB 1070: State Spends $640,000 on Police Training."

9 Author interview, circa January 14, 2004.

10 Author interview, January 5, 2004.

11 For accounts of policing on the Tohono O'odham reservation see Todd Miller, *Border Patrol Nation.*

12 U.S. Census Bureau, *U.S. Census 2010.*

13 Author interview, July 16, 2010.

14 See Meissner et al., *Immigration Enforcement.*

15 Author interview, January 5, 2004.

16 U.S. Census Bureau, *U.S. Census 2010.*

17 Ibid.

18 Cadava, "Borderlands of Modernity," p. 368.

19 Ibid., p. 381.

20 Author interview, Tucson, AZ, November 15, 2002.

21 Author interview, Tucson, AZ, January 20, 2003.

22 U.S. General Accounting Office, *Illegal Immigration.*

23 Immigration and Naturalization Service, "Programs and Activities (INS) Operation Safeguard," USCIS Library, Washington, DC, 1995.

24 Author interview, Douglas, AZ, November 11, 2002.

25 Author interview, mayor of Douglas, AZ, January 13, 2003.

26 Author interview, U.S. Border Patrol, January 4, 2004.

27 Fieldnotes, Nogales, AZ, December 14, 2002.

28 U.S. Customs and Border Protection, *National Border Patrol Strategy* (Washington, DC: Office of the Border Patrol and the Office of Policy and Planning, 2004).

29 Author interview, January 15, 2004.

30 Author interview, Douglas, AZ, November 6, 2002.

31 The Border Patrol continues to foster community support through outreach programs. In 2012, the Border Patrol established a Citizen's Academy in which participants learn about "the history of the Border Patrol; criminal and immigration law; tracking skills; firearms, as well as horse patrol and interdiction scenarios." See Maldonado, "Local Citizens Graduate."

32 For analysis of national coverage see Chavez, *Covering Immigration*.

33 Author interview, Tucson, AZ, November 15, 2002.

34 On crime and insecurity in Nogales, Sonora, Mexico, see Rosas, *Barrio Libre*.

35 Southeast Arizona Economic Development Group Report, on file with the author.

36 Nogales Chamber of Commerce Report, on file with the author.

37 Two main drainage systems link Nogales, Sonora, and Nogales, Arizona, which also serve as throughways for clandestine crossing. During my fieldwork, the papers regularly reported on the discovery of new tunnels. See Stellar, "Nogales Tunnel Opens into Grave"; Swedlund, "Tunnels Found in Nogales Tied to Smuggling"; Gutierrez, "Illegal Traffic in Tunnels."

38 Author interview, Tucson, AZ, January 20, 2003.

39 The Southern Border Communities Coalition reports that since 2010, there have been six fatal Border Patrol shootings in Southern Arizona alone, some involving rock-throwing incidents, and three nonfatal shootings. See also Santos, "Shootings by Agents"; Trevizo, "Mexican Government Objects."

40 Fieldnotes, Douglas, AZ, September 28, 2002.

41 Fieldnotes, Douglas, AZ, October 19, 2003.

42 Fieldnotes, Douglas, AZ, October 17, 2003.

43 Fieldnotes, Nogales, AZ, January 4, 2003.

44 Author interview, Douglas, AZ, January 13, 2003.

45 Fieldnotes, Douglas, AZ, October 3, 2002.

46 Fieldnotes, Douglas, AZ, November 9, 2002.

47 Fieldnotes, Douglas, AZ, October 17, 2002.

48 Fieldnotes, Nogales, AZ, November 7, 2002.

49 A shooting of a nineteen-year-old native of Douglas, Arizona, in 2011 suggests that such incidents are recurring. See "Border Patrol Agents Shoot Douglas 19-year-old."

50 Author interview, Douglas, AZ, November 11, 2002.

51 Fieldnotes, Douglas, AZ, September 28, 2002.

52 Eagly, "Local Immigration Prosecution."

53 Author interview, January 14, 2003.

54 Telephone interview with federal public defender, District of Arizona, March 29, 2013; see also Lucas, "144 Border Agents"; United States Government Accountability Office, "Border Security."

55 See Table 6: Demographic characteristics of federal defendants charged in US District Court with Criminal Immigration, in Motivans, "Immigration Offenders."

56 Fieldnotes, Nogales, AZ, November 7, 2002.

57 Author interview, Nogales, AZ, December 14, 2002.

58 See Stevens, "US Government Unlawfully Detaining and Deporting US Citizens."

59 The EIOR website explicitly states that "[i]n coordination with DHS and correctional authorities in all 50 states, Puerto Rico, the Commonwealth of the Northern Mariana Islands, the District of Columbia, selected municipalities, and Federal Bureau of Prisons facilities, immigration judges conduct on-site hearings to adjudicate the immigration status of alien inmates while they are serving sentences for criminal convictions." See Office of the Chief Immigration Judge, http://www.justice.gov/eoir/ocijinfo.htm, accessed May 9, 2013.

60 Author interview, Nogales, AZ, December 14, 2002.

61 See Beckett and Herbert, *Banished*; Manza and Uggen, *Locked Out*; Wacquant, "Race as Civic Felony."

62 Fieldnotes, Douglas, AZ, November 5, 2002.

63 Fieldnotes, Douglas, AZ, October 17, 2003.

64 Fieldnotes, Douglas, AZ, September 28, 2002.

65 Fieldnotes, Nogales, AZ, February 1, 2003.

66 See Arizona State Legislature, 32–1471: "Health care provider and any other person; emergency aid; nonliability. http://www.azleg.gov/FormatDocument. asp?inDoc=/ars/32/01471.htm&Title=32&DocType=ARS, accessed January 4, 2016.

67 Although this case occurred well before I conducted my own fieldwork, I include it because it highlights shifting practices of border security in the post–civil rights era.

68 Quoted in Mark Day, "Sweeping up Aliens."

69 Ibid.

70 See Coutin, *Culture of Protest*.

71 Huicochea and Barrios, "2 Samaritans Charged in Transporting Entrants." On September 1, the charges were officially dropped after a court ruling that the defendants had not violated the law and that further prosecution would violate their due process rights.

72 See Innes, "Border Activists Say They Knew Law"; Portillo, "'05 Border Bill Punishes Those Aiding Illegal Entrants."

73 Grossman, "'No More Deaths' Volunteer Charges Tossed."

74 Fieldnotes, Douglas, AZ, October 3, 2002.

75 Fieldnotes, Douglas, AZ, November 9, 2002.

76 Hammer-Tomizuka and Allen, "Hate or Heroism."

77 Durkheim, *Division of Labor in Society*.

78 See Doty, *Law into Their Own Hands*; Brown, *Strain of Violence*.

79 Doty, *Law into Their Own Hands*, p. 24.

80 Bell, *Race, Racism, and American Law*.

81 Minutemen Project website.

82 Bosniak, "Membership, Equality, and the Difference That Alienage Makes."

83 Despite the racial rhetoric, investigations of the Minutemen Project have found no direct links to hate groups. See Doty, *Law into Their Own Hands*, p. 59; Hammer-Tomizuka and Allen, "Hate or Heroism," p. 9.

84 Minutemen Project website.

85 See Hall and O'Driscoll, "Border Patrols Growing in Arizona"; "Nazis, Racists Join Minutemen Project"; Holthouse, "Playing Army."

86 Eagly, "Local Immigration Prosecution," p. 1756.

87 Eagly, "Local Immigration Prosecution," p. 1770

88 Kil, Menjivar, and Doty, "Securing Borders."

89 Author interview, Douglas, AZ, January 13, 2003. Document on file with author.

90 Border Action Network, Press Release, Tucson, AZ, November 22, 2006, on file with author.

91 Kil, Menjivar, and Doty, "Securing Borders," p. 298.

92 What interests me about this disturbing case is the way it captures the blending of elements of overtly racially motivated vigilantism with a post–civil rights variety of vigilantism that draws on rights frameworks and crime control.

93 *U.S. v. Patrick Hanigan*, U.S. Court of Appeals, Ninth Circuit, No. 81–1262, 681 F.2d 1127, 10 Fed. R. Evid. Serv. 1553, July 19, 1982. See also Cadava, "From *Hanigan* to SB 1070."

94 Cacho refers to this as "an ideology of white injury." See Cacho, *Social Death*.

95 Author interview, January 15, 2004.

CHAPTER 6. A NEW ENFORCEMENT TERRAIN

1 Corella, "Activists Block Tucson Courthouse"; #Not1More, "Breaking: Tucson Blocking Deportation Buses Right Now," October 10, 2013. http://www.notone-moredeportation.com/2013/10/10/tucson/.

2 Bogado, "Undocumented Activists Take a Giant Risk to Return Home."

3 Preston, "9 in Deportation Protest Are Held."

4 Bogado, "The Dream 9 Come Home."

5 Simon, *Governing through Crime*, p. 37.

6 Law, *The Immigration Battle in American Courts*; Salyer, *Laws as Harsh as Tigers*.

7 Kanstroom, "Discretion, Jurisdiction Stripping, and Retroactivity, 1965–2006," in *Deportation Nation*.

8 Aguilar, "Managing Borders in North America"; Papademetiou and Collett, "A New Architecture for Border Management."

9 Skolnick, "Democratic Order and the Rule of Law," in *Justice without Trial*.

10 See Richie, *Arrested Justice*; Rios, *Punished*; Alexander, *The New Jim Crow*.

11 Rios, *Punished*; Wacquant, "Race as a Civic Felony."

12 Johnson, "Intersection of Race and Class"; Romero, "Racial Profiling and Immigration Law Enforcement."

13 De Genova, "Legal Production of Mexican/Migrant 'Illegality'"; Hernandez, *Migra!*

14 Rios, *Punished*; Goffman, *On the Run*; Alexander, *The New Jim Crow*.

15 Muhammad, *Condemnation of Blackness*.

16 Eagly, "Criminal Justice for Noncitizens."

17 Gordon, *Mainstreaming Torture*; Margulies, *Guantanamo*; Cacho, *Social Death*.

18 In 2014, the Jeh Johnson memo rescinded enforcement priorities under the 2011 John Morton memos. See "Policies for the Apprehension, Detention, and Removal of Undocumented Immigrants," http://www.dhs.gov/sites/default/files/publications/14_1120_memo_prosecutorial_discretion.pdf.

19 Ibid.

20 Ibid.

21 Rosenblum, "Understanding the Potential Impact of Executive Action on Immigration Enforcement."

22 Papademetiou and Collett, "A New Architecture for Border Management"; Aguilar, "Managing Borders in North America: Charting the Future."

23 Castells, "The Perverse Connection: The Global Criminal Economy," in *End of Millenium: The Information Age*.

24 Gordon, *Mainstreaming Torture*, p. 56.

25 Margulies, *What Changed When Everything Changed*; Demleitner, "Misguided Prevention"; Stumpf, "The Crimmigration Crisis."

26 Gonzales, *Reform without Justice*; Calavita, "Contradictions of Immigration Lawmaking."

27 Undocumented antideportation activists publicly expressed this critique during a speech that President Obama gave in Chicago, shortly after introducing the new Priority Enforcement Program, taking executive action on immigration, and announcing that new enforcement priorities would target "felons, not families." They directly challenged criminal enforcement priorities and the criminal alien mandate that has thrived and proliferated through bipartisan consensus.

28 Waters, *Black Identities*.

29 Wacquant, "Race as a Civic Felony."

30 Bell, *Race, Racism, and American Law*.

REFERENCES

Aguilar, David. "Managing Borders in North America: Charting the Future." Panel discussion, Migration Policy Institute, Washington, DC. February 7, 2014. http://www.migrationpolicy.org/multimedia/managing-borders-north-america-charting-future.

Alba, Francisco, and Manuel Angel Castillo. *New Approaches to Migration Management in Mexico and Central America.* Washington, DC: Migration Policy Institute, 2012.

Aleinikoff, T. Alexander, David A. Martin, and Hiroshi Motomura. *Immigration and Citizenship, Process and Policy,* 7th ed. New York: Thomson Reuters, 2003.

Alexander, Michelle. *The New Jim Crow: Mass Incarceration in the Age of Colorblindness.* New York: New Press, 2012.

Amnesty International. *In Hostile Terrain: Human Rights Violations in Immigration Enforcement in the US Southwest.* New York: Amnesty International, 2012. http://www.amnestyusa.org/sites/default/files/ai_inhostileterrain_032312_singles.pdf.

Andreas, Peter. *Border Games: Policing the US-Mexico Divide.* Ithaca, NY: Cornell University Press, 2012.

Associated Press. "Arizona Immigration Law SB1070: State Spends $640,000 on Police Training." Associated Press, October 28, 2012. http://www.abc15.com/news/state/arizona-immigration-law-sb1070-state-spends-640000-on-police-training.

———. "Santa Cruz County Readies Newer, Bigger Jail." *Arizona Capitol Times,* February 24, 2011. http://azcapitoltimes.com/news/2011/02/24/santa-cruz-county-readies-newer-bigger-jail/.

Balderrama, Francisco E., and Raymond Rodriguez. *Decade of Betrayal: Mexican Repatriation in the 1930s.* Albuquerque: University of New Mexico Press, 1995.

Beckett, Katherine. *Making Crime Pay: Law and Order in Contemporary American Politics.* Studies in Crime and Public Policy. New York: Oxford University Press, 1997.

Beckett, Katherine, and Steve Herbert. *Banished: The New Social Control in Urban America.* New York: Oxford University Press, 2009.

Bell, Derrick. *Race, Racism, and American Law.* New York: Aspen, 2004.

Benton-Cohen, Katherine. *Borderline Americans: Racial Division and Labor War in the Arizona Borderlands.* Cambridge, MA: Harvard University Press, 2011.

Berg, Robert. "Manufacturing in Arizona." In *Arizona's Changing Economy: Trends and Prospects,* edited by Bernard Ronan. Phoenix: Arizona Chamber of Commerce, 1986.

Biggers, Jeff. "The Arizonification of America." *New York Times*, October 15, 2012. http://campaignstops.blogs.nytimes.com/2012/10/15/the-arizonification-of-america/.

Bigo, Didier. "Security and Immigration: Toward a Critique of the Governmentality of Unease." *Alternatives: Global, Local, Political* 27.1 (2002): 63–92.

Bigo, Didier, and Elspeth Guild. *Controlling Frontiers: Free Movement into and within Europe*. Aldershot, UK: Ashgate, 2005.

Bogado, Aura. "The Dream 9 Come Home." *Colorlines*, August 8, 2013. http://www.colorlines.com/articles/dream-9-come-home.

———. "Undocumented Activists Take a Giant Risk to Return Home." *Colorlines*, July 23, 2013.

"Border Patrol Agent Shoots Douglas 19-Year-Old." *Douglas Dispatch*, March 23, 2011. http://www.douglasdispatch.com/news/border-patrol-agent-shoots-douglas-year-old/article_a6f50ccd-903a-54e1-9116-68f7cd458f8b.html.

Bosniak, Linda S. "Membership, Equality, and the Difference That Alienage Makes." *New York University Law Review* 69.6 (December 1994): 1047–1149.

Bourdieu, Pierre, and John B. Thompson. *Language and Symbolic Power*. Cambridge, MA: Harvard University Press, 1991.

Brotherton, David, and Philip Kretsedemas. *Keeping Out the Other: A Critical Introduction to Immigration Enforcement Today*. New York: Columbia University Press, 2008.

Brown, Anna, and Eileen Patten. "Latinos in the 2014 Election: Arizona." Pew Research Center, October 2, 2014.

Brown, Richard Maxwell. *Strain of Violence: Historical Studies of American Violence and Vigilantism*. New York: Oxford University Press, 1975.

Broyles, Bill, and Mark H. Haynes. *Desert Duty: On the Line with the U.S. Border Patrol*. Austin: University of Texas Press, 2010.

Butterfield, Fox. "With Cash Tight, States Reassess Long Prison Terms." *New York Times*, November 10, 2003.

Cacho, Lisa Marie. *Social Death: Racialized Rightlessness and the Criminalization of the Unprotected*. New York: NYU Press, 2012.

Cadava, Geraldo L. "Borderlands of Modernity and Abandonment: The Lines within Ambos Nogales and the Tohono O'odham Nation." *Journal of American History* 98.2 (2011): 362–83.

———. "From *Hanigan* to SB 1070: How Arizona Got to Where It Is Today." *History News Network*, August 22, 2010. http://historynewsnetwork.org/article/130543.

———. *Standing on Common Ground*. Cambridge, MA: Harvard University Press, 2013.

Calavita, Kitty. *Inside the State: The Bracero Program, Immigration, and the INS*. New York: Routledge, 1992.

———. "The Contradictions of Immigration Lawmaking: The Immigration Reform and Control Act of 1986." *Law & Policy* 11.1 (1989): 17–47.

Caldeira, Teresa Pires do Rio. *City of Walls: Crime, Segregation, and Citizenship in Sao Paulo*. Berkeley: University of California Press, 2001.

Camayd-Freixas, Erik. "Interpreting after the Largest ICE Raid in US History: A Personal Account." *New York Times*, July 14, 2008. http://graphics8.nytimes.com/images/2008/07/14/opinion/14ed-camayd.pdf.

Capps, Randolph, Rosa Marie Castaneda, Ajay Chaudry, and Robert Santos. "Paying the Price: The Impact of Immigration Raids on America's Children." Washington, DC: Urban Institute, October 31, 2007. http://www.urban.org/research/publication/paying-price-impact-immigration-raids-americas-children.

Castells, Manuel. *The Information Age: Economy, Society, and Culture.* Vol. 3, *End of Millennium*. Malden, MA: Blackwell, 1998.

Castro, Gustavo Lopez. "Coyotes and Alien Smuggling." In *Migration between Mexico and the United States: Binational Study* 3: 965–74. Mexico City: Mexican Ministry of Foreign Affairs, 1998. https://www.utexas.edu/lbj/uscir/binpapers/v3a-6lopez.pdf.

Ceyhan, Ayse, and Anastassia Tsoukala. "The Securitization of Migration in Western Societies: Ambivalent Discourses and Policies." *Alternatives: Global, Local, Political* 27.1 (2002): 21–39.

Chacón, Jennifer M. "Border Exceptionalism in the Era of Moving Borders." *Fordham Urban Law Journal* 38 (2010): 129.

———. "Managing Migration through Crime." *Columbia Law Review* 109 (2009): 135–48.

———. "Unsecured Borders: Immigration Restrictions, Crime Control, and National Security." *Connecticut Law Review* 39.5 (2007): 1827.

———. "Whose Community Shield: Examining the Removal of the Criminal Street Gang Member." *University of Chicago Legal Forum* 2007 (2007): 317–58.

Chavez, Leo R. *Covering Immigration: Popular Images and the Politics of the Nation.* Berkeley: University of California Press, 2001.

Chemerinsky, Erwin, and Laurie L. Levenson, *Criminal Procedure*, 2nd ed. New York: Aspen, 2013.

Clear, Todd R., and Natasha A. Frost. *The Punishment Imperative: The Rise and Failure of Mass Incarceration in America.* New York: NYU Press, 2013.

Cole, David. *Enemy Aliens: Double Standards and Constitutional Freedoms in the War on Terrorism.* New York: New Press, 2003.

Cooper, Bo. "INS Exercise of Prosecutorial Discretion." July 11, 2000. National Immigrant Women's Advocacy Project. http://niwaplibrary.wcl.american.edu/reference/additional-materials/immigration/enforcement-detention-and-criminal-justice/government-documents/Bo-Cooper-memo%20pros%20discretion7.11.2000.pdf/view.

Corella, Hipolito. "Activists Block Tucson Courthouse, Immigration Hearings Canceled for the Day." *Arizona Daily Star*, October 11, 2013. http://tucson.com/news/local/activists-block-tucson-courthouse-immigration-hearings-canceled-for-the-day/article_884dc9da-3287-11e3-918e-0019bb2963f4.html.

Cornelius, Wayne A. "Impacts of Border Enforcement on Unauthorized Mexican Migration to the United States." *Border Battles: The U.S. Immigration Debates*, September 26, 2006. http://borderbattles.ssrc.org/Cornelius/.

Coutin, Susan Bibler. "Contesting Criminality: Illegal Immigration and the Spatialization of Legality." *Theoretical Criminology* 9.1 (2005): 5–33.

——. *Legalizing Moves: Salvadoran Immigrants' Struggle for U.S. Residency.* Ann Arbor: University of Michigan Press, 2003.

——. *The Culture of Protest: Religious Activism and the US Sanctuary Movement.* Boulder, CO: Westview, 1993.

D'Appollonia, Ariane Chebel. *Frontiers of Fear: Immigration and Security in Europe and the United States.* Ithaca, NY: Cornell University Press, 2012.

Davis, Angela J. *Arbitrary Justice: The Power of the American Prosecutor.* New York: Oxford University Press, 2007.

Davis, Scott G., and Tronstad E. Russell. *Arizona's Traditional Economy.* Tucson: University of Arizona Economic and Business Research Center, 2002.

Day, Mark. "Sweeping Up the Aliens." *Nation,* February 5, 1977, 146–48.

De Genova, Nicholas P. "Migrant 'Illegality' and Deportability in Everyday Life." *Annual Review of Anthropology* 31 (2002): 419–47.

——. "The Legal Production of Mexican/Migrant 'Illegality.'" *Latino Studies* 2.2 (2004): 160–85.

De Genova, Nicholas, and Nathalie Mae Peutz. *The Deportation Regime: Sovereignty, Space, and the Freedom of Movement.* Durham, NC: Duke University Press, 2010.

Demleitner, Nora V. "Misguided Prevention: The War on Terrorism as a War on Immigrant Offenders and Immigration Violators." *Criminal Law Bulletin* 40 (2004): 550.

Department of Homeland Security. "Criminal Alien Program | ICE." *Immigration Enforcement.* Accessed September 6, 2015. http://www.ice.gov/criminal-alien-program.

Diaz, Gabriela, and Gretchen Kuhner. *Women Migrants in Transit and Detention through Mexico.* Washington, DC: Migration Policy Institute, 2007.

Dolbeare, Cushing. *Detention of Undocumented Aliens: Actions by the INS prior to Adoption of the Immigration Reform and Control Act of 1986.* Vol. 1. Washington, DC: Center for National Security Studies, 1990.

Doty, Roxanne Lynn. *The Law into Their Own Hands: Immigration and the Politics of Exceptionalism.* Tucson: University of Arizona Press, 2009.

Dowling, Julie, and Jonathan Inda. *Governing Immigration through Crime: A Reader.* Redwood City, CA: Stanford University Press, 2013.

Dunn, Timothy J. *Blockading the Border and Human Rights: The El Paso Operation That Remade Immigration Enforcement.* Inter-America Series. Austin: University of Texas Press, 2009.

——. *The Militarization of the U.S.-Mexico Border.* Austin: University of Texas Press, 1996.

Durand, Jorge, Douglas S. Massey, and Nolan J. Malone. *Beyond Smoke and Mirrors: Mexican Immigration in an Era of Economic Integration.* New York: Russell Sage Foundation, 2002.

Durkheim, Émile. *The Division of Labor in Society.* New York: Free Press, 1997.

Eagly, Ingrid V. "Criminal Justice for Noncitizens: An Analysis of Variation in Local Enforcement." *New York University Law Review* 88 (2013): 1126–23.

———. "Local Immigration Prosecution: A Study of Arizona before SB 1070." *UCLA Law Review* 58.1749 (2011): 1749–1817.

———. "Prosecuting Immigration." *Northwestern University Law Review* 104.4 (2010).

———. "Remote Adjudication in Immigration." *Northwestern University Law Review* 109.4 (2015): 1–87.

Eagly, Ingrid V., and Steven Shafer. "A National Study of Access to Counsel in Immigration Court." *University of Pennsylvania Law Review* 165 (2015).

Faist, Thomas. "*Extension du domaine de la lutte*': International Migration and Security before and after September 11, 2001." *International Migration Review* 36.1 (2002): 7–14.

Farb, Jessica. "The U Visa Unveiled: Immigrant Crime Victims Freed from Limbo." *Human Rights Brief* 15 (2007): 26–57.

"Federal Courts Hit Hard by Increased Law Enforcement on Border: Defendants Charged in the Border District Courts and Courts Affected." *Third Branch*, July 2008. http://www.uscourts.gov/ttb/2008-07/article02_1.cfm.

Feeley, Malcolm M., and Jonathan Simon. "The New Penology: Notes on the Emerging Strategy of Corrections and Its Implications." *Criminology* 30.4 (1992): 449–74.

Flamm, Michael W. *Law and Order: Street Crime, Civil Unrest, and the Crisis of Liberalism in the 1960s.* New York: Columbia University Press, 2005.

Foley, Elise. "Latino Vote Could Tip the Scales for Democrats in Arizona," *Huffington Post*, March 4, 2014.

Foner, Nancy, Rubén G. Rumbaut, and Steven Gold, eds. *Immigration Research for a New Century: Multidisciplinary Perspectives.* New York: Russell Sage Foundation, 2003.

Fredrickson, George M. *Racism: A Short History.* Princeton, NJ: Princeton University Press, 2009.

Gainsborough, Jenni, and Marc Mauer. "Diminishing Returns: Crime and Incarceration in the 1990s." Washington, DC: Sentencing Project, 2000.

Galindo, René, and Jami Vigil. "Are Anti-Immigrant Statements Racist or Nativist? What Difference Does It Make?" *Latino Studies* 4.4 (2006): 419–47.

García, Juan Ramon. *Operation Wetback: The Mass Deportation of Mexican Undocumented Workers in 1954.* Contributions in Ethnic Studies no. 2. Westport, CT: Greenwood, 1980.

Garcia-Villegas, Mauricio. "Symbolic Power without Violence? Critical Comments on Legal Consciousness Studies." *International Journal for the Semiotics of Law* 16.4 (2003): 363–93.

Garland, David. *Punishment and Modern Society: A Study on Social Theory.* Chicago, University of Chicago Press, 1990.

———. *The Culture of Control: Crime and Social Order in Contemporary Society.* Chicago: University of Chicago Press, 2001.

Giblin, Paul. "Hiring Freeze Puts Squeeze on Federal Prosecutors in Arizona." *Arizona Republic*, January 5, 2014.

Goffman, Alice. *On the Run: Fugitive Life in an American City.* Chicago: University of Chicago Press, 2014.

Golash-Boza, Tanya Maria. "Racism and the Consequences of U.S. Immigration Policy." In *Immigration Nation: Raids, Detentions, and Deportations in Post-9/11 America.* Boulder, CO: Paradigm, 2012. http://www.acslaw.org/acsblog/201204?page=6.

Golash-Boza, Tanya Maria, and Pierrette Hondagneu-Sotelo. "Latino Immigrant Men and the Deportation Crisis: A Gendered Racial Removal Program." *Latino Studies* 11.3 (2013): 271–92. doi:10.1057/lst.2013.14.

Gonzales, Alfonso. *Reform without Justice: Latino Migrant Politics and the Homeland Security State.* New York: Oxford University Press, 2013.

Gonzalez, Gilbert G. *Mexican Consuls and Labor Organizing: Imperial Politics in the American Southwest.* Austin: University of Texas Press, 1999.

Gordon, Charles. "Powers and Responsibilities of Immigration Officers." *American Bar Association Journal* 59 (1973): 64.

Gordon, Rebecca. *Mainstreaming Torture: Ethical Approaches in the Post-9/11 United States.* New York: Oxford University Press, 2014.

Greenhouse, Linda. "Crack Cocaine Limbo." *New York Times*, January 5, 2014.

Grossman, Djamila. "'No More Deaths' Volunteer Charges Tossed." *Arizona Daily Star*, September 2, 2006. http://tucson.com/news/local/border/no-more-deaths-volunteer-charges-tossed/article_86d4dcod-ddf7–5b9c-9f8e-e5303d83edb2.html.

Guerette, Rob T. *Migrant Death: Border Safety and Situational Crime Prevention on the US-Mexico Divide.* New York: LFB Scholarly Pub., 2007.

Gutierrez, Genevieve. "Illegal Traffic in Tunnels Shows Dramatic Decline." *Nogales International*, October 31, 2001. http://www.nogalesinternational.com/news/illegal-traffic-in-tunnels-shows-dramatic-decline/article_86c1eea2–208f-5303–90e7–3bbea23877a8.html.

Gutman, Daniel. "The Criminal Gets the Breaks." *New York Times*, November 29, 1964.

Hagan, John. *Who Are the Criminals: The Politics of Crime Policy from the Age of Roosevelt to the Age of Reagan.* Princeton, NJ: Princeton University Press, 2010.

Hall, Mimi, and Patrick O'Driscoll. "Border Patrols Growing in Arizona." *USA Today.com*, March 29, 2005. http://usatoday30.usatoday.com/news/nation/2005–03–29-borders_x.htm.

Hammer-Tomizuka, Zoe. *Criminal Alienation: Arizona Prison Expansion, 1993–2003.* 2004. Available at http://arizona.openrepository.com/arizona/handle/10150/290137.

Hammer-Tomizuka, Zoe, and Jennifer Allen. "Hate or Heroism: Vigilantes on the Arizona-Mexico Border." Tucson: Border Action Network, December 2002.

Hansenfeld, Yeheskel. "People Processing Organizations: An Exchange Approach." *American Sociological Review* 37.3 (1972): 256–63.

Hanson, Anna. "The U-Visa: Immigration Law's Best Kept Secret." *Arkansas Law Review* 63 (2010): 177.

Harcourt, Bernard E. *Against Prediction: Profiling, Policing, and Punishing in an Actuarial Age*. Chicago: University of Chicago Press, 2008.

Hart, Bill. *Arizona's Emerging Latino Vote*. Tucson: Morrison Institute for Public Policy, Arizona State University, 2012.

Harwood, Edwin. "Arrests without Warrant: The Legal and Organizational Environment of Immigration Law Enforcement." *U.C. Davis Law Review* 17 (1984): 505.

———. *In Liberty's Shadow: Illegal Aliens and Immigration Law Enforcement*. Stanford, CA: Hoover Institution Press, Stanford University, 1986.

Hernandez, Kelly Lytle. *Migra! A History of the US Border Patrol*. Berkeley: University of California Press, 2010.

Heyman, Josiah McConnell. *Life and Labor on the Border: Working People of Northeastern Sonora, Mexico, 1886–1986*. Tucson: University of Arizona Press, 1991.

———. "Putting Power in the Anthropology of Bureaucracy: The Immigration and Naturalization Service at the Mexico–United States Border." *Current Anthropology* 362 (1995): 261–87.

———. "US Immigration Officers of Mexican Ancestry as Mexican Americans, Citizens, and Immigration Police." *Current Anthropology* 43.3 (2002): 479–507.

Hing, Bill Ong. *Defining America: Through Immigration Policy*. Philadelphia: Temple University Press, 2004.

———. "Providing a Second Chance." *Connecticut Law Review* 39.5 (2006): 1893–1910.

Hollifield, James. *Immigrants, Markets, and States: The Political Economy of Postwar Europe*. Cambridge, MA: Harvard University Press, 1999.

Hollifield, James F., Valerie F. Hunt, and Daniel J. Tichenor. "The Liberal Paradox: Immigrants, Markets, and Rights in the United States." *Southern Methodist Law Review* 26.1 (2008).

Hollifield, James, Martin Philip, and Pia Orrenius. *Controlling Immigration: A Global Perspective*. Stanford, CA: Stanford University Press, 2014.

Holthouse, David. "Playing Army: In Arizona, Minutemen Leaders and Their Volunteers Spouted Racist Rhetoric." *Fort Worth Weekly*, August 17, 2005. http://www.fwweeklyarchives.com/content.asp?article=2721.

Huicochea, Alexis, and Joseph Barrios. "2 Samaritans Charged in Transporting Entrants." *Arizona Daily Star*, July 10, 2005. http://tucson.com/news/local/border/samaritans-charged-in-transporting-entrants/article_3de6deof-3b10-5d6d-b667-1954a0912349.html.

Human Rights Watch. "Forced Apart: Families Separated and Immigrants Harmed by United States Deportation Policy." Washington DC: Human Rights Watch, July 17, 2007. https://www.hrw.org/reports/2007/us0707/.

———. "US: Mandatory Deportation Laws Harm American Families." *Human Rights Watch*, July 17, 2007. Accessed September 14, 2015. https://www.hrw.org/news/2007/07/17/us-mandatory-deportation-laws-harm-american-families.

Huysmans, Jef. *The Politics of Insecurity: Fear, Migration, and Asylum in the EU*. London: Routledge, 2006.

Ibrahim, Maggie. "The Securitization of Migration: A Racial Discourse." *International Migration* 43.5 (2005): 163–87.

Innes, Stephanie. "Border Activists Say They Knew Law." *Arizona Daily Star*, December 15, 2005. http://tucson.com/news/local/border/border-activists-say-they-knew-law/article_61aa3349–015a-5d0d-822d-bf2e2b76d3ca.html.

Isacson, Adam, and Maureen Meyer. "Beyond the Border Buildup: Security and Migrants along the U.S.-Mexico Border." Washington, DC: Washington Office on Latin America, 2012. Available at http://senatorjoserodriguez.com/wp-content/uploads/2012/04/wola-report1.pdf.

Israel, Jerald H. "Criminal Procedure, the Berger Court, and the Legacy of the Warren Court." *Michigan Law Review* 75 (1977): 1319–425.

Jacobson, Michael. "Reversing the Punitive Turn: The Limits and Promise of Current Research." *Criminology & Public Policy* 5.2 (2006): 277–84.

Johnson, Kevin. *The Huddled Masses Myth: Immigration and Civil Rights*. Philadelphia: Temple University Press, 2004.

———. "The Intersection of Race and Class in US Immigration Law and Enforcement." *Law and Contemporary Problems* 72 (2009): 1–35.

Johnson, Kevin R., and Bernard Trujillo. *Immigration Law and the US–Mexico Border*. Tucson: University of Arizona Press, 2011.

Kamisar, Yale. "When the Cops Were Not 'Handcuffed.'" *New York Times*, November 7, 1965.

Kanstroom, Daniel. *Aftermath: Deportation Law and the New American Diaspora*. New York: Oxford University Press, 2012.

———. *Deportation Nation: Outsiders in American History*. Cambridge, MA: Harvard University Press, 2007.

———. "Deportation, Social Control, and Punishment: Some Thoughts about Why Hard Laws Make Bad Cases." *Harvard Law Review* 113.8 (2000): 1890–1935.

Kerwin, Donald, and Kristen McCabe. "Arrested on Entry: Operation Streamline and the Prosecution of Immigration Crimes." *Migration Information Source*, April 29, 2010. http://www.migrationpolicy.org/article/arrested-entry-operation-streamline-and-prosecution-immigration-crimes.

Kil, Sang H., Cecilia Menjivar, and Roxanne L. Doty. "Securing Borders: Patriotism, Vigilantism, and the Brutalization of the US American Public." In *Immigration, Crime, and Justice*. Sociology of Crime Law and Deviance, volume 13, edited by W. McDonald, 297–312. Bingley, UK: Emerald Group Publishing, 2009.

King, Ryan D., Michael Massoglia, and Christopher Uggen. "Employment and Exile: US Criminal Deportations, 1908–2005." *American Journal of Sociology* 117.6 (2012): 1786–1825.

Koulish, Robert. "Entering the Risk Society: A Contested Terrain for Immigration Enforcement." In *Social Control and Justice: Crimmigration in the Age of Fear*, edited by Maria João Guia and Maartje Amalia van der Woude, 61–86. The Hague: Eleven International Publishing, 2013. http://dialnet.unirioja.es/servlet/articulo?codigo=4058094.

Kovandzic, Tomislay, and Lynn M Vieretis. "The Effect of County-level Prison Population on Crime Rates." *Criminology & Public Policy* 5.2 (2006): 213–44.

Kubrin, Charis, Elizabeth Martínez, and Marjorie Sue Zatz. *Punishing Immigrants: Policy, Politics, and Injustice.* New Perspectives in Crime, Deviance, and Law Series. New York: NYU Press, 2012.

Kukino, Douglas. "Arizona's Growing Service Sector." In *Arizona's Changing Economy: Trends and Prospects,* edited by Bernard Ronan. Phoenix: Arizona Chamber of Commerce, 1986.

Lakhani, Sarah Morando. "From Problems of Living to Problems of Law: The Legal Translation and Documentation of Immigrant Abuse and Helpfulness." *Law & Social Inquiry* 39.3 (2014): 643–65.

———. "Producing Immigrant Victims' 'Right' to Legal Status and the Management of Legal Uncertainty." *Law & Social Inquiry* 38.2 (2013): 442–73.

Larkin, Micaela Ann. "Southwestern Strategy: Mexican Americans and Republican Politics in the Arizona Borderlands." In *Barry Goldwater and the Remaking of the American Political Landscape,* edited by Elizabeth Tandy Shermer. Tucson: University of Arizona Press, 2013.

Latino Policy Forum. "Un-'Clogging the System' Obama Administration Announces 'Common-Sense,'" August 19, 2011. http://www.latinopolicyforum.org/news/8.19.11 CommonSenseEnforcement.pdf.

Law, Anna O. *The Immigration Battle in American Courts.* Cambridge: Cambridge University Press, 2010.

Legomsky, Stephen H. "The New Path of Immigration Law: Asymmetric Incorporation of Criminal Justice Norms." *Washington and Lee Law Review* 469 (2007): 471–73.

Lipsky, Michael. *Street-level Bureaucracy: Dilemmas of the Individual in Public Services.* New York: Russell Sage Foundation, 1980.

Liptak, Adam. "Blocking Parts of Arizona Law, Justices Allow Its Centerpiece." *New York Times,* June 25, 2012. http://www.nytimes.com/2012/06/26/us/supreme-court-rejects-part-of-arizona-immigration-law.html.

Light, Michael T., Mark Hugo Lopez, and Ana Gonzales-Barrera. "The Rise of Federal Immigration Crimes: Unlawful Reentry Drives Growth, 2014." Pew Research Center's Hispanic Trends Project. Available at http://www.pewhispanic.org/2014/03/18/the-rise-of-federal-immigration-crimes/.

Lopez, Mark Hugo, and Michael T. Light. "A Rising Share: Hispanics and Federal Crime." Washington, DC: Pew Hispanic Center, February 18, 2009. Available at http://www.pewhispanic.org/2009/02/18/a-rising-share-hispanics-and-federal-crime/.

Lorey, David E., and UCLA Program on Mexico. *United States–Mexico Border Statistics since 1900.* Vol. 1990. Los Angeles: UCLA Latin American Center Publications, 1993.

Lucas, Fred. "144 Border Agents Charged with Alien, Drug Smuggling and Corruption since 2005." *Cnsnews.com,* January 10, 2013. http://cnsnews.com/news/article/144-border-agents-charged-alien-drug-smuggling-and-corruption-2005.

Luntz, Bruno. "Guía del Migrante Mexicano: análisis sociológico de la historieta de la Secretaría de Relaciones Exteriores." *Contribuciones desde Coatepec* 16 (2009): 91–113.

Lydgate, Joanna. "Assembly-Line Justice: A Review of Operation Streamline." University of California, Berkeley Law School: Chief Justice Earl Warren Institute on Race, Ethnicity & Diversity, January 2010. https://www.law.berkeley.edu/files/Operation_Streamline_Policy_Brief.pdf.

Lynch, Mona Pauline. *Sunbelt Justice: Arizona and the Transformation of American Punishment.* Stanford, CA: Stanford Law Books, 2009.

Mac Donald, Heather. "Mexico's Undiplomatic Diplomats: It's Time for Mexican Consulates to Stop Aiding and Abetting Illegal Immigration." *City Journal*, Autumn 2005. http://www.city-journal.org/html/15_4_mexico.html

Maldonado, Trisha. "Local Citizens Graduate from Douglas Border Patrol Station Citizens Academy." *Douglas Dispatch*, December 5, 2012. http://www.douglasdispatch.com/news/local-citizens-graduate-from-douglas-border-patrol-station-citizens-academy/article_69962356-a7f0-54a5-8c35-dboe6cf47993.html.

Manza, Jeff, and Christopher Uggen. *Locked Out: Felon Disenfranchisement and American Democracy.* New York: Oxford University Press, 2006.

Margulies, Joseph. "Coming out of the Turn: Charting a New Course in Criminal Justice." *Verdict*, January 22, 2014. https://verdict.justia.com/2014/01/22/coming-turn-charting-new-course-criminal-justice.

———. *Guantanamo and the Abuse of Presidential Power.* New York: Simon & Schuster, 2007.

———. *What Changed When Everything Changed: 9/11 and the Making of National Identity.* New Haven, CT: Yale University Press, 2013.

Martin, David A. "A Defense of Immigration-Enforcement Discretion: The Legal and Policy Flaws in Kris Kobach's Latest Crusade." *Yale Law Journal Online*, December 20, 2012. Virginia Public Law and Legal Theory Research Paper No. 2013-01. Available at SSRN: http://ssrn.com.

Martinez, Roberto, Jr., and Abel Valenzuela Jr., eds. *Immigration and Crime: Race, Ethnicity, and Violence.* New York: NYU Press, 2006.

McGirr, Lisa. *Suburban Warriors: The Origins of the New American Right.* Princeton, NJ: Princeton University Press, 2002.

Medina, Maria Isabel. "The Criminalization of Immigration Law: Employer Sanctions and Marriage Fraud." *Immigration & Nationality Law Review* 18 (1997): 643.

Meeks, Eric V. *Border Citizens: The Making of Indians, Mexicans, and Anglos in Arizona.* Austin: University of Texas Press, 2007.

Meissner, Doris. "Exercising Prosecutorial Discretion Memo." U.S. Department of Justice, November 17, 2000. http://iwp.legalmomentum.org/reference/additional-materials/immigration/enforcement-detention-and-criminal-justice/government-documents/22092970-INS-Guidance-Memo-Prosecutorial-Discretion-Doris-Meissner-11-7-00.pdf/view.

Meissner, Doris, Donald M. Kerwin, Muzaffar Chishti, and Claire Bergeron. *Immigration Enforcement in the United States: The Rise of a Formidable Machinery*. Washington, DC: Migration Policy Institute, 2013. http://www.immigrationresearch-info.org/report/migration-policy-institute/immigration-enforcement-united-states-rise-formidable-machinery.

Melossi, Dario. "Punishment and Social Action: Changing Vocabularies of Punitive Motive within a Political Business Cycle." *Current Perspectives in Social Theory* 6 (1985): 169–97.

Menjivar, Cecilia, and Olivia Salcido. "Gendered Paths to Legal Status: The Case of Latin American Immigrants in Phoenix, Arizona, Immigration Policy Center." Washington, DC: American Immigration Council, May 29, 2013.

Miller, Teresa A. "Blurring the Boundaries between Immigration and Crime Control after September 11th." *Boston College Third World Law Journal* 25.1 (2005): 81–123.

———. "Citizenship & Severity: Recent Immigration Reforms and the New Penology." *Georgetown Immigration Law Review* 10 (2003): 611.

Miller, Todd. *Border Patrol Nation: Dispatches from the Front Lines of Homeland Security*. San Francisco: City Lights Publishers, 2014.

Minuteman Project: Bringing National Awareness to the Illegal Alien Invasion. Accessed September 15, 2015. http://minutemanproject.com/.

Montgomery, David. *Workers' Control in America: Studies in the History of Work, Technology, and Labor Struggles*. New York: Cambridge University Press, 1979.

Montini, Ed, and Bob Ortega. "Border Killings: 46 People Killed, No Agents Disciplined." *Arizona Republic*, September 14, 2014. Available at http://www.azcentral.com/story/news/arizona/investigations/2014/09/14/border-deaths-agents-transparency-secrecy/15616933/.

Morawetz, Nancy. "Rethinking Retroactive Deportation Laws and the Due Process Clause." *NYU Law Review* 73 (1998).

———. "Understanding the Impact of the 1996 Deportation Laws and the Limited Scope of Proposed Reforms." *In Defense of the Alien* 23 (2000): 1–30.

Morton, John. "Civil Immigration Enforcement: Priorities for the Apprehension, Detention, and Removal of Aliens." United States Immigration and Customs Enforcement, 2011. http://www.ice.gov/doclib/news/releases/2011/110302washingtondc.pdf.

———. "Exercising Prosecutorial Discretion Consistent with the Civil Immigration Enforcement Priorities of the Agency for the Apprehension, Detention, and Removal of Aliens." U.S. Immigration and Customs Enforcement, June 17, 2011. http://www.ice.gov/doclib/secure-communities/pdf/prosecutorial-discretion-memo.pdf.

Motivans, Mark. "Immigration Offenders in the Federal Justice System, 2010." Bureau of Justice Statistics, July 18, 2012. http://www.bjs.gov/index.cfm?ty=pbdetail&iid=4392.

Motomura, Hiroshi. "Prosecutorial Discretion in Context: How Discretion Is Exercised throughout Our Immigration System." Immigration Policy Center: American Immigration Council, April 2012. http://www.immigrationpolicy.org/special-reports/

prosecutorial-discretion-context-how-discretion-exercised-throughout-our-immigration.

———. "The Curious Evolution of Immigration Law: Procedural Surrogates for Substantive Constitutional Rights." *Columbia Law Review* 92.7 (1992): 1625–1704.

———. "The Discretion That Matters: Federal Immigration Enforcement, State and Local Arrests, and the Civil-Criminal Line." *UCLA Law Review* 58.6 (2010): 1819–58.

Muhammad, Khalil Gibran. *The Condemnation of Blackness: Race, Crime, and the Making of Modern Urban America*. Cambridge, MA: Harvard University Press, 2010.

Murakawa, Naomi. *The First Civil Right: How Liberals Built Prison America*. New York: Oxford University Press, 2014.

Murolo, Priscilla, A. B. Chitty, and Joe Sacco. *From the Folks Who Brought You the Weekend: A Short Illustrated History of Labor in the United States*. New York: New Press, 2001.

Nadelhoff, Maile. *Benchmarks: Arizona's Agricultural Sector*. Tucson: University of Arizona Economic and Business Research Center, 2002.

National Immigrant Justice Center. "Immigration Detention Bed Quota Timeline," 2014. http://immigrantjustice.org/sites/immigrantjustice.org/files/Immigration%20Detention%20Bed%20Quota%20Timeline%20Spring%202014_0.pdf.

"Nazis, Racists Join Minuteman Project." *Southern Poverty Law Center*, April 22, 2005. https://www.splcenter.org/news/2005/04/22/nazis-racists-join-minuteman-project.

Nevins, Joseph. *Operation Gatekeeper and Beyond: The War on "Illegals" and the Remaking of the US–Mexico Boundary*. New York: Routledge, 2010.

Nevins, Joseph, and Mizue Aizeki. *Dying to Live: A Story of US Immigration in an Age of Global Apartheid*. San Francisco: City Lights Books, 2008.

Newton, Lina. *Illegal, Alien, or Immigrant: The Politics of Immigration Reform*. New York: NYU Press, 2008.

Ngai, Mae M. *Impossible Subjects: Illegal Aliens and the Making of Modern America*. Princeton, NJ: Princeton University Press, 2004.

No More Deaths Coalition. *A Culture of Cruelty, Abuse, and Impunity in Short-Term U.S. Border Patrol Custody*. No More Deaths Coalition, 2011.

Office of Immigration Statistics. "Yearbook of Immigration Statistics 2013." Washington, DC: U.S. Department of Homeland Security, August 2014. http://www.dhs.gov/yearbook-immigration-statistics.

"Office of the Chief Immigration Judge | EOIR | Department of Justice." Accessed May 9, 2013. http://www.justice.gov/eoir/office-of-the-chief-immigration-judge.

Padilla v. Kentucky, 559 U.S. 356 (2010).

Pallares, Amalia, and Nilda Flores-Gonzalez. *Marcha: Latino Chicago and the Immigrant Rights Movement*. Champaign: University of Illinois Press, 2010.

Papademetriou, Demetrios G., and Elizabeth Collett. "A New Architecture for Border Management." Washington, DC: Migration Policy Institute, 2011.

PBS. "Border Patrol Series Prompts OIG Investigation | Need to Know | PBS." *I Know on PBS*, October 22, 2012. http://www.pbs.org/wnet/need-to-know/security/border-patrol-series-prompts-oig-investigation/15204/.

Perla, Hector, Jr., and Susan Bibler Coutin. "Legacies and Origins of the 1980s US–Central American Sanctuary Movement." In *Sanctuary Practices in International Perspectives: Migration, Citizenship, and Social Movements*, edited by Randy K. Lippert and Sean Rehaag, 73–91. New York: Routledge, 2012.

Petintseva, Olga. "Social Control and Justice: Crimmigration in the Age of Fear." *Panopticon* 34.3 (2013): 229–36.

Phillips, Scott, Jacqueline Maria Hagan, and Nestor Rodriguez. "Brutal Borders? Examining the Treatment of Deportees during Arrest and Detention." *Social Forces* 85.1 (2006): 93–109.

Pollack, Andrew. "2 Illegal Immigrants Win Arizona Ranch in Court Fight." *New York Times*, August 19, 2005, sec. A, col. 1.

Portes, Alejandro. *City on the Edge: The Transformation of Miami*. Berkeley: University of California Press, 1994.

Portillo, Ernesto, Jr. "'05 Border Bill Punishes Those Aiding Entrants, Foes Contend." *Arizona Daily Star*, January 26, 2006. http://tucson.com/news/local/ernesto-portillo-jr-border-bill-punishes-those-aiding-entrants-foes/article_88c959cd-e958-541a-9a8d-0b4d88b0d2a6.html.

Preston, Julia. "9 in Deportation Protest Are Held in Bid to Re-Enter U.S." *New York Times*, July 23, 2013. http://www.nytimes.com/2013/07/24/us/9-in-deportation-protest-are-held-in-bid-to-re-enter-us.html.

Provine, Doris Marie, and Paul G. Lewis. "Shades of Blue: Local Police, Legality, and Immigration Law." In *Constructing Immigrant "Illegality": Critiques, Experiences, and Responses*, edited by Cecilia Menjívar and Daniel Kanstroom. New York: Cambridge University Press, 2013.

Redburn, Steve, Peter Reuter, and Malay Majmundar, eds. *Budgeting for Immigration Enforcement: A Path to Better Performance*. Washington, DC: National Academies Press, 2011.

Richie, Beth. *Arrested Justice: Black Women, Violence, and the Prison Nation*. New York: NYU Press, 2012.

Rios, Victor M. *Punished: Policing the Lives of Black and Latino Boys*. New York: NYU Press, 2011.

Robbins, Ted. "Border Patrol Program Raises Due Process Concerns." *Morning Edition*. National Public Radio, September 13, 2010, "Hear from the Judges" section. http://www.npr.org/templates/story/story.php?storyId=129780261.

Romero, Mary. "Racial Profiling and Immigration Law Enforcement: Rounding Up of Usual Suspects in the Latino Community." *Critical Sociology* 32.2–3 (2006): 447–73.

Rosas, Gilberto. *Barrio Libre: Criminalizing States and Delinquent Refusals of the New Frontier*. Durham, NC: Duke University Press, 2012.

Rosenblum, Marc R. *Border Security: Immigration Enforcement between Ports of Entry.* Washington, DC: Congressional Research Service, 2012. http://www.fas.org/sgp/crs/homesec/R42138.pdf.

———. "Understanding the Potential Impact of Executive Action on Immigration Enforcement." Washington, DC: Migration Policy Institute, 2015. https://www.fairus.org/DocServer/GR/Understanding_the_Potential_Impact_of_Executive_Action_on_Immigration_Enforcement_July2015.pdf.

Rubio-Goldsmith, Raquel, M. Melissa McCormick, Daniel Martinez, and Inez Magdalena Duarte. "The 'Funnel Effect' and Recovered Bodies of Unauthorized Migrants Processed by the Pima County Office of the Medical Examiner, 1990–2005." Report submitted to the Pima County Board of Supervisors by the Binational Migration Institute, Mexican American Studies and Research Center at the University of Arizona, Tucson, Arizona, October 2006. doi=10.1.1.368.7800.

Rumbaut, Rubén G., Walter A. Ewing, and Immigration Policy Center. *The Myth of Immigrant Criminality and the Paradox of Assimilation: Incarceration Rates among Native and Foreign-Born Men.* Washington, DC: Immigration Policy Center, American Immigration Law Foundation, 2007.

Salant, Tanis J. *Border Impact: Criminal Illegal Immigrants on the Law Enforcement & Criminal Justice System in Santa Cruz County, Arizona.* Nogales, AZ: Santa Cruz County Board of Supervisors, 1999.

———. *Fighting the Drug Wars: Fiscal Impacts on Santa Cruz County, Arizona.* Tucson: Office of Community and Public Service, University of Arizona, 1991.

———. *Illegal Immigrants in Arizona's Border Counties: The Costs for Law Enforcement, Criminal Justice, and Emergency Medical Services: Santa Cruz County, Pima County, Cochise County, Yuma County.* Tucson: Institute for Local Government, School of Public Administration and Policy, Eller College of Business and Public Administration, University of Arizona, 2000.

Salant, Tanis J., Christine Brenner, Nadia Rubaii-Barrett, and John R. Weeks. *Illegal Immigrants in US/Mexico Border Counties: The Costs of Law Enforcement, Criminal Justice, and Emergency Medical Services.* Tucson: Institute for Local Government, University of Arizona, 2001.

Salyer, Lucy. *Laws as Harsh as Tigers: Chinese Immigrants and the Shaping of Modern Immigration Law.* Chapel Hill: University of North Carolina Press, 1995.

Sandoval, Carlos, and Catherine Tambini. *The State of Arizona.* DVD. Camino Bluff Productions, 2013.

Santos, Fernanda. "Shootings by Agents Increase Border Tensions." *New York Times,* June 10, 2013. http://www.nytimes.com/2013/06/11/us/shootings-by-agents-increase-border-tensions.html.

Savage, Charlie, and Erica Goode. "Two Powerful Signals of a Major Shift on Crime." *New York Times,* August 12, 2013. http://www.nytimes.com/2013/08/13/us/two-powerful-signals-of-a-major-shift-on-crime.html.

Scheingold, Stuart A. *The Politics of Law and Order: Street Crime and Public Policy.* New Orleans: Quid Pro Books, 2010.

Schuck, Peter. "Removing Criminal Aliens: The Pitfalls and Promises of Federalism." *Harvard Journal of Law & Public Policy* 22 (1999): 367–463.

———. "The Transformation of Immigration Law." *Columbia Law Review* (1984): 1–90.

Schwartz, David. "Judge Orders Sheriff Joe Arpaio to Undergo Training to Stop Racial Profiling." *Huffington Post*, Oct. 29, 2014.

Semple, Kirk. "Immigrants Released Ahead of Automatic Budget Cuts." *New York Times*, February 26, 2013. http://www.nytimes.com/2013/02/27/us/immigrants-released-ahead-of-automatic-budget-cuts.html.

Shahani, Aarti, and Judith Greene. "Local Democracy on ICE: Why State and Local Governments Have No Business in Federal Immigration Law Enforcement." Justice Strategies Report, 2009. http://justicestrategies.net/sites/default/files/publications/JS-Democracy-On-Ice.pdf.

Shear, Michael D. "Obama, Citing a Concern for Families, Orders a Review of Deportations." *New York Times*, March 13, 2014. http://www.nytimes.com/2014/03/14/us/obama-orders-review-of-deportations.html.

Shermer, Elizabeth Tandy, ed. *Barry Goldwater and the Remaking of the American Political Landscape*. Tucson: University of Arizona Press, 2013.

———. "Drafting a Movement: Barry Goldwater and the Rebirth of the Arizona Republican Party." In *Barry Goldwater and the Remaking of the American Political Landscape*, edited by Elizabeth Tandy Shermer. Tucson: University of Arizona Press, 2013.

———. *Sunbelt Capitalism: Phoenix and the Transformation of American Politics*. Philadelphia: University of Pennsylvania Press, 2013.

Simon, Jonathan. *Governing through Crime: How the War on Crime Transformed American Democracy and Created a Culture of Fear*. New York: Oxford University Press, 2007.

———. "Refugees in a Carceral Age: The Rebirth of Immigration Prisons in the United States." *Public Culture* 10.3 (1998): 577–607.

Siskin, Alison. "Immigration-Related Detention: Current Legislative Issues." Washington, DC: Congressional Research Service, January 12, 2012. http://digitalcommons.ilr.cornell.edu/key_workplace/882/.

Siulc, Nina, Zhifen Cheng, Arnold Son, and Olga Byrne. "Improving Efficiency and Promoting Justice in the Immigration System: Lessons from the Legal Orientation Program." New York: Vera Institute of Justice: Center on Immigration and Justice, May 2008. http://www.vera.org/sites/default/files/resources/downloads/LOP_Evaluation_May2008_final.pdf.

———. "Legal Orientation Program Evaluation and Performance and Outcome Measurement Report." Vera Institute of Justice, New York, May 2008.

Skolnick, Jerome H. *Justice without Trial: Law Enforcement in Democratic Society*. New Orleans: Quid Pro Books, 2011.

Smith, Dennis. "Program Streamlining Immigration Enforcement." *Frontline*, November 2010.

———. "Technology Speeds Judicial Process." *Frontline*, November 2010.

Spelman, William. "What Recent Studies Do (and Don't) Tell Us about Imprisonment and Crime." In *Crime and Justice: A Review of Research*, edited by Michael Tonry. Chicago: University of Chicago Press, 2000.

Spener, David. *Clandestine Crossings: Migrants and Coyotes on the Texas-Mexico Border.* Ithaca, NY: Cornell University Press, 2009.

Stellar, Tim. "Nogales Tunnel Opens into Grave: Possible Entry to Smuggling Route." *Arizona Daily Star*, January 18, 2003.

Stevens, Jacqueline. "US Government Unlawfully Detaining and Deporting US Citizens as Aliens." *Virginia Journal of Social Policy and the Law* 18.3 (2011): 606.

Stumpf, Juliet P. "Introduction." In *Social Control and Justice: Crimmigration in the Age of Fear*, edited by Maria João Guia and Maartje Amalia van der Woude, 7–16. The Hague: Eleven International Publishing, 2013.

———. "The Crimmigration Crisis: Immigrants, Crime, and Sovereign Power." *American University Law Review* 56 (2006): 367.

Sunnucks, Mike. "Arizona Budget Deficit Labeled Country's Worst." *Phoenix Business Journal.* Accessed February 28, 2016. http://www.bizjournals.com/phoenix/stories/2008/02/25/daily29.html.

Swedlund, Eric. "Deputies Tie Body of Crosser to Hood." *Arizona Daily Star*, September 14, 2002. http://www.highbeam.com/doc/1P2-26964116.html.

———. "Tunnels Found in Nogales Tied to Smuggling." *Arizona Daily Star*, January 3, 2004.

"Technology Speeds Judicial Process." *Frontline*, November 2010.

"The Rights of the Guilty." *Wall Street Journal*, April 26, 1965.

Thompson, Ginger. "In Border Town, Migrant Crackdown Rankles." *New York Times*, June 5, 2003, sec. World. http://www.nytimes.com/2003/06/05/world/in-border-town-migrant-crackdown-rankles.html.

Tichenor, Daniel. *Dividing Lines: The Politics of Immigration Control in America.* Princeton, NJ: Princeton University Press, 2002.

Tonry, Michael, and Joan Petersilia. "American Prisons." In *Prisons*, edited by Michael Tonry and Joan Petersilia. Chicago: University of Chicago Press, 1999.

Transactional Records Access Clearinghouse: Immigration. "Federal Prosecutors along Southwest Border Overwhelmed by Soaring Arizona Drug Cases." April 19, 2010. http://trac.syr.edu/immigration/reports/230/.

———. "FY 2009 Federal Prosecutions Sharply Higher: Surge Driven by Steep Jump in Immigration Filings." December 21, 2009. http://trac.syr.edu/tracreports/crim/223/.

Trevizo, Perla. "ICE Says Most Released in Arizona Weren't Criminals." *Arizona Daily Star*, March 16, 2013. http://tucson.com/news/local/border/ice-says-most-released-in-ariz-weren-t-criminals/article_846f3067-64cb-5f57-857c-a52055317765.html.

———. "Mexican Government Objects Justice Department's Decision on BP Shootings." *Arizona Daily Star*, August 16, 2013. http://tucson.com/news/local/border/mexican-government-objects-justice-department-s-decision-on-bp-shootings/article_965d3b2b-fada-5af9-a11a-f58bd85419d1.html.

"Undocumented Activists Take a Giant Risk to Return Home." *Colorlines*, July 23, 2013. http://www.colorlines.com/articles/undocumented-activists-take-giant-risk-return-home.

United States Commission on Civil Rights. *The Tarnished Golden Door: Civil Rights Issues in Immigration*. Washington, DC: U.S. Government Printing Office, 1980.

United States Department of Homeland Security. *Yearbook of Immigration Statistics: 2011*. Washington, DC: U.S. Department of Homeland Security, Office of Immigration Statistics, 2012.

United States General Accounting Office. "Illegal Immigration: Southwest Border Strategy Results Inconclusive; More Evaluation Needed." Washington, DC: United States General Accounting Office, December 1997. http://www.gao.gov/products/GGD-98-21.

United States Government Accountability Office. "Border Security: Additional Actions Needed to Strengthen CBP Efforts to Mitigate Risk of Employee Corruption and Misconduct." Report to Congressional Requesters. Washington, DC: United States Government Accountability Office, December 2012. http://www.gao.gov/products/GAO-13-59.

United States Sentencing Commission. *2011 Sourcebook of Federal Sentencing Statistics*. Washington, DC: United States Sentencing Commission, 2011. http://www.ussc.gov/research-and-publications/annual-reports-sourcebooks/2011/sourcebook-2011.

———. *2012 Sourcebook of Federal Sentencing Statistics*. Washington, DC: United States Sentencing Commission, 2012. http://www.ussc.gov/research-and-publications/annual-reports-sourcebooks/2012/sourcebook-2012.

Urrea, Luis Alberto. *The Devil's Highway: A True Story*. Boston: Little, Brown, 2004.

Vialet, Joyce. "Brief History of United States Immigration Policy." Washington, DC: Congressional Research Service, 1989.

Wacquant, Loïc. "Crafting the Neoliberal State: Workfare, Prisonfare, and Social Insecurity." *Sociological Forum* 25.2 (2010): 197–220.

———. "For an Analytic of Racial Domination." *Political Power and Social Theory* 11.1 (1997): 221–34.

———. *Punishing the Poor: The Neoliberal Government of Social Insecurity*. Durham, NC: Duke University Press, 2009.

———. "Race as Civic Felony." *International Social Science Journal* 57.183 (2005): 127–42.

Warner, Judith Ann. "The Social Construction of the Criminal Alien in Immigration Law, Enforcement Practice, and Statistical Enumeration: Consequences for Immigrant Stereotyping." *Journal of Social and Ecological Boundaries* 1.2 (2005): 56–80.

Waslin, Michele L. "Driving while Immigrant: Driver's License Policy and Immigration Enforcement." In *Outside Justice*, 3–22. New York: Springer, 2013.

———. "The Impact of Immigration Enforcement Outsourcing on ICE Priorities." In *Social Control and Justice: Crimmigration in the Age of Fear*, edited by Maria João Guia, Maartje Van der Woude, and Joanne Van der Leun. The Hague: Eleven International Publishing, 2013.

"Watergate Scandal Key Players." *Washington Post*, June 5, 2012. http://www.washingtonpost.com/politics/watergate-scandal-key-players/2012/06/05/gJQAkn1jLV_gallery.html.

Waters, Mary C. *Black Identities: West Indian Immigrant Dreams and American Realities*. New York: Russell Sage Foundation, 2001.

Weaver, Vesla. "Frontlash: Race and the Development of Punitive Crime Policy." *Studies in American Political Development* 21 (2007): 230–65.

Welch, Michael. *Detained: Immigration Laws and the Expanding I.N.S. Jail Complex*. Philadelphia: Temple University Press, 2002.

———. "Panic, Risk, Control: Conceptualizing Threats in a Post-9/11 Society." In *Punishing Immigrants: Policy, Politics, and Injustice*, edited by Charis Kubrin, Marjorie S. Zatz, and Ramiro Martinez, 17–41. New York: NYU Press, 2012.

Western, Bruce. *Punishment and Inequality in America*. New York: Russell Sage Foundation, 2007.

Whitaker, Matthew C. *Race Works: The Rise of Civil Rights in the Urban West*. Lincoln: University of Nebraska Press, 2005.

Wildes, Leon. "The Nonpriority Program of the Immigration and Naturalization Service Goes Public: The Litigative Use of the Freedom of Information Act." *San Diego Law Review* 14 (1976): 42–75.

———. "The Operations Instructions of the Immigration Service: Internal Guides or Binding Rules." *San Diego Law Review* 17.1 (1979): 99–120.

Young, Jock. *The Exclusive Society: Social Exclusion, Crime, and Difference in Late Modernity*. London: Sage, 1999.

Zadvydas v. Davis, 533 U.S. 678 (2001).

Zatz, Marjorie S., and Nancy Rodriguez. "The Limits of Discretion: Challenges and Dilemmas of Prosecutorial Discretion in Immigration Enforcement." *Law & Social Inquiry* 39.3 (2014): 666–89. doi:10.1111/lsi.12083.

INDEX

Administrative Procedures Act (1946), 184n60

African Americans, 10, 27, 155, 170. *See also* Black(s)

American Civil Liberties Union (ACLU), 27, 43, 45, 48, 65

Anti-Drug Abuse Act (1986), 58, 59

anti-immigration, 5, 11, 33, 38, 39, 80, 140, 153, 155, 159; 163; anti-immigrant rights groups, 32, 154, 155, 163. *See also* vigilantism

Arizona, 31, 34, 94, 114, 118, 124, 133, 138, 149, 155, 156, 181n13, 193n73; and advocacy, 151–152; anti-deportation activism, 40, 160–161; changing demographics, 25, 32; 80, 163; Cochise County, 30, 36, 37, 83–84, 88, 156–157; Department of Corrections, 27, 28, 38; economic restructuring, 30, 33, 92; and immigration politics, 3, 10, 24, 25, 27, 38–39, 170; Good Samaritan laws, 151; immigration to, 31, 16, 29, 80, 84; Florence, Arizona, 6, 27, 124, 126, 149, 160; law and order politics, 21, 24, 26, 32, 49, 50, 51, 62, 71, 75; ; and migrant deaths, 97–98; Naco, 35, 93, 114, 115, 137, 140; Phoenix, 6, 12, 25, 26, 28, 29, 30, 31, 33, 39, 40, 52, 86, 95, 115, 116–117, 124, 125, 151; political restructuring, 25–26, 32–34; prison, 1, 27, 88; prison overcrowding, 1, 3, 9, 11, 27, 54–61, 63, 75, 91, 169, 163; punitive state, 11, 35, 36, 38, 79, 167; Rehnquist, William, 33; Republican Party, 26, 32, 33–34; residents feelings of victimiza-

tion, 80; Santa Cruz County, 28, 78, 88; Sasabe, 6, 16, 94, 115, 116; SB1070, 6, 38–39, 88, 133–134, 174n18; Southern Arizona, 3, 5, 28, 36, 37, 38, 86, 102, 137; "tent cities," 41; Tucson, 1, 5, 6, 15, 26, 29, 30, 39, 34, 35, 77, 86, 92, 95, 97, 98, 100, 103, 104, 116, 124, 135, 153, 167

Arizona Coalition for Human Rights/ Coalición de Derechos Humanos, 37

Army Corps of Engineers, 140

Arpio, Joe, 38, 41, 190n9

arrests, 36, 40, 49, 52, 54, 86, 112, 133, 174n18, 191n33; activists, 10, 152–153, 161; border residents, 2, 11, 12, 42, 51, 66, 109, 126, 132–133, 135, 139, 143, 144–145, 154, 158, 165; criminal aliens, 1, 18, 38, 39, 112, 135, 129, 144–145; criminal background checks, 1, 191n33; migrant apprehensions, 1, 18, 97, 113, 128, 129, 139; of U.S. citizens, 2, 11, 12, 47, 132, 144, 152, 155, 156, 158, 164; vigilantes, 36, 114, 154, 155–156. *See also* Border Patrol (U.S.); border policing

Ashcroft, John (Attorney General), 67

"*bajadores*", 84–85, 131, 163, 194n27

Barnett, Roger, 36–37, 156–157

biometric technology, 1, 3, 10, 72, 75, 85, 119–120, 128, 129, 167, 170

Black(s), 52, 82, 178n49; anti-Black criminalization, 46, 164, 168, 170; criminalization of, 10, 46, 167, 183n39; hyperincarceration of, 27, 58, 62, 68, 75, 169; violence against, 22, 164, 165

167, 201n27; overreach of, 158–159; and U.S. Attorney's Office, 95–96. *See also* border enforcement; immigration enforcement; Priority Enforcement Program

Executive Office for Immigration Review (EOIR), 35, 40, 59, 64, 68, 69 103, 117, 120–121, 186n90, 199n59; Board of Immigration Appeals (BIA), 64, 68; immigration courts, 35, 40, 63, 65, 68, 70, 71, 91, 103, 168, 170, 186n90, 193n73; and judicial review, 52, 61, 65, 111, 161, 162; and Notice to Appear (NTA), 90

Fair Sentencing Act (2010), 18
Federal Bureau of Investigations (FBI), 30, 51, 119, 128

Goldwater, Barry, 26, 32–33, 49, 62
Grupo Beta, 5, 35, 99, 100. *See also* Mexican government: anti-smuggling
Guía del Migrante Mexicano, 101. *See also* Mexican government

Hanigan, Patrick and Thomas, 157
Herbert Hoover's National Commission on Law Observance and Enforcement (Wickersham Commission), 48

IIRIRA (Illegal Immigration Reform and Immigrant Responsibility Act) (1996), 2, 9, 61–68, 90, 103, 111, 169–170, 65; aggravated felony category, 61, 176n17; constraints on judicial review, 52, 61, 65, 111, 161, 162; and "criminal aliens," 61, 62, 63, 66, 69, 90, 126, 166, 176n17; "Fix 96" campaign, 65; letter to Attorney General Janet Reno, 66; mandatory detention, 63; Meissner memo on prosecutorial discretion, 66; provisions of, 61, 166; punitive aspects of, 62; restructuring deportation and detention, 61–62; retroactive deporta-

tions, 61, 62, 170; secret evidence, 61, 65, 167. *See also* deportations; detention

illegalization, 10, 46, 164, 177n47. *See also* criminalization

immigrant rights, 1, 3, 9, 11, 23, 25, 32, 34, 41, 43, 51, 62, 65, 76, 79, 80, 111, 127, 128, 131, 157, 159, 163, 167, 168, 177n44; and antideportation protests, 41, 42, 160, 161, 162, 201n27; border-rights movement, 37, 39; Border Summit, 37; and early reformers, 43–44; grassroots activists, 36–38, 161; immigrant rights movement, 167–168; "know your rights" workshops, 6, 103–104, 151

(im)migration/migrants: changing patterns, 31, 141; criminalization of, 9, 10, 22, 43, 72, 76, 94, 113, 119; early twentieth century, 2, 43; fear of, 37, 84, 126, 143, 147, 150; long distance, long-distance migrants, 31, 193n2; migrant workers, 2, 3, 21, 25, 31, 33, 43, 51, 81, 82, 89, 100, 101, 112, 114, 116, 163, 162, 165; migration control, 9, 10, 11, 17, 21, 24, 75, 79, 161, 169; migration flows, 20, 21, 31, 36, 72, 79, 193n2; politics and policymaking, 10, 11, 19, 20, 41; regional/seasonal, 25, 31, 141, 154, 193n2; restrictions on, 62, 64, 81, 82, 96, 98; unauthorized, 8, 37, 94, 135, 101, 135, 171; undocumented,15, 23, 38, 47, 51, 82, 83, 90, 96, 97, 112, 118, 119, 121, 125, 128,130–131, 133, 134, 150, 155, 156, 157, 158, 164. *See also* anti-immigration

Immigration Act (1924), 42, 43, 47
Immigration Act (1929), 17
Immigration Act (1965), 48–49, 154
Immigration and Customs Enforcement (ICE), 5, 8, 38, 40, 41, 68, 70, 71, 104, 118, 121, 129, 149, 173; agency funding, 74, 75; criminal removals, 72, 73, 127, 129; enforcement priorities, 73, 75, 105, 120; ICE attorneys, 92, 93, 104–105;

non-Mexican nationals. *See* 'Other than Mexicans'

Obama, Barak, 72, deportations, 41, 73, 161; and immigration reform 41; executive action, 161, 201n27; felons not families, 13, 201n27; prosecutorial discretion, 193n4
Office of Enforcement and Removal Operations, *See* Immigration and Customs Enforcement
Office of the Mexican Consulate. *See* Mexican Consulate
Operation Safeguard, 1, 35–36, 98, 99, 137, 139; and "criminal alien removal, 1, 35"; escalation of Border Patrol, 135, 158
Operation Streamline, 15, 17, 70, 72, 76, 88, 94, 96, 160, 192n49; activists shut down, 160; adoption of priorities under, 76, 88, 94, 95, 96; Del Rio, TX, 90, 91; "flip flop" cases, 124; funding for, 72, 88, 92; mass hearings, 12, 16, 92, 192n49; migrants prosecuted for illegal entry and reentry, 6, 16, 91, 92, 93, 96, 124; Ninth Circuit Court of Appeals, 192n49; *Padilla v. Kentucky*, 195n53; plea bargain, 92, 124–125; "race-blind" language, 91–92, 141; the Tucson sector, 98, 103, 167; U.S. Marshals, 40, 63, 69, 91, 94; *See also* criminal prosecutions; U.S. Attorney's Office
'Other than Mexicans' (OTMs), 90, 91, 100, 101. *See also* Central America

PATRIOT Act (2001), 67
Pearce, Russell, 38
Priority Enforcement Program, 13, 165–167, 193n5, 201n27. *See also* enforcement priorities of DHS; prosecutorial discretion
prisons: deportation as a pathway to, 12; prison boom, 24, 42, 54–61; prison construction, 4, 27, 55, 58; and over-crowding, 1, 3, 9, 11, 27, 54–61, 63, 75, 91, 169. *See also* U.S. Bureau of Prisons
Proposition 200 (Arizona), 38
prosecution. *See* criminal prosecution
prosecutor: 30, 51, 79, 96, 97, 120, 133
prosecutorial approaches: to migration control, 11,111, 129, 153, 155, 162, 164, 165, 167, 168, 169, 170; prosecutorial rhetoric, 45, 50, 79, 100, 101, 156, 152, 159
prosecutorial discretion: early twentieth century, 46, 48–49; enforcement discretion of agents, 24, 83, 89, 111,112, 109, 120, 124, 159; and 2012 government sequestration, 118; and humanitarian considerations, 114, 165, 166; immigration context, 41, 70, 129, 160–161, 165, 166, 167; under IRCA, 60; Johnson, Jeh, memo, 193n5; legislative discretion, 68, 70, 88; Meissner, Doris, memo, 66–67; Morton, John, memo, 109–110; non-priority program, 40, 53, 60; Obama administration and, 193n4, 193n5; Priority Enforcement Program, 13, 165–167, 193n5, 201n27; struggles over, 160–162; "vulnerable groups," 18, 22, 66, 105. *See also* Border Patrol (U.S.); enforcement priorities of DHS; immigration enforcement

Quota Act (1921) (early restrictive immigration law), 42

race, 2, 6, 20, 26, 43, 134, 168; anti-black criminalization, 46, 114, 164; anti-racist struggle, 48, 168; and the carceral state, 22, 24; caste, 167, 174n26; and citizenship, 13 154, 170; civil rights, 3, 6, 21; colorblind constitutionalism, 171; criminal stigma, 3, 10, 167–168, 170, 174n26; critical race theory, 171; and democracy, 13, 21; and immigration law, 22, 42, 48, 130, 159; nondiscrimination, 49, 91; "race-blind," 22,

24, 62, 91; "race-neutral" criminal classifications, 12, 22, 66, 141, 171; racial criminalization, 18, 23, 78, 158; racial disparities, 18, 20; racial justice, ix, 46; racial liberalism, 22; racial profiling, 12, 36, 78, 102, 133, 134, 150, 164, 190n9; racial violence, 22, 80, 131, 157, 159; and slavery, 170, 171

raids, 36, 50, 52, 70, 126, 152, 173n4; litigation, 52; Palmer Raids, 43, 48

Reagan, Ronald, 27, 32, 33, 34, 54, 56, 169; Anti-Drug Abuse Act (1986), 58, 59; Comprehensive Crime Control Act (1984), 27, 54, 60, 169

reentry after deportation. *See* criminal prosecution; deportations; mass incarceration; Operation Streamline

Refugee Act (1980), 34, 56, 194n33

Refugees, 20, 34, 56, 57, 64, 149, 152

removals, *See* deportations

Republican Party (GOP), 26, 32, 33, 41, 131, 168, 170

rights: and citizenship, 77, 13, 131, 150, 152, 154, 159, 173n12; and claims-making, 77, 79, 104, 171; coaction with criminalization, 9, 10, 13, 22, 23, 24, 25, 43, 62, 102, 105, 130–131, 133, 170; and equality, 22, 24, 79, 133; freedom of mobility, 7, 99, 100, 158, 165; human-rights, 2, 5, 10, 11, 36, 37, 98, 99, 100, 115, 116, 126, 133, 170, 194n33; as individual freedoms, 7, 34, 52, 79; as legal guarantees, 6, 23, 52, 53, 56, 78, 79, 93, 94, 99, 103, 119, 133, 149, 159, 165; as moral principles, 21, 34, 53, 133, 154; procedural, 9, 18, 22, 52, 63, 111, 119, 128, 130, 131, 175n9, 196n62; protection from violence, 18, 22, 37, 48, 79, 80, 98, 126, 131, 158, 159, 196n62; as protection of crime, 2, 3, 20, 21, 23, 24, 26, 49, 53, 79, 80, 100, 105, 128–131, 154, 155, 157; rights in the criminal justice system, 17, 18, 22, 23, 24, 36, 37, 43, 47–48, 76, 102, 105, 111, 128, 131, 165,

171; rights in the immigration system, 3, 9 17, 18, 22–23, 24, 36, 118–119, 128, 133, 162, 165, 167–168. 170, 171; "racialized rightlessness," 13, 23; as safety and freedom from fear, 1, 20, 24, 79; substantive, 17, 23, 62, 119, 175n9; victim's rights, 94, 79, 105, 135, 155, 162. *See also* civil rights; Constitution (U.S.)

Sanctuary movement, 34, 37–38, 57, 152–153, 179n89

SB1070 ("Papers Please" law), 6, 38–39, 88, 133–134, 174n18

smuggling, 1, 7, 14, 19, 20, 31, 32, 38, 41, 42, 47, 78, 84, 85, 89, 140, 151, 163, 174n14, 178n72; activists charged with, 152–153, 159; antismuggling operations, 5, 49, 132, 139, 140, 144, 147; Arizona's 2005 smuggling law, 38, 147, 156, 159; control of tunnels on border, 86; crimes against migrants, 94, 99, 100, 101, 105, 113, 115, 153, 158; "criminal networks," 29, 134; drug smuggling, 12, 29, 84, 119, 136, 157; human smuggling, 29, 30, 36, 38, 60, 83, 118, 135, 136, 137, 144, 147, 148, 152, 159; residents targeted as, 2, 12, 132, 134, 144, 145, 147; self-smuggling, 19, 38, 148, 156; and unauthorized immigrants, 96, 114, 125, 130, 132, 184n57

street-level bureaucrats, 129, 162

Supreme Court (U.S.), 33, 39, 183n39; Chinese Exclusion Act, 180n7; on deportation, 52; Fourth Amendment rights on the border, 17: on indefinite detention (*Zadvydas v. Davis*), 67; raids, 52; on the rights of criminal defendants, 128; SB1070, 133; the Warren Court, 52; search and seizure, 52, 180n7

terrorism, *See* War on Terror

Tohono O'odham Nation, 79, 80, 83, 97, 190n16, *See also* Native Americans

"tunnel kids." See *"bajadores"*

ABOUT THE AUTHOR

Patrisia Macías-Rojas is Assistant Professor of Sociology and Latin American and Latino Studies at the University of Illinois at Chicago. She received her PhD in sociology at the University of California, Berkeley.